KV-051-829

Form-focused Instruction and Teacher Education

Studies in honour of ROD ELLIS

Editors

SANDRA FOTOS

HOSSEIN NASSAJI

OXFORD

UNIVERSITY PRESS

OXFORD

UNIVERSITY PRESS

Great Clarendon Street, Oxford OX2 6DP

Oxford University Press is a department of the University of Oxford.
It furthers the University's objective of excellence in research, scholarship,
and education by publishing worldwide in

Oxford New York

Auckland Cape Town Dar es Salaam Hong Kong Karachi
Kuala Lumpur Madrid Melbourne Mexico City Nairobi
New Delhi Shanghai Taipei Toronto

With offices in

Argentina Austria Brazil Chile Czech Republic France Greece
Guatemala Hungary Italy Japan Poland Portugal Singapore
South Korea Switzerland Thailand Turkey Ukraine Vietnam

OXFORD and OXFORD ENGLISH are registered trade marks of
Oxford University Press in the UK and in certain other countries

© Oxford University Press 2007

The moral rights of the author have been asserted
Database right Oxford University Press (maker)

First published 2007

2011 2010 2009 2008 2007

10 9 8 7 6 5 4 3 2 1

No unauthorized photocopying

All rights reserved. No part of this publication may be reproduced,
stored in a retrieval system, or transmitted, in any form or by any means,
without the prior permission in writing of Oxford University Press,
or as expressly permitted by law, or under terms agreed with the appropriate
reprographics rights organization. Enquiries concerning reproduction
outside the scope of the above should be sent to the ELT Rights Department,
Oxford University Press, at the address above

You must not circulate this book in any other binding or cover
and you must impose the same condition on any acquirer

Any websites referred to in this publication are in the public domain and
their addresses are provided by Oxford University Press for information only.
Oxford University Press disclaims any responsibility for the content

ISBN-13: 978 0 19 442250 5

Typeset by Data Standards Ltd, Frome, Somerset, UK
Printed in China

THE EDITORS, AUTHORS, AND OXFORD UNIVERSITY PRESS are pleased to publish this book in honour of Rod Ellis for his outstanding contribution to the field of second language teaching and learning.

THE EDITORS AND THE PUBLISHER would like to thank the authors for their excellent chapters, and are grateful to Alister Cumming, Henry Widdowson, and David Nunan for their helpful comments and suggestions. The editors would like to thank Laura Hawkes for her assistance.

Contents

Introduction

THIS BOOK is edited in honor of Rod Ellis, whose contributions to the field of second language acquisition (SLA) and teacher education have been of tremendous significance over the past three decades. Rod's work and ideas have advanced our understanding of many areas within SLA, including form-focused instruction (FFI), task-based teaching and learning, classroom research, and the role of input and interaction. Throughout his career, Rod's commitment to teacher education through linking research with classroom pedagogy stands out as especially significant. Because he began his career as an English teacher, he has extensive experience with and knowledge of classroom teaching and the challenges facing teachers. This background, coupled with his expertise in SLA research and applied linguistics, has enabled him to connect theory and practice effectively and to make outstanding contributions to various areas of teacher education, including curriculum development, teaching methodology, and classroom research. Rod's contributions in these areas have appeared in numerous journal articles, conference presentations, workshops, and teacher education textbooks and monographs. By editing this Festschrift, we wish to express our appreciation of what Rod has done over the course of his academic and teaching career for second and foreign language (FL) teachers, researchers, and teacher educators.

The book has been designed to focus on current areas of research, theory, and practice in FFI and teacher education. The contributors are Rod's colleagues and friends and those who have worked with him over the years and have inspired or been inspired by his work. The range of topics covered reflects the breadth and depth of Rod's expertise and interests.

In line with Rod's work, the volume addresses FFI from the perspective of informing teachers of the role that formal instruction plays in communicative contexts. It considers both theoretical and empirical issues as well as classroom use of form-focused activities in communicative pedagogy. Since many SLA researchers and teacher educators now recognize the important role of FFI in language learning theory, teaching, and learning, a volume that combines theoretical concerns, classroom practices, and teacher education constitutes an important contribution to the field.

Overview of the volume

The book is organized into three parts: 'Theoretical issues of focus on form', 'Focus on form and classroom practice', and 'Focus on form and teacher education'. All sections address FFI with particular reference to Rod's work, and the last two discuss its classroom applications, again drawing upon Rod's many contributions to the field. The first section contains four chapters addressing theoretical considerations including an overview of focus on form (FoF), consciousness, cognitive processing, explicit knowledge and sociocultural theory, the relationship between task research and language teaching pedagogy, and FoF as psycholinguistic and sociolinguistic phenomena.

Chapter 1, 'Issues in form-focused instruction and teacher education' by Hossein Nassaji and Sandra Fotos, introduces the volume by examining the theoretical aspects of FoF and reviewing the various types of FFI in classroom practice. This chapter also discusses current insights from FFI research and theory and their relevance for teachers and teacher education. Chapter 2, 'The weak interface, consciousness, and form-focused instruction: mind the doors' by Nick Ellis, examines the interface between implicit and explicit knowledge and compares the roles of consciousness in SLA and psychology. N. Ellis suggests that current theories of the role of consciousness correspond to the 'weak interface' theory proposed by Rod (R. Ellis 1994b) whereby explicit knowledge plays a facilitating role in SLA.

Chapter 3, 'Conceptual knowledge and instructed second language learning: a sociocultural perspective' by James Lantolf, considers the implications of sociocultural theory for second language (L2) instruction, arguing that conceptual knowledge is likely to have a more powerful impact on grammatical development than traditional approaches which focus less on meaning and more on formal grammatical features. Chapter 4, 'Task research and language teaching: reciprocal relationships' by Peter Skehan, begins with a comprehensive review of task research, particularly examining the sequence and implications of pre-task, task, and post-task activities and relating the research findings to current pedagogical practice. Skehan notes that a task-based approach has much to offer FFI.

The second section, 'Focus on form and classroom practice', examines research-based FFI activities in the (L2) classroom. Chapter 5, by Merrill Swain and Sharon Lapkin, is titled 'The distributed nature of second language learning: Neil's perspective'. The authors review research on the distributed nature of learning as a situated local phenomenon, then present an analysis of a French immersion student's transcripts during performance of multi-task activities, suggesting that the participant's L2 learning is mediated by his own languaging. Chapter 6, 'Recontextualizing focus on form' by Rob Batstone, examines the ongoing, discourse-based nature of FoF and the critical roles of framing and negotiation of form. The shift from meaning to form is reconsidered, with particular focus on the processes by which learners develop alertness and attentional capacity.

Chapter 7, 'The prior and subsequent use of forms targeted in incidental focus on form' by Shawn Loewen, investigates the effectiveness of incidental FoF in promoting L2 learning by examining the use of targeted linguistic items in classroom interaction both before and after FFI took place. The author emphasizes the need for various measures of learners' L2 knowledge. Chapter 8, 'Reactive focus on form through negotiation on learners' written errors' by Hossein Nassaji, examines the role of negotiation taking place during oral feedback on English as a second language (ESL) learners' written errors. The results indicated that negotiated feedback occurred more frequently than non-negotiated feedback, and was more effective in helping students identify and correct their L2 writing errors than non-negotiated feedback. Chapter 9, 'Form-focused instruction and output for second language writing gains' by Sandra Fotos and Eli Hinkel, reviews research indicating that, without FFI, even advanced L2 learners write text with simple grammatical and lexical features. Classroom pedagogy consisting of FFI, output opportunities, feedback, and learner revision is recommended, and activities in an English as a foreign language (EFL) writing class are described.

The third section, 'Focus on form and teacher education', integrates FFI with teacher education and practice. Chapter 10, 'Materials development and research: towards a form-focused perspective' by Jack Richards, discusses research and theory in materials development, including the writer's goals, the focus of the materials, and the syllabus. Richards suggests that development of successful teaching material is not dependent on research but rather on how the material is received by teachers and students, and whether it meets their needs.

Chapter 11, 'Time, teachers, and tasks in focus on form instruction' by Teresa Pica, addresses time as a factor in teachers' selection of target forms, their decision when to focus attention on the forms, and their practices for form mastery. Recommendations are given for designing tasks which are consistent with FFI and curriculum requirements. Brian Tomlinson's Chapter 12, 'Using form-focused discovery approaches', describes various types of discovery approaches and investigates teacher attitudes and adoption practices. The author's experience of introducing discovery approaches to teachers around the world is presented, and suggestions are offered regarding the use of discovery approaches in the future.

Chapter 13, 'Learning or measuring? Exploring teacher decision-making in planning for classroom-based language assessment' by Pauline Rea-Dickins, recognizes the need to understand language assessment practices within the social and cultural context in which they take place. The chapter explores decisions that teachers make in relation to classroom-based assessment and to the different phases in the assessment cycle.

Chapter 14, 'Learning through the looking glass: teacher response to form-focused feedback on writing', by Tricia Hedge, examines teacher responses to their writing tutor's taped FFI and commentary on their writing. The teachers responded positively to the taped feedback in comparison to face-to-face interaction or written commentary. Chapter 15, 'Explicit language knowledge and focus on form: options and obstacles for TESOL teacher trainees', by Catherine Elder, Rosemary Erlam, and Jenefer Philp, examines TESOL teacher trainees' explicit knowledge and their ability to deliver FoF options. The authors also suggest that if FoF interventions are to be effective, teacher education programs must help teacher trainees develop strategies to tailor their instructional approaches to their level of metalinguistic knowledge.

The primary theme running through the chapters in this collection is that FFI is necessary in language classrooms. Written from the viewpoint of language teachers, the chapters attempt to demonstrate, either theoretically or empirically, options for integrating form and meaning in language classrooms. The theoretical concerns which should underlie an integrated curriculum are discussed, and specific techniques are examined, with suggestions for their application in language teaching and teacher education.

Sandra Fotos
Hossein Nassaji

Part One
Theoretical issues of focus on form

1

Issues in form-focused instruction and teacher education

HOSSEIN NASSAJI and SANDRA FOTOS

IN RECENT YEARS the role of FFI in language teaching has become an important issue in the field of SLA. Research suggests that traditional instruction on isolated grammar forms is insufficient to promote their acquisition (Long 1991; Long and Robinson 1998), yet purely communicative approaches have been found inadequate for developing high levels of target language (TL) accuracy (Harley and Swain 1984; Swain 1985, 1998; Swain and Lapkin 1998). Two general solutions have been proposed in the research literature: one is to encourage learners to attend to target forms by noticing them in input (Schmidt 1990, 1993; Doughty and Williams 1998a; R. Ellis 1994a, 2001a), thus assisting in their processing. The other is to provide learners with opportunities to produce output containing target forms, again enabling learners to notice the gap between their current TL ability and the correct use of the target form (Swain 1985, 2005).

Teacher education: the gap between SLA research and pedagogy

Regarding past and current approaches to teacher education, the point has often been made (Crandall 2000: 35) that traditional approaches have usually been top-down, viewing teachers as passive knowledge recipients, whereas current constructivist approaches emphasize active roles for teacher cognition, reflection, and research. Widdowson (1990: 62) distinguishes between teacher training and teacher education, arguing that training has traditionally been viewed as 'a process of preparation towards the achievement of a range of outcomes which are specified in advance', and the development of skills for predictable situations. Teacher education, however, allows for unpredictability and equips prospective teachers for 'situations which cannot be accommodated into preconceived patterns of response but which require a reformulation of ideas and the modification of established formulae' (ibid.: 62). This view of teacher education as the flexible development of professional knowledge to be applied when needed is emphasized in the present volume.

Two areas of SLA have been identified by R. Ellis (1997a) as having particular relevance for teacher education. One is the role of input and interaction, and the other is the role of FFI. R. Ellis (2001a) considers FFI to be any instructional activity, planned or incidental, that is used to draw the learner's attention to language forms. A number of studies have investigated the role of FFI in SLA and their findings have been reviewed extensively (for example, Long 1983; Larsen-Freeman and Long 1991; R. Ellis 1994a, 1997a, 2001a, 2001b; Spada 1997; Doughty and Williams 1998a; Norris and Ortega 2000, 2001). However, despite these reviews, there has often been a gap between SLA research and its successful application to language pedagogy (Stenhouse 1981, 1983; Widdowson 1990; Crookes 1997a, 1997b, 1998; R. Ellis 1997a, 1997b, 2001a; Lightbown 2000; Liu and Master 2003; Nassaji 2005). For example, surveying English as a second/foreign language teachers, Nassaji (2005) found that while many teachers acknowledged the importance of SLA research, few mentioned that they regularly read such research. One reason for this could be that research results are often published in venues not easily accessible (Crookes 1997a; R. Ellis 1997a). In addition research reports are often perceived as too theoretical, with findings not directly applicable to classroom practice. Robbins (2003: 59) stated:

> To date, much SLA research remains within categorical lists, little
> of which have been translated into teaching materials, learner
> expectancies, or topics in teacher training courses. To some degree
> this trend has resulted in theory for theory's sake.

The purpose of the current book is to address this gap by providing chapters authored by SLA experts who are language teachers or teacher educators. The main theme is how theory and research in FFI can inform classroom pedagogy and teacher education. However, for theory and research to be useful to teachers, their connection with pedagogy should be made explicit so that they can be conceived of as relevant. For example, with respect to pedagogical grammars, defined as 'the types of grammatical analysis and instruction designed for the needs of second language students' (Odlin 1994: 1), it has been noted that grammar can be taught as prescription, description, an internalized system or as an axiomatic system, the latter being the kind of pedagogical grammar needed for teacher education (Fotos 2005). As the articles in a recent book on grammar teaching in teacher education emphasize (Liu and Master 2003), although teachers believe that pedagogical grammar is essential for the language classroom, many find it challenging—not only because it is difficult to learn and teach, but also partially because of the emphasis on communicative pedagogy many received during their training. Thus, the questions the authors have addressed in this volume are those asked by language teachers, and the research reported has been conducted from the vantage point of informing L2 pedagogical practices.

Theoretical research in language pedagogy

Considerable research has been conducted over the past few decades on the ways in which second languages can be best taught. R. Ellis (2001a) provides an overview of these studies outlining their origins, the research questions they have addressed, and the research methods they have used. (See also Lightbown 2000; Mitchell 2000; see Fotos 2005, for a historical survey.) As R. Ellis points out, much of the early SLA research has been method-driven with the aim of comparing language teaching methods that differed in the extent to which they taught language forms explicitly or implicitly (for example the large scale experimental research projects conducted in the 1960s and 1970s). However, these studies did not indicate that one method of teaching was superior to another. Subsequent research has become more theory-driven in focus and is now mainly conducted to test theoretical claims about second language (L2) acquisition processes (R. Ellis 2001a). These claims include those related to the role of attention and noticing in SLA (Schmidt 1993, 1995, 2001; Tomlin and Villa 1994; Leow 1998, 2001a), the relationship between instructed SLA and developmental sequences (Pienemann 1984, 1989), and the relationship between explicit and implicit knowledge and the effects of frequency on cognition and SLA (for example, Reber 1976, 1989, 1993; Bialystok 1990, 1994; N. Ellis 1993, 1994, 2002a, 2002b; DeKeyser 1995, 1997, 1998, 2005a; Robinson 1996; R. Ellis 2002a).

Although theory-based research has not been directly concerned with pedagogical issues, it has produced many new insights regarding effective L2 instruction. It has increased our understanding of the complexity of the processes underlying the learning of second languages and how they are affected by formal instruction. For example, research into the role of attention has shown that although noticing or attention to form is a crucial factor in learning an L2, it is not clear what constitutes attention and how attention functions in learning (Sharwood Smith 1981, 1993; Schmidt 1990, 1993, 1995, 2001; Tomlin and Villa 1994; Robinson 1995, 2001; Leow 1997, 2001a, 2001b, 2002; Wong 2001). Moreover, it has been shown that attention and noticing interact with the learning task and context, as well as with various cognitive processing variables (Robinson 1995, 2001, 2005; Skehan 1996b, 1998; N. Ellis 2002a, 2002b). Findings from studies on developmental sequences have indicated that, although instruction may have facilitative effects on SLA, its effectiveness may be constrained by the learner's developmental readiness (Pienemann 1984, 1989, 1998; Williams and Evans 1998; Spada and Lightbown 1999), which may be further mediated by first language (L1) transfer or other L1-based factors (Spada and Lightbown 1999).

As for the relationship between explicit and implicit knowledge, one of the main debates concerns the extent to which explicit knowledge gained through formal instruction can lead to the development of implicit knowledge underlying spontaneous and naturalistic L2 use. Some researchers in the past have argued that there is no relationship between the two forms of knowledge (for example, Krashen 1981, 1985, 1993; Schwartz 1993). However, many SLA researchers now believe that a relationship exists, particularly through: (1) performance of activities that promote the learner's attention to target forms while processing input (for example, R. Ellis 1982, 1990, 1994a, 1997c, 2003, 2005c; VanPatten 1990; Robinson 1995, 1996, 2001; Doughty and Williams 1998a; White 1998; Williams 2001), or (2) through repeated practice and increased exposure (for example, McLaughlin 1978, 1990; McLeod and McLaughlin 1986; N. Ellis 1994, 1995, 2002a, 2002b; DeKeyser 1998), although N. Ellis cautions (2002b) that rote practice alone does not necessarily facilitate spontaneous TL production, or (3) through making the learning process more efficient by helping learners attend to features in the input that they would not otherwise notice (R. Ellis 1997a, 2003; Doughty and Williams 1998a; Williams and Evans 1998).

Empirical studies on the relationship between explicit and implicit knowledge, however, indicate the existence of a complex relationship between the two types of knowledge suggesting that, while explicit rule learning may be advantageous over implicit rule learning, its advantages depend on a number of linguistic and psycholinguistic variables. For example, some studies have found that explicit instruction may be more effective than implicit instruction when learning involves simple rules (for example, DeKeyser 1995; Robinson 1996; de Graaff 1997). Other studies suggest that the relative benefits of explicit instruction may be more related to factors such as the extent of instruction, the kind of task involved, the amount, nature and timing of planning (see articles in R. Ellis 2005c), the learners' differences in their cognitive abilities, their stages of L2 learning, frequency effects (see N. Ellis 2002a, 2002b; R. Ellis 2002a, 2002c), and even L2 learning aptitude (Robinson 2005).

FFI research in language pedagogy

One line of SLA research that has had substantial impact on our under-standing of the role of FFI in promoting language acquisition is classroom-based research. Such research has brought teachers and researchers together and has led to findings that have more direct relevance for teachers and teacher educators than the theory-driven research described above. This research has addressed various issues related to the role of formal instruc-tion including that of student–student or student–teacher interaction, error correction, comprehension and production practices, communicative and instructional activities, and input and output processes, including learner revision, and has led to important findings (for example, Lightbown and Spada 1990; VanPatten 1990; Fotos and Ellis 1991; Fotos 1993, 1994, 1998, 2002; VanPatten and Cadierno 1993; Williams 1995, 2005a; DeKeyser and Sokalski 1996; Lyster and Ranta 1997; Doughty and Varela 1998; Lyster 1998b; Swain 1998, 2000, 2005; White 1998; R. Ellis, Basturkmen, and Loewen 2001a; Swain and Lapkin 2001; Pennington 2003).

With respect to the role of FFI, this research has produced convincing evidence that instruction including some kind of FFI is more effective than instruction that focuses only on meaning. This evidence has been confirmed by the results of a meta-analysis of 49 FFI studies (Norris and Ortega 2000, 2001) from which the researchers concluded that: (1) in general, FFI pro-duces substantial gain of the target structure over the course of the study, (2) the effects of FFI seem to be sustained over time, (3) instruction that contains explicit instructional techniques results in more positive effects than that involving implicit techniques, and (4) the effectiveness of the instructional treatments depends on the methodological approaches adopted, particularly the assessment procedures utilized to measure the effectiveness of FFI.

FFI taxonomies and definitions

The evidence reviewed above relates to the overall effectiveness of FFI. However, current FFI research is concerned with issues that go beyond the question of mere effectiveness. FFI refers to a wide range of activities that differ from one another in important ways and a number of elements must be considered such as: (a) the continuum of implicit versus explicit FFI, with formal, rule-based instruction at one end, and embedding of the target structure in authentic discourse at the other; (b) the timing of FFI during the lesson; (c) the teacher's role and intention; (d) task-based FFI; (e) the existence of input enhancement during communicative lessons designed to draw learner attention to the form; and (f) output-based FFI. Thus, a crucial question for both research and pedagogy concerns the nature of these elements and the effects they have on language learning.

A number of SLA researchers have proposed various FFI taxonomies and classifications (for example, Williams 1995, 2005a; Doughty and Williams 1998b, 1998c; Lightbown 1998; Long and Robinson 1998; Nassaji 1999; Doughty 2001; Nassaji and Fotos 2004). One of the first classifications, which has been widely cited and has had a considerable impact on our understanding of the concept of FFI, is the distinction that Long (1991) made between *focus on form* (FoF) and *focus on forms* (FoFs). FoFs, according to Long (1991, 2000; Long and Robinson 1998), is based on traditional structural and synthetic approaches to language teaching (Wilkins 1976) in which language is segmented into discrete items and is then presented to the learners in an isolated and decontextualized manner. FoF, on the other hand, involves drawing the learner's attention to linguistic forms 'as they arise incidentally in lessons whose overriding focus is on meaning or communication' (Long 1991: 46). Long (2000) believes that FoF instruction is advantageous over FoFs instruction because FoF is learner-centered, is tuned to the learner's internal syllabus, and occurs when needed. However, FoFs does not match learning processes, is not needs-based, and often results in boring lessons.

Since its conception, the idea of FoF has been widely advocated in the SLA literature. However, the construct has been interpreted and used differently by different researchers. For example, while, as we have seen above, Long (1991) and Long and Robinson (1998) conceptualized FoF mainly as *reactive* responses to communication problems, occurring after the event, Doughty and Williams (1998c) have suggested that FoF can also be achieved *proactively*; that is, the teacher can also plan in advance to introduce FoF. Lightbown (1998) notes that FoF can be either integrated into a communicative context or delivered in the form of mini lessons. Within this FFI framework, advanced planning to teach a particular grammar point is considered to match the notion of FoF as long as the focus is 'triggered by an analysis of learner need rather than being imposed externally by a linguistic syllabus' (Doughty and Williams 1998b: 5).

According to Doughty and Williams (1998b), a central feature of FoF is that 'meaning and use must already be evident to the learner at the time that attention is drawn to the linguistic apparatus needed to get the meaning across' (p. 4). Some researchers have reacted to this assumption, arguing that focus of form should not be limited to situations in which form is focused on during communicative activities or only when learners are engaged with meaningful activities (Sheen 2002; Swain 2005). R. Ellis (2001a), for example, argued that, although the reactive/proactive distinction is useful as both constitute occasions where learners are invited to FoF while their primary attention is on meaning, the proactive perspective does not meet the incidental characteristic of FoF as posited in Long's (1991) original definition. Thus, according to R. Ellis, proactive FoF can result in repeated opportunities for attention to a pre-selected language form or *intensive* instruction whereas incidental FoF (see below) results in *extensive* instruction in that a range of linguistic forms including grammatical, lexical, phonological, pragmatic forms may compete for learner attention. This then, 'raises the question as to whether language learning benefits most from focusing on a few problematic linguistic forms intensively or from a scatter-gun approach where multitudinous problematic forms are treated randomly and cursorily and where the treatment may or may not be repeated' (p. 16).

To address some of these problems, R. Ellis has distinguished among three types of FFI: *FoFs, planned FoF*, and *incidental FoF*. Considering FFI as any instructional activity that is used to draw the learner's attention to language forms (see also Spada 1997), R. Ellis has characterized *FoFs* as instruction that involves pre-selected forms presented to the learners either explicitly and implicitly. This can be achieved explicitly through teaching rules or implicitly through exercises allowing the learners to infer the rules (for example, structured input or production practice) (R. Ellis 2001a), thus creating a FFI continuum ranging from structure-based instruction to communicative lessons containing the target form. *Planned FoF* is defined as instruction that involves treatment of pre-selected forms with the difference that the treatment occurs while the learner's primary focus is on processing meaning (for example, communicative input containing the form, textual enhancement, or communicative tasks using the form). *Incidental FoF* differs from planned FoF in that the form is not pre-selected and attention occurs incidentally while the learner's primary focus is on meaning (for example, recasts and negotiation of meaning during communicative interaction).

The incidental FoF construct is very similar to Long's (1991) and Long and Robinson's (1998) notion of FoF. However, it is also different in that R. Ellis' concept of FoF can also involve *explicit attention* to form as well as responses to anticipated 'need,' in addition to communicative 'problems' (Williams 2005a). Thus, in addition to the reactive/proactive distinction, R. Ellis (2001a) has also made a distinction between reactive and *preemptive* FoF. (See also Williams 2001, 2005a.) As mentioned before, reactive FoF involves the teacher's reaction to an actual or perceived problem in the course of communication (for example, Lyster and Ranta 1997; Doughty and Varela 1998; Lyster 1998b; McDonough and Mackey 2000). *Preemptive FoF*, on the other hand, involves taking time out from a communicative activity, either by the teacher or by the student, to respond to a form that is anticipated to be problematic although no actual error has taken place (for example, R. Ellis, Basturkmen, and Loewen 2001a, 2001b). Similarly, Nassaji (1999) has suggested that focus of form can be realized in language classrooms through both *process* and *design*. The former refers to FoF created incidentally when both the teacher and the learners' attention is on processing meaning whereas the latter occurs intentionally through designing communicative grammar tasks in which attention to form becomes an essential component of carrying out the task (for example, Loschky and Bley-Vroman 1993b; Fotos 1993, 1998). Here the learner needs to attend to the target form while attempting to either comprehend (for example, R. Ellis 1995) or produce it (for example, Swain 1998).

Regarding this typology, Williams (2005a) observes that if problematicity (i.e. reaction to an actual or perceived problem or error) is considered to be a criterion for FoF, it may be difficult to regard pre-emptive treatments as FFI (Williams 2005a). She also discusses the concept of obtrusiveness, or whether reactive/preemptive FFI could impact negatively on learner processing of the meaningful activity (2005a: 676). However, Lightbown (1998, 2000) suggests that when the form is significant for comprehension of meaning, a focus on both the form and the meaning is advantageous. Additional research (Ellis, Basturkmen, and Loewen 2001a; Nassaji in press; Lyster and Mori 2006) suggests that learners performing meaning-focused activities can actually benefit by shifting their attention momentarily towards form, and that such a shift can promote interlanguage restructuring.

In terms of calling the learners' attention to target structures, R. Ellis (2003) has particularly recommended *task-based FFI*. Here form-focused tasks may appear to be purely communicative yet the input has been crafted to contain the target form and its use is required to complete the task (Loschky and Bley-Vroman 1993b; Nobuyoshi and Ellis 1993; R. Ellis 1995). Other tasks incorporate the target form more explicitly, such as the grammar consciousness raising task where the learners' task objective is to solve a grammar problem using the target structure or to generate grammar rules (Fotos and Ellis 1991; Sheen 1992; Fotos 1993; Leow 2001a). In addition, planning before or during the task is also seen as important (R. Ellis 2003, 2005c) for noticing and production.

Input enhancement has also been used to develop learner awareness of target forms. Structures have been made physically salient through highlighting, underlining, or other treatments (Fotos 1993, 1994; White 1998;

Williams and Evans 1998; Nassaji in press). A different approach has been to provide learners an input 'flood', which has been defined by Williams and Evans (1998: 141) as 'an artificially increased incidence of the form in focus'. (Also see Trahey 1996.)

In terms of output as FFI, Swain (1985, 1995, 2005) emphasized the importance of production to develop learner awareness of the gap between current TL production ability and the TL. Collaborative output tasks (Swain and Lapkin 1998, 2001; Swain 2001b; Nassaji and Tian 2005) require learners to produce the TL cooperatively and one type in particular, the dictogloss (Wajnryb 1990; Swain and Lapkin 1998, 2001; Swain 2000), has been noted to improve learner accuracy in the use of the target form since learners reconstruct a TL dictation and thereby increase their awareness of the target structure. In a survey of the role of frequency effects in promoting SLA, Nick Ellis suggests that both input and output containing target forms can favorably affect their acquisition (N. Ellis 2002b).

Conclusion

If the goal of L2 classroom activities is to develop both accuracy and fluency, it is clear that meaningful activities must be integrated with form-focused activities, particularly those requiring output. The FFI taxonomies reviewed in this section contribute to our understanding of FFI, its elements, and the various ways in which it can be implemented in L2 classrooms. This framework provides a useful conceptual tool that can guide teachers, teacher educators, and researchers in their selection and investigation of various aspects of FFI in both research and pedagogy (R. Ellis 2001a; Williams 2005a). Although the types differ, they share the common assumption that some kind of attention to form is necessary in L2 classrooms. The following chapters in this volume address many of the key issues in FFI and explore their contributions to teaching and teacher education.

2

The weak interface, consciousness, and form-focused instruction: mind the doors

NICK C. ELLIS

If the doors of perception were cleansed every thing would appear to man as it is, infinite. For man has closed himself up, till he sees all things thru' narrow chinks of his cavern.

(William Blake 1790: plate 14)

THIS CHAPTER examines the theoretical backgrounds of form-focused instruction (FFI) in language education, applied linguistics, psychology, and cognitive science, these disciplines all being concerned with the differences between implicit and explicit knowledge and the ways in which these might interact. It argues that although much of first language (L1) acquisition involves implicit learning, these mechanisms do not suffice for second language acquisition (SLA) because of learnt attention and transfer from the L1. SLA must therefore overcome the processing habits of the L1 by recruiting additional resources of explicit learning. The interface is dynamic: it happens transiently during conscious processing, but the influence upon implicit cognition endures thereafter. The various roles of consciousness in SLA include: learners noticing negative evidence; their attending to language, their perception focused by social scaffolding or explicit instruction; their voluntary use of pedagogical grammatical descriptions and analogical reasoning; their reflective induction of meta-linguistic insights about language; and their consciously guided practice which results, eventually, in unconscious, automatized skill. Consciousness creates access: its contents are broadcast throughout the brain to the vast array of our unconscious sources of knowledge, and by these means, consciousness is the interface (N. Ellis 2005). Current cognitive theories of the role of consciousness in learning (Baars 1997; Baars and Franklin 2003) correspond well with the weak interface theory of second language (L2) instruction proposed by Rod Ellis (R. Ellis 1994b) whereby explicit knowledge plays a role in SLA by facilitating the processes of 'noticing', of 'noticing the gap', and of consciously guided output practice form. (See Chapter 1.)

Implicit and explicit language learning and knowledge

Children acquire their L1 by engaging with their caretakers in natural meaningful communication. From this 'evidence' they automatically acquire complex knowledge of the structure of their language. Yet paradoxically they cannot describe this knowledge, the discovery of which forms the object of the disciplines of theoretical linguistics, psycholinguistics, and child language acquisition. This is a difference between explicit and implicit knowledge—ask a young child how to form a plural and she says she does not know; ask her 'here is a wug, here is another wug, what have you got?' and she is able to reply, 'two wugs'. The acquisition of L1 grammar is implicit and is extracted from experience of usage rather than from explicit rules—simple exposure to normal linguistic input suffices and no explicit instruction is needed. Adult acquisition of an L2 is a different matter in that what can be acquired implicitly from communicative contexts is typically quite limited in comparison to native speaker norms, and adult attainment of L2 accuracy usually requires additional resources of consciousness and explicit learning.

Theoretical dissociations between implicit and explicit knowledge of language evolved relatively independently in language education and applied linguistics and in psychology and cognitive neuroscience.[1] From various divisions of cognitive science and education we know that implicit and explicit learning are distinct processes, that humans have separate implicit and explicit memory systems, that there are different types of knowledge of and about language, that these are stored in different areas of the brain, and that different educational experiences generate different types of knowledge.

The history of the interface in language education and applied linguistics

Differing assumptions about the nature of language representation and its promotion motivated different teaching traditions (Kelly 1969). Traditional grammar translation foreign language (FL) instruction and the cognitive code method popular in the 1960s and 1970s capitalized on the formal operational abilities of older children and adults to think and act in a rule-governed way. This allowed their instruction, through the medium of language, in pedagogical grammar rules, with lessons focusing on language forms such as, for example, particular tenses and inflectional patterns. These explicit methods were motivated by the belief that perception and awareness of L2 rules necessarily precedes their use. In contrast, FL and L2 teaching methods like 'audiolingualism' which held sway during the Second World War, and more recent 'natural' and 'communicative' approaches, maintained that adult language learning is, like L1 acquisition, implicit. Since language skill is very different from knowledge about language, they consequently renounced explicit grammar-based instruction. The defining distinction between implicit acquisition and explicit learning of L2 was that of Krashen (1982). He argued that adult L2 students of grammar-translation methods, who can tell more about a language than a native speaker, yet whose technical knowledge of grammar leaves them totally in the lurch in conversation, testify that conscious learning about language and subconscious acquisition of language are different things, and that any notion of a 'strong interface' between the two must be rejected. Krashen's Input Hypothesis, an extreme 'non-interface' position, thus countered that (1) subconscious acquisition dominates in L2 performance; (2) learning cannot be converted into acquisition; and (3) conscious learning can be used only as a monitor, i.e. an editor to correct output after it has been initiated by the acquired system. In Krashen's theory, SLA, just like L1 acquisition, comes naturally as a result of implicit processes occurring while the learner is receiving comprehensible L2 input. The Input Hypothesis was the theoretical motivation behind natural and communicative approaches to instruction.

These foundations suggest that language learning can take place implicitly, explicitly, or, because we can communicate using language, it can be influenced by declarative statements of pedagogical rules (explicit instruction). There are at least some mutual influences in their development too. Consider, for example, that from implicit to explicit knowledge: although in native language acquisition implicit learning is primary, the development of self-awareness allows reflective examination, analysis, and re-organization of the products of implicit learning, resulting in redescription at a higher level and the formation of new independent and explicit representations. Thus an older child can make a good stab at explaining how to form a plural in English because they have realized the relevant metalinguistic insight of 'add -s' from observing themselves forming plurals in this way (Bialystok 1982). But what about the other direction? The central issue of the 'interface question' is just how much do explicit learning and explicit instruction influence implicit learning, and how can their symbiosis be optimized? Subsequent research took up this theme.

Empirical analyses of learners in 'grammar-free' communicative, natural, or immersion L2 and FL programmes demonstrated significant shortcomings in the accuracy of their language (Lightbown et al. 1993). Critical theoretical reactions to Krashen's Input Hypothesis (for example, McLaughlin 1987), together with demonstrations that it is those language forms which are attended that are subsequently learnt, prompted Schmidt (1990) to propose that conscious cognitive effort involving the subjective experience of noticing is a necessary and sufficient condition for the conversion of input to intake in SLA. Schmidt's Noticing Hypothesis was the theoretical motivation for subsequent research efforts, both in laboratory experiments (Hulstijn and DeKeyser 1997) and in the classroom (Doughty and Williams 1998a), into the role of consciousness in SLA. Together, the shortcomings in uptake, the consequently limited endstate of naturalistic learners, and the demonstrable role of noticing in SLA, obliged in turn the rejection of the extreme 'no interface' position.

Applied linguistics was thus left with something in-between, some form of a weak interface position (Long 1991; R. Ellis 1994b) whereby explicit knowledge plays various roles (1) in the perception of, and selective attending to, L2 form by facilitating the processes of 'noticing' (i.e. paying attention to specific linguistic features of the input), (2) by 'noticing the gap' (i.e. comparing the noticed features with those the learner typically produces in output), and (3) in output, with explicit knowledge coaching practice, particularly in initial stages, with this controlled use of declarative knowledge guiding the proceduralization and eventual automatization of language processing, as it does in the acquisition of other cognitive skills.

As this volume attests, the weak interface position motivated renewed interest in explicit instruction, but the pendulum didn't swing back all the way to the decontextualized and often meaningless grammar drills of traditional grammar translation instruction, which Long (1991) termed 'focus on forms'. Instead, instruction was to be integrated into the meaningful communication afforded by more naturalistic approaches: learner errors should be picked up by a conversation partner and corrected in the course of meaningful, often task-based, communication by means of negative evidence which offers some type of explicit focus on linguistic form (R. Ellis 1990, 1994a, 2000, 2001a, 2002a; Doughty and Williams 1998a). The period from 1980–2000 was a time of concerted research to assess the effectiveness of different types of explicit and implicit L2 instruction. Reviews of these investigations (Lightbown et al. 1993; Long 1983; N. Ellis and Laporte 1997; Hulstijn and DeKeyser 1997; Spada 1997; Doughty and Williams 1998a), particularly the comprehensive meta-analysis of Norris and Ortega (2000) that summarized the findings from 49 unique sample studies of experimental and quasi-experimental investigations into the effectiveness of L2 instruction, demonstrate that focused L2 instruction results in large target-oriented gains, that explicit types of instruction are more effective than implicit types, and that the effectiveness of L2 instruction is durable.

Implicit and explicit knowledge and their interface in psychological research

These developments ran in parallel to research in psychology demonstrating the dissociations of implicit and explicit memory, and of implicit and explicit learning (N. Ellis 1994). The separation between explicit and implicit memory was evidenced in anterograde amnesic patients who, as a result of brain damage, lost the ability to consolidate new explicit memories (those where recall involves a conscious process of remembering a prior episodic experience) to update their autobiographical record with their daily activities, to learn new concepts, or to learn to recognize new people or places. Nevertheless, amnesiacs maintained implicit memories (those evidenced by the facilitation of the processing of a stimulus as a function of a recent encounter with an identical or related stimulus but where the person at no point has to consciously recall the prior event) and were able to learn new perceptual skills (such as mirror reading) and new motor skills (Schachter 1987; Squire and Kandel 1999). They also showed normal classic conditioning—hence the famous anecdote of the amnesic patient who, having once been pricked by a pin hidden in the hand of her consultant, refused thereafter to shake him by his hand while at the same time denying ever having met him before.

The dissociation between explicit and implicit learning was made by Reber (1976) who had people learn complex letter strings (for example, MXRMXT, VMTRRR) generated by an artificial grammar. In the course of studying these for later recognition, they unconsciously abstracted knowledge of the underlying regularities, so to be able to later distinguish between novel strings which either accorded or broke the rules of the underlying grammar. However, like young children who can pass 'wug tests' in their native language, these adult participants too were unable to explain their reasoning. Such research illustrated quite different styles of learning, varying in the degree to which acquisition is driven by conscious beliefs, as well as in the extent to which they give rise to explicit verbalizable knowledge: implicit learning is acquisition of knowledge about the underlying structure of a complex stimulus environment by a process which takes place naturally, simply, and without conscious operations. Explicit learning is a more conscious operation where the individual attends to particular aspects of the stimulus array and volunteers and tests hypotheses in a search for structure.

In brain science, neuropsychological investigations of the results of brain damage demonstrated that different areas of the brain are specialized in their function and that there are clear separations between areas involved in explicit learning and memory and those involved in implicit learning and memory (A. Ellis and Young 1988). Explicit learning is supported by neural systems in the prefrontal cortex involved in attention, the conscious apperception of stimuli, and working memory; the consolidation of explicit memories involves neural systems in the hippocampus and related limbic structures. In contrast, implicit learning and memory are localized, among other places, in various areas of perceptual and motor cortex.

In psychology, subsequent research in implicit and explicit learning of artificial languages, finite-state systems, and complex control systems showed: (1) When the material to be learnt is simple, or where it is relatively complex but there is only a limited number of variables and the critical features are salient, then learners gain from being told to adopt an explicit mode of learning where hypotheses are to be explicitly generated and tested and the model of the system updated accordingly. As a result they are also able to verbalize this knowledge and transfer to novel situations. (2) When the material to be learnt is more randomly structured with a large number of variables and when the important relationships are not obvious, then explicit instructions only interfere and an implicit mode of learning is more effective. This learning is instance-based but, with sufficient exemplars, an implicit understanding of the structure will be achieved. Although this knowledge may not be explicitly available, the learner may none the less be able to transfer to conceptually or perceptually similar tasks and to provide default cases on generalization ('wug') tasks. (3) Whatever the domain, learning the patterns, regularities, or underlying concepts of a complex problem space or stimulus environment with explicit instruction, direction, and advanced clues, heuristics, or organizers is always better than learning without any cues at all (Reber *et al.* 1980; MacWhinney 1997a). (4) Although Reber had emphasized that the results of implicit learning were abstract, unconscious, and rule-like representations, subsequent research showed that there was a very large contribution of concrete memorized knowledge of chunks and sequences of perceptual input and motor output that unconscious processes tally and identify to be frequent across the exemplars experienced in the learning set (Stadler and Frensch 1998).

On the broader stage of cognitive science, the period from 1980–2000 showed a parallel shift away from an almost exclusively symbolic view of human cognition to one which emphasized the overwhelming importance of implicit inductive processes in the statistical reasoning which sums prior experience and results in our generalizations of this knowledge as schema, prototypes, and conceptual categories. Everything is connected, resonating to a lesser or greater degree, in the spreading activation of the cognitive unconscious, and categories emerge as attractor states in the conspiracy of related exemplars in implicit memory. These are the aspects of cognition that are readily simulated in connectionist models (Rumelhart and McClelland 1986; Elman *et al.* 1996) and which subsequently have had considerable influence upon our understanding of implicit knowledge of language and its acquisition (Christiansen and Chater 2001).

In cognitive neuroscience technological advances in functional brain imaging using electro-encephalographic (EEG) and functional Magnetic Resonance Imaging (fMRI) triangulated the findings of earlier cognitive neuropsychological studies of brain areas involved in implicit and explicit memory. Subsequent improvements in the temporal and spatial resolution of these techniques afforded much more detailed descriptions of the dynamics of brain activity, promoting a shift of emphasis from knowledge as static representation stored in particular locations to knowledge as processing involving the dynamic mutual influence of inter-related types of information as they activate and inhibit each other over time (Eichenbaum 2002; Frackowiak *et al.* 2004)—as Charles Sherrington had put it 60 years previously, 'an enchanted loom, where millions of flashing shuttles weave a dissolving pattern, always a meaningful pattern though never an abiding one; a shifting harmony of subpatterns' (Sherrington 1941: 225).

Thus, in the latter part of the twentieth century, research in these various disciplines converged on the conclusion that explicit and implicit knowledge of language are distinct and dissociated—they involve different types of representation, they are substantiated in separate parts of the brain, and yet they can come into mutual influence in processing.

Implicit and explicit knowledge and their interface in SLA

What is the nature of the implicit knowledge which allows fluency in phonology, reading, spelling, lexis, morphosyntax, formulaic language, language comprehension, grammaticality, sentence production, syntax, and pragmatics? How are these representations formed? How are their strengths updated so to statistically represent the nature of language, and how do linguistic prototypes and rule-like processing emerge from usage? These difficult and complex issues are certainly not resolved and they remain the focus of the disciplines of linguistics, psycholinguistics, and child language acquisition. Nevertheless, there has been a growing consensus over the last 20 or 30 years that the vast majority of our linguistic processing is unconscious, its operations tuned by the products of our implicit learning which has supplied a distributional analysis of the linguistic problem space, that is, a statistical sampling of language over our entire history of prior usage. Frequency of usage determines availability of representation and tallies the likelihoods of occurrence of constructions and the relative probabilities of their mappings between aspects of form and their relevant interpretations. Generalizations arise from conspiracies of memorized utterances collaborating in productive schematic linguistic constructions (Rumelhart and McClelland 1986; Bybee and Hopper 2001; Christiansen and Chater 2001; N. Ellis 2002a; Bod *et al.* 2003). Implicit learning collates the evidence of language, and the results of this tallying provide an optimal solution to the problem space of form-function mappings and their contextualized use, with representational systems modularizing over thousands of hours on task (N. Ellis 2002a).

But if these implicit learning processes are sufficient for L1 acquisition, why not for second? One part of the answer must be transfer. Transfer phenomena pervade SLA (Weinreich 1953; Lado 1957; C. James 1980; Odlin 1989; MacWhinney 1997b). Our neural apparatus is highly plastic in its initial state. It is not entirely an empty slate, since there are broad genetic constraints upon the usual networks of system-level connections and upon the broad timetable of maturation and myelination, but nevertheless the cortex of the brain is broadly equipotent in terms of the types of information it can represent (Elman *et al.* 1996; Kandel *et al.* 2000). In contrast to the newborn infant, the L2 learner's neocortex has already been tuned to the L1, incremental learning has slowly committed it to a particular configuration, and it has reached a point of entrenchment where the L2 is perceived through mechanisms optimized for the L1. Thus L1 implicit representations conspire in a 'learnt attention' to language and in the automatized processing of L2 in non-optimal ways. In this view, the limitations of SLA result from psychodynamic tensions in the unconscious mind of the L2 speaker— not the psychodynamics of Freudian psychology, but those of a more psycholinguistic kind. It is basic principles of associative and connectionist learning which yield the limited endstate, whereby features in the L2 input, however available as a result of frequency, recency, or context, fall short of intake because their processing is shaped by the L1. Further details of these constituent processes of contingency, cue competition, salience, interference, overshadowing, blocking, and perceptual learning can be found in N. Ellis (2006a, b).

Gathering these strands together, we can conclude:

1 Implicit and explicit learning are distinct processes.
2 Implicit and explicit memory are distinguished in their content, their form, and their brain localizations.
3 There are different types of knowledge of and about language, stored in different areas of the brain, and engendered by different types of educational experience.
4 A large part of acquisition involves the implicit learning of language from usage.
5 L1 transfer, learnt attention, and automatization all contribute to the more limited achievements of exclusive implicit learning in SLA than in L1 acquisition.
6 Pedagogical responses to these shortcomings involve explicit instruction, recruiting consciousness to overcome the implicit routines that are non-optimal for L2.
7 Evaluation research in language education demonstrates that such FoF instruction can be effective.

What then are the detailed mechanisms of interface? How do the explanations of weak interface as proposed over a decade ago (Long 1991; R. Ellis 1994b) stand up in the light of subsequent research? What are the various psychological and neurobiological processes by which explicit knowledge of form-meaning associations impacts upon implicit language learning? In the remainder of this chapter, I will bring to bear current research in cognitive neuroscience as it relates to this question. I believe that this research broadly supports the weak interface position and that additionally it provides an important emphasis for our understanding of language learning and instruction, namely that we must concentrate on dynamic processes (Larsen-Freeman and N. Ellis 2006a, b) rather than on static conceptualizations of language, representation and physical interface. The interface, like consciousness, is dynamic, situated, and contextualized: it happens transiently during conscious processing, but the influence upon implicit cognition endures thereafter (N. Ellis 2005).

Consciousness provides the weak interface

Learning is a dynamic process; it takes place during processing, as Hebb (1949), Craik and Lockhart (1972), Pienemann (1998), and O'Grady (2003) have all reminded us from their neural, cognitive, and linguistic aspects on learning. In fluency in our native language, both language processing and language tallying (N. Ellis 2002a) are typically unconscious; our implicit systems automatically process the input, allowing our conscious selves to concentrate on the meaning rather than the form. Implicit, habitual processes are highly adaptive in predictable situations. But the more novelty we encounter, the more the involvement of consciousness is needed for successful learning and problem-solving (Baars 1997). As with other implicit modules, when automatic capabilities fail, there follows a call recruiting additional collaborative conscious support (Baars and Franklin 2003): We only think about walking when we stumble, about driving when a child runs into the road, and about language when communication breaks down. In unpredictable conditions, the capacity of consciousness to organize existing knowledge in new ways is indispensable. 'The particulars of the distribution of consciousness, so far as we know them, point to them being efficacious ... ' (W. James 1890/1983 Vol. 1: 141–2).

The psychological processes of interface are exactly that—they are dynamic processes, synchronous with consciousness (N. Ellis 2005). The last 10 years have seen significant advances in our scientific study of consciousness and its roles in learning and memory[2] (Baars et al. 2003). There have been three major strands of development: (1) cognitive neuroscientific investigation of the neural correlates of consciousness (NCC) (see Koch 2004 for review); (2) cognitive analysis of consciousness (particularly Global Workspace Theory: Baars 1988, 1997); and (3) computational modelling of the events underlying the emergence of self-amplifying resonances across a global network of neuronal coalitions, the dynamic competition among the massively parallel constituency of the unconscious mind that elects (Koch 2004: 24, 173) the current oneness of the fleeting stream of conscious experience (Dehaene et al. 2003; Dehaene and Changeux 2004). These developments inform three issues relating to the Weak Interface: the neurobiology of implicit tallying, NCC, and the role of consciousness in learning.

The neurobiology of implicit tallying

For the first time, it is now possible, using fMRI and ERP techniques, to image the implicit processing of words which, despite being presented below the threshold for conscious noticing, nevertheless result in subsequent implicit memory effects. The implicit statistical tallying that underlies subsequent priming effects can be seen to take place in various local regions of primary and secondary sensory and motor cortex (Dehaene and Changeux 2004; Dehaene et al. 2004).

The NCC

The NCC is a huge, difficult, and fascinating question, and it is generating a correspondingly massive collaborative research effort. A lot more will have been discovered in another 10 years. But what is already known is potent enough in its implications for the interface: implicit learning occurs largely within modality and involves the priming or chunking of representations or routines within a module; it is the means of tuning our *zombie agents*, the menagerie of specialized sensori-motor processors, such as those identified in Dehaene's research, that carry out routine operations in the absence of direct conscious sensation or control (Koch 2004: Chapter 12). In contrast, conscious processing is spread wide over the brain and unifies otherwise disparate areas in a synchronized focus of activity. Conscious activity affords much more scope for focused long-range association and influence than does implicit learning. It brings about a whole new level of potential associations.

Consciousness and learning: the collaborative mind

Compared to the vast number of unconscious neural processes happening in any given moment, conscious capacity evidences a very narrow bottleneck. But the narrow limits of consciousness have a compensating advantage: consciousness seems to act as a gateway, creating access to essentially any part of the nervous system. Consciousness creates global access (Baars 1997).

Baars (1988, 1997) introduced 'Global Workspace Theory' by describing the likenesses between our cognitive architecture and a working theatre. The entire stage of the theatre corresponds to working memory, the immediate memory system in which we talk to ourselves, visualize places and people, and plan actions. In the working theatre, focal consciousness acts as a 'bright spot' on the stage. Conscious events hang around, monopolizing time 'in the limelight'. The bright spot is further surrounded by a 'fringe' (Mangan 1993) or 'penumbra' (W. James 1890; Koch 2004: Chapter 14) of associated, vaguely conscious events. Information from the bright spot is globally distributed to the vast audience of all of the unconscious modules we use to adapt to the world. A theatre combines very limited events taking place on stage with a vast audience, just as consciousness involves limited information that creates access to a vast number of unconscious sources of knowledge. Consciousness is the publicity organ of the brain. It is a facility for accessing, disseminating, and exchanging information and for exercising global coordination and control: consciousness is the interface. 'Paying attention—becoming conscious of some material—seems to be the sovereign remedy for learning anything, applicable to many very different kinds of information. It is the universal solvent of the mind' (Baars 1997, Section 5: 304).

Note that in this view, consciousness is not the director, neither is it the author of the play. The contents of consciousness are hugely constrained by top-down processes. But the stream of consciousness is the reflection of thoughts, not the thoughts themselves. Consciousness has no more access to the implicit workings of the prefrontal cortex and other regions involved in the evaluation of different courses of action, decision making, and planning than it does to the implicit workings of the lower perceptual levels of primary perceptual cortex. The theatre in Global Workspace Theory is all of our unconscious modules; there is no one place in the brain to which the unconscious modules send their results for ultimate conscious appreciation by the audience, as in a Cartesian theatre (Dennett 2001). In Freud's (1966) terms, the id and the super-ego are both unconscious. In Koch's (2004: Chapter 18), the homunculus is nonconscious. In Jackendoff's (1987), consciousness is an intermediate level: Thinking—the manipulation of sensory data, concepts, and more abstract patterns—is largely unconscious; what is conscious about thoughts are images, tones, silent speech, and other feelings associated with intermediate-level sensory representations. And at any one time, our state of mind reflects complex dynamic interactions of implicit and explicit knowledge:

> In the human brain information (as a marginally coupled, phase-locked state) is created and destroyed in the metastable regime of the coordination dynamics, where tendencies for apartness and togetherness, individual and collective, segregation and integration, phase synchrony and phase scattering coexist. New information is created because the system operates in a special regime where the slightest nudge will put it into a new coordinated state. In this way, the (essentially nonlinear) coordination dynamics creates new, informationally meaningful coordination states that can be stabilized over time. The stability of information over time is guaranteed by the coupling between component parts and processes and constitutes a dynamic kind of (nonhereditary) memory.
>
> (Scott Kelso 2002: 369)

Global Workspace Theory and parallel research into NCC illuminates the mechanisms by which the brain interfaces functionally and anatomically independent implicit and explicit memory systems involved variously in

motoric, auditory, emotive, or visual processing and in declarative, analogue, perceptual, or procedural memories, despite their different modes of
processing, which bear upon representations and entities of very different
natures. Biological adaptations tend to be accretive (Gould 1982). The
speech system, for example, is overlaid on a set of organs that in earlier
mammals supports breathing, eating, and simple vocalization. Language is
overlaid upon systems for the visual representation of the world. Yet, however different the symbolic representations of language and the analogue
representations of vision are, they interact so that through language, we
create mental images in our listeners that might normally be produced only
by the memory of events as recorded and integrated by the sensory and
perceptual systems of the brain (Jerison 1976). Likewise, it may be that the
global broadcasting property of the consciousness system is overlaid on
earlier functions that are primarily sensori-motor. In his major review
culminating a lifetime's pioneering work in human neuropsychology, Luria
(1973), having separately analysed the workings of the three principal functional units of the brain (the unit for regulating tone or waking, the unit for
obtaining, processing, and storing information, and the unit for program-
ming, regulating, and verifying mental activity), emphasized that it would
be a mistake to imagine that each of these units carry out their activity
independently:

> Each form of conscious activity is always a *complex functional*
> *system* and takes place through the *combined working of all three brain*
> *units*, each of which makes its own contribution ... *all three principal*
> *functional brain units work concertedly*, and it is only by studying
> their interactions when each unit makes its own specific
> contribution, that an insight can be obtained into the
> nature of the cerebral mechanisms of mental activity.

(Luria 1973: 99–101, italics in original)

Some component processes of the weak interface

This, then, is the broad framework: language representation in the brain
involves specialized localized modules, largely implicit in their operation,
collaborating via long-range associations in dynamic coalitions of cell
assemblies representing—among others—the phonological forms of words
and constructions and their sensory and motor groundings (Barsalou 1999;
Pulvermüller 1999, 2003). L1 uses tunes and automatizes them to perform in
particular ways, resulting in our highly specialized L1 processing modules.

To break out of these routines, to consolidate the new connections, networks and routines necessary for L2 processing, consciousness is necessary.

The weak interface theory of L2 instruction proposed that explicit processing plays a role in SLA by means of 'noticing', 'noticing the gap', and guided output practice. The remainder of this chapter outlines relevant research on each in turn.

Noticing

The primary conscious involvement in SLA is the explicit learning involved in the initial registration of pattern recognizers for constructions that are then tuned and integrated into the system by implicit learning during subsequent input processing. Neural systems in the prefrontal cortex involved in working memory provide attentional selection, perceptual integration, and the unification of consciousness. Neural systems in the hippocampus then bind these disparate cortical representations into unitary episodic representations. ERP and fMRI imaging confirm these NCC, a surge of widespread activity in a coalition of forebrain and parietal areas interconnected via widespread cortico-cortico and cortico-thalamic feedback loops with sets of neurons in sensory and motor regions that code for particular features, and the subsequent hippocampal activity involved in the consolidation of novel explicit memories. These are the mechanisms by which Schmidt's noticing helps solve Quine's problem of referential indeterminacy (N. Ellis 2005).

This means is most relevant where the language form is of low salience and where L1 experience has tuned the learner's attention elsewhere: 'since many features of L2 input are likely to be infrequent, non-salient, and communicatively redundant, intentionally focused attention may be a practical (though not a theoretical) necessity for successful language learning' (Schmidt 2001: 23). Instruction is thus targeted at increasing the salience of commonly ignored features by firstly pointing them out and explaining their structure, and secondly by providing meaningful input that contains many instances of the same grammatical meaning-form relationship (Terrell 1991). Once consolidated into the construction, it is this new cue to interpretation of the input whose strengths are incremented on each subsequent processing episode. The cue does not have to be repeatedly noticed thereafter; once consolidated, mere use in processing for meaning is enough for implicit tallying. A natural corollary is that if explicit knowledge is to be effective, it must be provided before relevant input that exemplifies it (Reber *et al.* 1980) if it is to affect the processing of the cue in question and become sufficiently associated with its relevant interpretation to become entrenched enough to influence implicit processing thereafter (as with the 'RuleandInstances' learners of N. Ellis 1993).

A meta-analysis of Norris and Ortega (2000) of 25 explicit form-focused treatments from a wide variety of studies with interventions including consciousness raising, input processing, compound FoF, metalinguistic task essentialness, and rule-oriented FoF, demonstrated an average effect size of these various treatments in excess of 1.2. More generally still, the same meta-analysis demonstrated average effect sizes in excess of 1.0 for 69 different explicit instructional treatments, whether they involved FoF or more traditional FoFs. It is true that explicit instruction evidences greater effect on outcome measures that are themselves more explicit and metalinguistic in content (Norris and Ortega 2000), but FFI results in a medium-sized effect on free constructed production measures too (Norris and Ortega 2000), with further studies reviewed by R. Ellis (2002a) confirming this route of influence of explicit knowledge on implicit learning. We need more studies to look at the effects of explicit instruction using outcome measures that particularly focus on different aspects of implicit knowledge and processing (Doughty 2004), but the weight of the evidence to date is in favour of significant interface by the means of attention being focused upon relevant form-meaning connections in the limelight of conscious processing.

Noticing the gap

A learner's flawed output can prompt negative feedback in the form of a 'corrective recast', that is, a reformulation of their immediately preceding erroneous utterance, replacing non-target-like (lexical, grammatical, etc.) items by the corresponding target-language forms. Recasts arguably present the learner with psycholinguistic data that is optimized for acquisition because they make the gap apparent—in the contrast between their own erroneous utterance and the recast they highlight the relevant element of form at the same time as the desired meaning-to-be-expressed is still active, and the language learner can engage in focused input analysis (Doughty 2001). Long (2006a) reviews over 40 descriptive, quasi-experimental, and experimental studies of the occurrence, usability, and use of recasts in classrooms, laboratory settings, and non-instructional conversation, showing that these techniques are generally effective in the promotion of uptake. There is some debate, however, concerning the degree to which attention should be focused upon the meaning or the message in the negotiations of recasting. Long holds that the focus of both interlocutors should always be on meaning so that any learning of form is implicit, whereas the review of Nicholas, Lightbown, and Spada (2001) raised questions as to the potential non-salience and/or ambiguity of recasts, concluding that recasts appear to be most effective in contexts where it is clear to the learner that the recast is a reaction to the accuracy of the form, not the content, of the original utterance. This is particularly so where the error is committed on a low salience form where the learner is unlikely to notice the variance between their production and the appropriate element in the form of the recast. More research is needed into the generality of the claim that, the less salient the gap, the more learners have to be made aware of it. As Long (2006: 41) concludes: 'Knowing which classes of problematic TL features can be addressed successfully via implicit negative feedback, and which, if any, require more explicit treatment would be both theoretically important, as it could help explain how recasts work, and pedagogically useful'.

Output practice

Explicit memories can guide the conscious building of novel linguistic utterances through processes of analogy. Formulas, slot-and-frame patterns, drills, and declarative pedagogical grammar rules can all contribute to the conscious creation of utterances whose subsequent usage promotes implicit learning and proceduralization. Thus, by various means, the learner can use explicit knowledge to consciously construct an utterance in working memory. 'Practice makes perfect' applies here as it does with other skills. Anderson's (1983, 1992, 1996) ACT model described the move from declarative to procedural knowledge as three broad stages: a cognitive stage, where a declarative description of the procedure is learnt; an associative stage, where the learner works on productions for performing the process; and an autonomous stage, where execution of the skill becomes rapid and automatic. McLaughlin (1987) described processes of L2 automatization, from the novice's slow and halting production by means of attentive control of construction in working memory to fluent automatic processing with the relevant programs and routines being executed swiftly and without reflection. Segalowitz and Segalowitz (1993), and DeKeyser (2001) provide more recent reviews of automatization and the ways that this conscious processing can result in the training of unconscious, automatic, zombie sensorimotor agents for L2 processing (Koch 2004: Chapter 14).

The balance of experimental findings supports the effectiveness for SLA of encouraging learners to produce output. Norris and Ortega (2000) summarized the results of six studies from before 1999 that involved explicit FoFs followed by output practice and that demonstrated a substantial average effect size of 1.39. DeKeyser *et al.* (2002) pulled together the results of five more recent studies, all of which substantiated that output-based treatments promoted learners to significant improvement on uses of the Spanish subjunctive, acquisition of Spanish copulas, interpretation and production of the Italian future tense, and acquisition of the French causative. Keck, Iberri-Shea, Tracy, and Wa-Mbaleka (2006) reported a quantitative meta-analysis of studies of the effects of interaction upon acquisition. Eight of the unique sample studies in this meta-analysis involved *pushed output*, where participants were required to attempt production of target features, often because they played the role of information-holders in jigsaw, information-gap, or narrative tasks. The effects of these treatments were compared with six other interaction studies that did not provide opportunities for pushed output. Tasks involving opportunities for pushed output ($d = 1.05$) produced larger effect sizes than tasks without pushed output ($d = 0.61$) on immediate post-tests. A lot more research is needed to get at the individual components, but taken together, these studies provide good reason to consider an interface of explicit knowledge upon implicit learning during output too.

Conclusion

Much of the problem of SLA stems from transfer, from the automatized habits of the L1 being inappropriately applied to the L2. The first step of FFI is, in the words of the London Underground, to 'mind the gap' and to realize this. The second step is for the learner to FoF again. In their songs of experience, the doors of perception can never be so clean as they were in their songs of innocence, but, through appropriately guided consciousness, the L2 learner can be usefully minded of language again, thus to allow an interface of explicit upon implicit knowledge.

Notes

1 In 1991, as I came to the issue of implicit and explicit SLA from a background in psycholinguistics, I searched out applied linguists who were of a more psychological and empirical persuasion. They were few enough that I resolved to try to visit them on an upcoming sabbatical, and to recruit them into an edited book on this topic (N. Ellis 1994). I was happy that Rod responded so quickly and positively and that I was able to visit him at Temple University in Japan in 1992. The few months I spent

there were an important part of my education in applied linguistics. I am grateful to Rod both for his enduring scholarship and his friendship.

2 The Association for the Scientific Study of Consciousness was established in 1996 and held its inaugural conference in 1997.

3

Conceptual knowledge and instructed second language learning: a sociocultural perspective

JAMES P. LANTOLF

ROD ELLIS (2005b: 214) points out that 'the value in teaching explicit knowledge of grammar has been and remains today one of the most controversial issues in language pedagogy'. The history of the controversy is effectively surveyed by the editors in the introduction to the present volume and there is no need to repeat it here. Suffice it to say that the debate, as R. Ellis's comment suggests, centers on how much attention, how frequent and what kind of attention must be given to the formal features of language in order for high levels of proficiency to be attained. DeKeyser and Sokalski (2001) for instance note that research points to the positive impact of some type of explicit learning on improved performance. They caution, however, along with R. Ellis (2004b), that there continues to be controversy over the specifics of just what optimal instruction should entail. For instance, is incidental FoF, as proposed by the interaction hypothesis, sufficient or must instructional programs provide extensive and explicit focus on the formal properties of language for successful learning to take place? (See Chapter 1 for a discussion of FoF.)

Although Norris and Ortega's (2000) meta-analysis revealed that both explicit form-focused and forms-focused instruction proved to be more effective than implicit instruction, the authors raise two important caveats that mitigate the force of these findings.[1] First, in many of the studies, the assessment instruments were biased toward more explicit types of instruction. Second, rule-based explicit instruction in either form-focused or forms-focused instruction did not result in strong learning effects. My focus of interest in this chapter is on the second caveat.

Among the problems associated with explicit rule-based instruction mentioned by Norris and Ortega is a lack of consistency across studies on rule presentation. In some, rules were provided paradigmatically 'with various forms and functions of a linguistic subsystem presented together' (Norris and Ortega 2000: 484), while in others the rules were presented in stages 'with aspects of a structure explained in small steps accompanied by intervening practice or exposure activities' (ibid.). Moreover, even though in the majority of studies rule-based explanations were presented prior to engaging learners in other instructional activities, in a few instances, explanations were available to learners during the instructional treatment.

DeKeyser (1998: 57) also expresses concerns about the type of explicit instruction learners received in studies which show little or no effect of formal instruction on so-called developmental sequences. He points out, for instance, that in none of the studies surveyed in his research was much attention given to techniques that promote the proceduralization of explicit knowledge (for example, use of appropriate communicative activities).

Although the design inconsistencies uncovered in Norris and Ortega's meta-analysis and the problems associated with proceduralization pointed out by DeKeyser's are not to be ignored, I believe there is another matter, no less important, that has been given short shrift in much of the research addressing the topic of explicit and implicit instruction—the quality of the explicit formal knowledge offered to learners. More often than not, formal linguistic knowledge is presented, particularly at the early stages of instruction, in a piecemeal, rule-of-thumb format rather than as coherent and theoretically informed conceptual knowledge. Rules of thumb are not necessarily wrong, but they generally describe concrete empirical occurrences of the relevant phenomenon in a fairly unsystematic fashion and, as a result, fail to reveal deeper systematic principles.

Rules of thumb in previous research

Textbooks produced for instruction in Romance languages generally adopt a reductive rule-of-thumb approach to explaining how verbal aspect functions in these languages. They typically discuss perfective and imperfective aspect in separate units and offer students a list of rules that supposedly characterize where each aspect is supposed to be used.

The following is a typical example of a rules-of-thumb explanation of Spanish aspect: the imperfect 'tells what was happening, recalls what used to happen, describes a physical, mental emotion, tells time in the past, describes the background and sets the stage upon which another action occurred', while the preterit 'records, reports and narrates' and in the case of certain verbs 'causes a change of meaning', which is relative to English and not a component of the concept of aspect (Whitley 1986).[2]

In an extensive study on teaching aspect to French immersion learners, Harley (1989: 340) provided teachers with a description of French aspect that was perhaps more extensive than that attributed by Whitley to Spanish textbooks, but was nevertheless a list of when perfective and imperfective forms are normally used, including in narrative genre, a feature missing in Whitley's example. Harley used the rules to explain aspect to the teachers whose classes participated in the study in order to assist them in implementing the activities designed to promote implicit discovery of the rules by their students.

As it turned out, some of the teachers reported that their students were unable to use empirical evidence to figure out how to use aspect and at least one of the teachers opted to explicitly explain the rule to her students. The results of Harley's study showed that the students who received some form of instruction, either discovery, inductive learning, or explicit instruction, out-performed students who had not received any form of instruction on the first two of the three performance measures used (i.e. cloze tests, oral interviews, compositions); however, the effect disappeared after three months.

In another study, which R. Ellis (2006) cites as evidence of learner ability to acquire explicit knowledge of complex grammatical rules, Macrory and Stone (2000) investigated the knowledge that classroom learners had of how to form and use the past tense in French. The researchers asked the students to describe how to form and when to use the present perfect. With regard to its formation, most students correctly indicated that the tense was formed with the past participle of the main verb accompanied by the auxiliary verb *avoir* 'to have' or *être* 'to be', although some confused *avoir* with *aller*, 'to go'. In a gap-filling task, the students were able to correctly form the required forms; however, in their spontaneous performance they frequently omitted the auxiliary verb, relying on the participle to convey the intended meaning. When they did use the auxiliary, they appeared to do so on the basis of verbal person rather than on the transitivity or intransitivity of the lexical verb.

More to the point for the present discussion, however, Macrory and Stone (2000: 74) note the mismatch between the students' spontaneous use of the perfective and their explicitly expressed knowledge. According to the authors, all of the students explicitly stated that they would use the perfective to talk about actions in the past—'what you did, what you've done, what you did last week/yesterday, and so on' (p. 66). This information is vague and in my view cannot be taken as strong evidence that the students had developed sophisticated explicit knowledge of how to use the perfective in French. It reflects the traditional rules-of-thumb approach to grammar instruction, where for example the form is ostensibly triggered by temporal adverbs, such as 'last week' or 'yesterday'.

Quality of explicit knowledge

Clearly, there is more than one source of imprecision that R. Ellis (2004a: 237) attributes to learners' explicit knowledge; however, a primary source of imprecision, in my view, is the lack of systematicity and completeness of the explicit information captured in rules-of-thumb. My argument, to be developed throughout the remainder of the chapter, is that for explicit knowledge to be maximally effective in promoting language development it must be systematically organized in accordance with the findings of linguistic theory and related research. (See for example, Bull 1971.) This type of highly structured knowledge, or what Vygotsky (1986) refers to as 'scientific concepts', should be the primary focus of classroom instruction. Because of their abstract and coherent properties, control of scientific concepts leads to the ability to freely and voluntarily use the object of study, in the case at hand, language, in a much wider array of circumstances than is permitted by spontaneous concepts, which are often invisible and closely connected to specific contexts (Vygotsky 1986: 148). While scientific concepts are a specific type of high quality explicit knowledge, spontaneous concepts closely parallel implicit knowledge acquired through a slow process of empirically based discovery learning.

My claim is not that scientific knowledge in itself is sufficient for successful learning. Learners must also engage in appropriate communicative activities, along with verbalization processes to be explained below, in order to proceduralize this knowledge. The basis of the argument to follow is found in Vygotsky's fundamental notion that the human mind is mediated by cultural artifacts, in particular those that are made or should be made available to students in the educational setting. I will first discuss the principle of mediation and the important distinction Vygotsky makes between spontaneous knowledge, on the one hand, and scientific knowledge, on the other. In so doing, I will also consider how these two concepts relate to implicit and explicit knowledge, the terms at the core of the form-focused debate in the L2 literature. Finally, I will briefly present some data from a study by Negueruela (2003), where Vygotsky's principle of instruction grounded in scientific concepts was implemented in an intermediate university L2 Spanish course.

Mediation and conceptual knowledge

The core of Vygotsky's theorizing is his proposal that uniquely human forms of mental processing (intentional memory and attention, rational thinking, planning and learning, and development) are mediated by cultural artifacts (for example, signs, symbols, numbers, arts, music, etc.) and culturally organized activities (for example, play, education, leisure, labor, etc.). These artifacts and activities, which do not operate in isolation from each other but interdependently in what Luria (1982) called 'functional systems', do not merely trigger or influence human development, but are the very *source* of this development (Vygotsky 1986). It is through the internalization of cultural affordances (see Van Lier 2004 for a fuller discussion), which occurs during participation in interpersonal activities that humans gain control (i.e. achieve self-regulation) over the psychological functions provided by their biological endowment, or what Vygotsky often called 'natural mind' (Yaroshevsky 1989: 230). Thus, unlike in the case of animals, the relationship between humans and their world is indirect because it is mediated by what culture creates and organizes and makes available to us for living, communicating, and thinking as humans.

According to Karpov and Haywood (1998), Vygotsky distinguished two types of mediation: meta-cognition, or self-regulation, and cognition, or mediation organized according to cultural concepts. Self-regulation is inwardly directed private or inner speech that is derived from social speech. The difference between social and self-regulatory speech resides in the nature of the interlocutors. In the former, interaction occurs between 'I' and 'You', while in the latter it takes place between 'I', who decides what to attend to and talk about, and 'Me' who interprets, critiques and evaluates 'I's' decisions (Vocate 1994: 12). We thus achieve self-regulation as a consequence of regulating others and of being ourselves regulated by others.

Cognitive mediation

Cognitive mediation is domain dependent and characterized by the quality of its content (Karpov and Haywood 1998: 29). Vygotsky (1986) distinguished two types of cognitive mediation—spontaneous and scientific knowledge. The former is comprised of concepts that are internalized in the activity of becoming a participant in one's community. Spontaneous concepts are formed during concrete practical experience and largely on the basis of 'an immediate observable property of an object' (Kozulin 1995: 123). They are empirically based and require lengthy periods of practical experience to develop. They are, however, at the heart of our lived experience as human beings and are, for the most part, more than adequate for carrying out our daily activities.

When asked to verbalize spontaneous knowledge, people usually produce accounts that are unsystematic, incomplete, and often erroneous. As a simple example, consider the fact that early in life, children frequently categorize whales as fish, solely on the basis of their immediately observable properties; for example, that they appear to have fins and swim in water. Later, especially when they enter school, they learn that whales belong to the same species, mammals, as do humans, and that this is so because they suckle their young. Children's understanding of a kinship term such as 'uncle' is also something that arises spontaneously and unconsciously, and it, along with other kinship terms, is something they have a hard time systematically explaining, other than through examples.

Vygotsky also recognized another type of concept that arises in daily life and this, following Piaget, to some degree, he called a non-spontaneous concept. Non-spontaneous concepts are intentionally taught and consciously acquired and include such activities as baking cakes, driving cars (I will return to this example a bit later), or serving an apprenticeship in butchery, carpentry, or becoming a stone mason. One does not need a deep understanding of chemistry to bake a cake, or of the physics of motion to drive a car, or of animal biology to become a butcher. Non-spontaneous concepts, in my view, are similar to rules-of-thumb typical of language classrooms. In both cases, the individual follows a set of behaviors on what to do under certain circumstances (for example, use the preterit in Spanish if a sentence contains an adverb such as 'yesterday', 'last week', etc.), and both are grounded in directly observable empirical evidence. Empirical knowledge, as Karpov (2003: 69 – 71) points out, 'may work if the common salient characteristics of objects or events reflect their significant, essential characteristics' but it runs into problems on several counts, such as when the observable common features of a set of objects are not the essential features of the entire class of objects under consideration.

Scientific concepts

Scientific concepts 'represent the generalizations of the experience of humankind that is fixed in science, understood in the broadest sense of the term to include both natural and social science as well as the humanities' (Karpov 2003: 66). These concepts, arise as a consequence of *theoretical learning*, which is domain specific and is 'aimed at selecting the essential characteristics of objects or events of a certain class and presenting these characteristics in the form of symbolic and graphic models' (Karpov 2003: 71). As already mentioned, the developmental value of theoretical knowledge is that it liberates learners from the constraints of their everyday experiences and allows them to function appropriately in any concrete circumstance in which they may find themselves. This is because theoretical knowledge empowers individuals to 'reproduce the essence of an object [physical or symbolic] in the mental plane' (Kozulin 1995: 124).

Consider the difference between the everyday understanding of circle as a property of objects that share a common feature of roundness—a wheel, a pancake, a bracelet—and the scientific concept of a circle as 'a figure that appears as the result of a movement of a line with one free and one fixed end' (Kozulin 1995: 124). The scientific definition, according to Kozulin, encompasses all possible circles and 'requires no previous knowledge of round objects to understand' (ibid.). Interestingly, as Kozulin points out (ibid.), teachers often introduce the concept of circle to their students through empirical observation by showing them examples of round objects, much in the way spontaneous learning happens in the everyday world.

Just as learners encounter difficulties in reaching appropriate generalizations on the basis of empirical concepts, Vygotsky characterized the converse problem associated with theoretical concepts as 'verbalism'; that is, because theoretical definitions are excessively abstract and 'detached from reality' (Vygotsky 1986: 148–9), memorizing them per se did not result in significant development. He argued, therefore, that the definition of a concept only marked the beginning and not the end of development (Vygotsky 1986: 159); but he did not offer any concrete pedagogical proposals in this regard other than to emphasize the importance of 'systematic cooperation' between teachers and their students in promoting the development of scientific concepts (Vygotsky 1986: 148).[3] Two of Vygotsky's students, Gal'perin and Davydov, however, did establish pedagogical programs designed to proceduralize scientific concepts. I will limit myself to consideration of Gal'perin's approach here.

Summary

To summarize the discussion so far, cultural mediation is the source of higher forms of human mental processes. Mediation is both a matter of process (i.e. self-regulation) and content (i.e. spontaneous and non-spontaneous everyday knowledge and scientific, theoretically informed knowledge). The primary responsibility of educational activity is to promote development through the appropriation of scientific concepts. From this perspective, teaching a language in the school setting in a way that attempts to privilege how learning occurs in the everyday world (either through spontaneous or non-spontaneous processes) is problematic. Schools are in general removed from the everyday world of empirical learning and as such have as their principal charge the development of theoretical understanding of the world. This is not to say that empirical learning does not occur in school; but, as Karpov argues, among other things, this type of learning is difficult to organize, it is slow and even though guided by a teacher, it can still result in inappropriate generalizations (2003: 75). For Vygotsky it makes little sense to expect students to 'rediscover' those scientific concepts 'already discovered by humankind' (Karpov 2006: 66). As Bruner (1966: 101) cogently remarked, 'culture ... is not discovered: it is passed on or forgotten' (cited in Karpov 2003: 75).

In the next section I will compare spontaneous and scientific know-ledge with implicit and explicit knowledge in order to bring to the fore similarities and important differences between these constructions.

Spontaneous/scientific vs. implicit/explicit knowledge and learning

Hulstijn (2005) points out that there exists greater consensus among L2 researchers on the definitions of implicit and explicit knowledge than on the definitions of implicit and explicit learning. R. Ellis (1994b: 85) defines implicit linguistic knowledge as intuitive knowledge 'in the sense that the learner is unlikely to be aware of having ever learnt it and is probably unaware of its existence'. Thus, it appears similar, if not identical to the linguistic knowledge that native speakers develop as they acquire their language during normal everyday communicative activity. Explicit linguistic knowledge, on the other hand, is 'knowledge that is analysed (in the sense that it exists independently of the actual instances of its use), abstract (in the sense that it takes the form of some underlying general-ization of actual linguistic behavior) and explanatory (in that the logical basis of the knowledge is understood independently of its application)'; 'it is available to the learner as an [sic] conscious representation', and it may or may not be couched in metalinguistic jargon (R. Ellis 1994b: 84). Explicit knowledge is often used synonymously with declarative knowledge (Hulstijn 2005: 131),[4] while implicit knowledge is at times equated with procedural knowledge (R. Ellis 2004b: 213). According to Hulstijn, implicit knowledge is automatically accessed while explicit knowledge requires more effort to access (p. 131).

Hulstijn (2005: 131) defines explicit learning as 'input processing with the conscious intention to find out whether the input information contains regularities and, if so, to work out the concepts and rules with which these regularities can be captured', while implicit learning is input processing characterized by the absence of intention and consciousness. Hulstijn also suggests that explicit learning is most effective when the rules to be discov-ered are not too complex or fuzzy (p. 133). R. Ellis (2002b: 19–20) seems to agree with the position, at least indirectly, in pointing out that formal instruction focusing on difficult grammatical features of the new language 'has little effect on performance in spontaneous language use'.

The most controversial of all issues relating to implicit/explicit knowledge and learning is the nature of the relationship between the two. According to R. Ellis (2005b: 144), there are three distinct positions on the nature of the implicit/explicit relationship represented in the SLA research literature: the non-interface position; the strong interface position, and the weak interface position, which in turn has three variants. The non-interface position, most notably represented in the work of Krashen (see Chapter 1), sees no connection between the two types of knowledge, with each controlled by distinct learning mechanisms. While implicit knowledge is responsible for spontaneous performance, explicit knowledge can serve to monitor this performance under the right conditions. The strong interface position contends that explicit knowledge can become implicit with the right kind of practice and without loss of the original explicit knowledge. According to R. Ellis, DeKeyser is a leading proponent of this position.[5] The weak interface position allows for the transformation of implicit into explicit knowledge with various subversions of the hypothesis taking a slightly different stance on the conditions under which the transformation happens. (See also Chapter 2.) Pienemann (1998), for example, claims that the conversion can occur only when learners are developmentally ready to acquire a particular form. N. Ellis (2005: 308), on the other hand, proposes that explicit knowledge can indirectly impact on implicit knowledge by focusing learners' attention on specific features in the input and by drawing their attention to the gap between their knowledge and the input; thus, 'declarative statements of pedagogical grammars along with memorized expressions, drills, and the like, can be pressed into service to construct novel utterances, which in turn 'partake in subsequent implicit learning and proceduralization'. The third version, which seems quite similar to the second, claims that explicit knowledge can be used to produce output that becomes 'auto-input' for implicit learning processes (R. Ellis 2005b: 144).

Making the comparison

Comparing Vygotskyan theory to the three interface positions, which for discussion purposes I will refer to as SLA positions, it appears that implicit knowledge is quite similar to spontaneous knowledge, in the sense that they are both automatically accessed and not easily open to conscious inspection and verbalization. Explicit knowledge, on the other hand, is not the same thing as scientific knowledge. The former may be systematic or not, it may be accurate or not, and it may entail rules or not. The latter, by definition is highly systematic and designed to reveal principles that are not usually observable to direct empirical observation. With regard to the interface matter, sociocultural theory (SCT) necessarily upholds the strong interface position and this is because, as I have stated earlier, all human development is culturally mediated and therefore passes through other individuals; this includes the symbolic artifacts (for example, grammatical rules) constructed by those individuals. Thus, all development, including spontaneous development, finds its source, not in the individual but in others. Education is a special kind of culturally-based development that differs in terms of the quality of its content and the intentional nature of its process; but as with everyday development, its source is the same—other members of the community.

The SLA position privileges the individual learner as an autonomous processor (R. Ellis 1997a: 244) as the source of development with the environment providing some 'resources that help the process move forward' (Lantolf and Thorne 2006: 157). With the individual positioned as the site and source of development it is not too surprising that implicit knowledge is also given privileged status, as something the individual constructs more or less alone. For this reason, education waits for the learner to become developmentally ready to receive instruction. The SCT position privileges cultural artifacts and activities as the source of development and therefore the site of development is the interaction between the learner and other persons who collaboratively engage in culturally organized activities and use culturally constructed artifacts. (See Newman, Griffin, and Cole 1989: 68.) At the outset, the person is socially and psychologically dependent on others and becomes an independent self-regulated individual as a consequence of the interaction. Since a self-regulated individual is not the premise but the result of education (Kozulin 1995: 121), education does not wait for the learner to reach the appropriate developmental level for instruction to be effective, but promotes learner development through instruction. The most effective instruction is that which takes account of the learner's Zone of Proximal Development. (See Aljaafreh and Lantolf 1994; Lantolf and Poehner 2004; Poehner and Lantolf 2005.)

More on proceduralization

DeKeyser (see discussion in Lantolf and Thorne 2006: 300) is 'non-committal' on whether or not proceduralized explicit knowledge becomes implicit or whether it becomes automatized and therefore remains accessible to consciousness. But he points out that the two (i.e. implicit and automatized explicit knowledge) may be functionally equivalent (Lantolf and Thorne 2006: 300).

For SCT there is a clear distinction between spontaneous and scientific knowledge owing to their different genetic histories. To make the point clearer, consider Leontiev's (1981) example of an individual learning how to shift gears when driving a car. Leontiev (1981) argues that the process entails transformation of conscious controlled knowledge into automatized knowledge. Shifting gears is usually first explained verbally and illustrated by someone else (for example, a driving instructor). The learner then carries out the procedure consciously under the other's control. It then comes under the conscious control of the learner. After a time, it becomes automatized as it no longer forms the object of the learner's goal directed activity but is subsumed under the higher-level activity of intentionally driving the car to a specific place. If however the driver unexpectedly encounters problems shifting gears, the behavior quickly jumps back into the driver's awareness as shifting gears again comes under the driver's conscious control. Once the problem is resolved, shifting gears again fades from the driver's consciousness and resumes its automatized status. Clearly, nothing analogous can happen with the spontaneous concept 'uncle', which is also automatically accessed, unless of course someone specifically explains to the child how kinship operates.

The classroom

In this section I will briefly compare the pedagogical implications of the SLA and the SCT positions. To do this, I will use the work of Rod Ellis, a proponent of the weak interface position, on the relationship between implicit and explicit knowledge. R. Ellis (2002a and 2004b) considers a set of principles and procedures for situating formal instruction in the language classroom. He is in favor of instruction in explicit knowledge, but argues that primary focus must be on building implicit knowledge (R. Ellis 2004b: 214), which is best developed through involving learners in communicative activities. Although R. Ellis acknowledges that things are far from settled regarding the strong versus weak interface positions, he does suggest that formal instruction may best promote acquisition (i.e. implicit knowledge) 'when it is linked with opportunities for natural communication' (R. Ellis 2002b: 20). He states that formal instruction may be most successful when its focus is on 'simple grammatical rules' such as English plural (R. Ellis 2002b: 20).[6] He also proposes that explicit grammatical knowledge is best developed through discovery (i.e. empirical) learning because it is assumed to be more motivating and prepares learners to eventually analyse data for themselves (R. Ellis 2002b: 30).

It would seem then that for R. Ellis explicit teaching of complex grammatical knowledge does not lead to the development of implicit knowledge. Such teaching, however, can enhance learner performance on assessment measures that allow 'for controlled, planned, language use' (R. Ellis 2002b: 20). He also recommends holding off teaching grammar to beginning students because the early stages of acquisition are primarily lexically rather than grammatically based (ibid.: 23) and because of the evidence from immersion programs that learners are able to acquire word order and 'salient inflection' without direct instruction (ibid.: 22). Once the foundation is established, grammar instruction can be introduced (ibid.: 31), but it is only effective when it is 'compatible with the natural processes of acquisition' (R. Ellis 2005b: 216). According to Ellis (ibid.), however, while instruction may not allow learners to 'beat' the built-in syllabus, it may still move acquisition forward provided the structure is 'not too far ahead of their developmental stage' (ibid.: 217).

SCT considers the educational setting to be a unique site where development does not mirror development in other settings, including above all spontaneous learning that occurs in everyday activities (Karpov 2003: 69). On the contrary, formal education, if properly organized around scientific concepts, results in a deeper understanding of, and control over, the object of study. These concepts must be taught from the outset of an instructional program, regardless of their complexity, and they must be taught explicitly and in their full form and not reduced to rules-of-thumb, which can mislead learners because, as I have said, they are descriptive lists of when particular features of the language may or may not be used. As such they often impart the impression that linguistic behavior is about following a strict and inflexible set of rules rather than about manipulating the affordances offered by a language in order to construct the meanings desired in concrete goal-directed communicative activity. Moreover, as Negueruela's (2003) study shows (discussed in the next section) once taught, rules-of-thumb become quite difficult for learners to overcome, even when presented with scientific concepts.

Finally, I return briefly to the matter of discovery learning. According to Karpov (2003), it can play a role in concept-based education, but not as a means for discovering a particular rule or principle, since this information is provided to learners by direct instruction, but as a means of discovering how the rule or principle functions and as a means of relating this to concrete practical activity. Vygotsky (1986: 148) captures this process nicely when he comments that in the development of a scientific concept, 'the primary role is played by *initial verbal definition* (italics in original), which being applied systematically, gradually comes down to concrete phenomena'. In terms of language instruction, it supports the argument for learner participation in extensive communicative (spoken and written) activity.

Implementing a concept-based instructional program

In this section I will briefly discuss some of the data reported by Negueruela (2003) following his implementation of a 16-week university course in Spanish as a FL organized around Gal'perin's approach to concept-based instruction known as systemic-theoretical instruction.[7] In the course, which more or less followed a traditional forms-focused syllabus as mandated by the Spanish program, Negueruela integrated a set of concept-based instructional units on aspect, mood, and tense. Space does not allow for a full exposé of the data and findings; instead I would like to focus on the verbalization data because it reveals the development of the learners' understanding of the concept. Negueruela documents improvement in the learners' spoken and written performance and shows how this relates to changes in their understanding, an indication that the concept was becoming proceduralized.

Materializing the concept

Systemic-theoretical instruction, as developed by Gal'perin and his students, implements a set of activities designed to proceduralize the relevant concept. Instruction begins with presentation of the concept in verbal form which is then materialized in a form that can be comprehended and used by learners. This process is referred to by Gal'perin as the 'Schema for the Orienting Basis of Action', or SCOBA, and functions to guide learner performance as they undertake learning activities to internalize the concept. For young children, materialization is best achieved through use of physical objects to represent the abstract concept. Karpova (1977), for example, was able to teach three-year-old Russian children the concept 'word' as well as grammatical categories in their native language by representing the words contained in sentences as different colored plates.[8] For adults, charts and diagrams are more effective means of materializing concepts. The SCOBA given in Figure 3.1 below was used by Negueruela and was based on the writings on aspect of William Bull (1965, 1971) and Dwight and Bolinger (1991).[9]

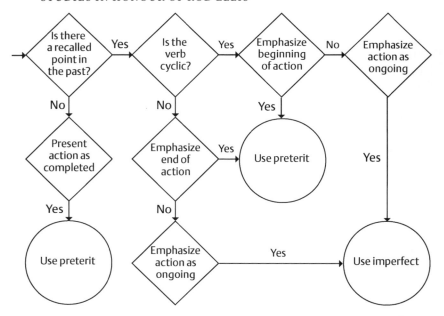

FIGURE 3.1 *SCOBA for Aspect in Spanish (based on Negueruela 2003)*

Verbalizing the concept

Following the presentation of the concepts and its materialization, as given in Figure 3.1, the concept must be verbalized by the learners, not from rote memory, but in their own words. It is here that the conflict between the new concept and the students' previously learned rules-of-thumb arose. In their verbalizations the students attempted to integrate the new conceptual information with their previously learned rules-of-thumb. They came to recognize the presence of a conflict and that their original understanding of the feature was inconsistent and often incoherent.

The student verbalization given in (1) was produced at the outset of the lesson on aspect and, according to Negueruela (2003), reveals a rule-of-thumb instructional history:

1   The idea behind imperfect and preterit is for expressing things in the past, I use preterit when it wants to express something that is finished, or that it has a definitive time. The imperfect is used to describe things that happened with frequency in the past, or general things, the imperfect is used in the past to describe characteristics of people, to tell age of a person, and also to tell time.

(Negueruela 2003: 295)

48

It is not the case that describing personal characteristics must be encoded through imperfective aspect and the preterit certainly can be used when discussing frequently occurring events. Most revealing is the student's assertion that imperfect is used to describe 'general things', a clear reflection of the student's vague and unsystematic understanding of the concept.

Toward the end of the instructional unit, the same student produced the account given in (2) below:

2 the *imperfecto* is used to describe a point in the past that isn't specific. It is also used when describing the background of a story. The *pretérito* is used when you are talking about a recalled point in the past, something specific that happened at a specific time.

(Negueruela 2003: 295)

Clearly, this account is lacking completeness, an important feature of conceptual understanding, but it is, as Negueruela points out, much more precise than the explanation given at time one. Moreover, the learner seems to appreciate that aspect marking depends on the user's perspective as well as on the user's intention and not some arbitrary property of the language.

A second student generated the confusing explanation of aspect use at the beginning of the unit, given in (3):

3 preterit is used when the action is finished. Both modes are in the past. The imperfect describes a habitual action or an action in progress, an example, '*(fuera)visitaba a mi abuela todos los veranos*' (I visit my grandma every summer). Then it is habitual because every summer I visit my grandma. An example with preterit: '*visité a mi abuela este verano*' (I visit my grandma this summer). This describes one time that I visit my grandma.

(Negueruela 2003: 308)

Negueruela argues that the definition and examples do not mesh. The English translations the learner gives of the different examples are also problematic. For one thing they are rendered in the present tense; for another, it puts the onus on the adverbial phases 'every summer' and 'this summer' rather on verbal aspect for marking the meaning difference. As I already mentioned, textbooks often advise students to decide on aspect selection on the basis of adverbial phrases. In fact, neither adverbial precludes use of either aspectual form.

Toward the end of the unit, the same learner produced the account of aspect given in (4):

4 First, the *pretérito* y *imperfecto* is to describe and/or explain
something that has already occurred, something in the past, obviously.
It is then taken a step further by understanding the
difference between an event that has occurred, and something that
may be habitual or describing something that has occurred. To do
this, it's important to look at each verb, decide what type of verb
it is, then use either *pretérito* or *imperfecto*.

(Negueruela 2003: 308)

According to Negueruela, the statement in (4) is more coherent and
systematic than what the learner produced in (3). User agency is emerging
but despite evidence of sensitivity to lexical aspect, she continues to manifest
residual influence of her earlier rule-of-thumb instruction when she
remarks that imperfect is used for 'describing something that has occurred'.

Finally, another student showed considerable development in terms of
her sensitivity to the importance of user intention and perspective in marking verbal aspect from time one to time two. Her initial characterization of
aspect given in (5), according to Negueruela, fails to explain the meaning of
aspect, but instead mentions its uses and as such reflects traditional rules-of-
thumb:

5 [preterit] is used a lot to report a story and to present
completed events that have happened. Imperfect is used for
description and to open a scene. It is like to say in English:
'I was something' when ...

(Negueruela 2003: 310)

At time two, however, the student appears on her way to understanding that
it is the user that determines the meaning to be conveyed through aspect and
she thus recognizes contextual overlap between the two aspectual forms:

6 there is no real time that you cannot use either or ... *pretérito* is
used for definite actions in the past when you are giving emphasis to
the fact that it is over or that it just began. Imperfect is used when
talking about the middle or giving background, it sets the scene
and shows that the action is in progress in the past

(Negueruela 2003: 311)

Proceduralizing the concept

To proceduralize their conceptual knowledge, Negueruela engaged the
students in a series of communicative activities based on interactive

scenarios as called for in Di Pietro's (1987) strategic interaction method. Scenarios are mini-dramas in which learners engage each other over a problem in which each has a different vested interest in its outcome (for example, a student trying to convince a professor to reconsider a course grade because he or she needs to have a high GPA to get into graduate school). The drama element arises from the fact that neither interlocutor (in more complex scenarios several interlocutors can be involved) knows what the other's interest and motivation are and therefore does not know what the conversational partner is likely to say. Learners can then generate derivative scenarios in written form where the problem remains constant but the motives and strategies change. In a sense, they are asked to create their own mini-dramas in writing.

Negueruela asked the students to retrospectively verbalize their reasons for using specific aspectual forms in their spoken and written performances. The purpose of this type of verbalization was to compel the learners to link their use of aspect with the concept as represented in the SCOBA and to make them aware through feedback when they were unable to make the appropriate connections. The example given in (7) illustrates one student's ability to make the appropriate connection to the concept to explain his use of perfective aspect:

7 El seis de junio fui a la escuela a mi dormitorio para comenzar mis clases. [June 6th, I went to school to my dorm to begin my classes]

   I used preterit there because it's referring to a recalled point: 'el seis de junio' and since 'fui' is a non-cyclic verb, it's referring to the beginning of the action.

   (Negueruela 2003: 430)

The same student, however, had problems explaining his performance later in the course and again, his rule-of-thumb instructional history intruded into his account:

8 *Siempre había mucho para comer.* [There was always a lot to eat] Imperfect because it's emphasizing an ongoing action because I am saying '*siempre*', so I use Imperfect cause it's a habitual action.

   (Negueruela 2003: 430)

The learner explains his use of imperfective aspect on the basis of the adverb 'always'; however, perfective aspect could easily have been used with the same adverb. The problem is that the student fails to appreciate that use of aspect is dependent on speaker perspective and not on co-occurring elements in an utterance. Over time, many of the learners were able to provide explanations that reflected the concept materialized in the SCOBA without direct use of the concrete diagram; according to Gal'perin (1967) an indication that the concept is undergoing internalization.

Conclusion

In this chapter I have considered the implications of SCT for L2 instruction. (For a fuller treatment, see Lantolf and Thorne 2006: Chapters 11 and 12.) Development in any activity, whether play, work or education arises from the types of mediation made available by the cultural affordances which engage the person in social activity that leads to the emergence of specifically human psychological processes as the person appropriates the affordances. Thus there exists a fundamental difference between how SLA and SCT perceive the person and the process of development. The former sees the source and site of development as the autonomous learner, while the latter locates the source and site of development in the culture and the interaction between the person and other members of the culture. Because of the difference in how development is theorized, the two approaches are led to make different assumptions about the role of education in language acquisition. While SLA debates the relationship between explicit and implicit knowledge and learning, SCT argues that formal education activity exercises a powerful influence on development. Neither the strong nor the weak SLA position has given sufficient attention to the quality of the explicit knowledge made available through intentional instruction. For SCT, education has the responsibility of grounding instruction in scientific concepts and for developing appropriate means for proceduralizing the concepts to enable learners to deploy the concepts to guide their behavior in concrete goal-directed activities. To date, the lion's share of SCT educational research has focused on instruction in sciences such as physics, biology, and chemistry as well as mathematics, giving much less attention to language instruction. Negueruela's (2003) study, briefly considered in this chapter, is one of only a handful of studies on concept-based L2 instruction. Clearly, SCT researchers need to pay more attention to effects of formal language instruction. The theory makes very clear claims in this regard but without the necessary implementation of its principles in educational practice there is no way of assessing its validity. As Vygotsky insisted, the true test of a theory is the extent to which it can make a difference in improving the practical activity of people.

Notes

1 As powerful as meta-analyses can be in integrating data from diverse studies with relatively small Ns, they must be considered with a bit of caution. For one thing, studies with a flawed research design can contaminate the meta-analysis. Norris and Ortega were cautious in setting up fairly conservative criteria for selecting the studies to be included in their research. It turns out that of the nearly 250 reports of studies that addressed the effect of instruction on learning over an 18-year period (1980–1998), the researchers were forced to eliminate 201 from their analysis either for flawed research design or because the studies did not fully report on their design, or because some of the reports were based on the same single study. Another significant problem facing meta-analysis research is what is called the 'file drawer' problem, which arises because studies reporting positive results are much more likely to be published, especially in the social sciences, than are studies that produce negative results and end up in someone's file drawer (Dallal http://www.tufts.edu/~gdallal/meta.htm).

2 Similarly, for Spanish adjective position, students are usually told that adjectives most often appear in post-nominal position and that there is a small set of modifiers that can be pre-posed. This is in fact not the case as most adjectives that appear in post-position can also appear in pre-position. Moreover, the meaning of the distinction between the two possibilities is normally not mentioned in most textbooks. (See Whitley 1986: 241–2.) *Los caballos blancos de mi amigo* ('my friend's white horses') refers to a subset of horses belonging to my friend, but *los blancos caballos de mi amigo* implies that my friend only has white horses. The difference can at times be expressed in English through restrictive and non-restrictive relative clauses, or through heavy stress on either the noun or adjective.

3 It is interesting that educators that support discovery learning stress the importance of active construction over passive reception of knowledge in the school setting. However, there is a third option, which is supported by Vygotsky's concept-based approach to education—active reception of knowledge whereby scientific concepts are not merely handed over to students but are acquired through the intensive and systematic cooperation between students and their teachers. This is a topic that merits further elaboration in future research.

4 However, according to Ullman (2005: 143) declarative knowledge only partly overlaps with explicit knowledge, since some forms of declarative

LIVERPOOL JOHN MOORES UNIVERSITY
LEARNING SERVICES

memory, in particular semantic memory which, for example, plays a role in lexical knowledge, are not easily made explicit.

5 Based on our reading of R. Ellis (2002b), Lantolf and Thorne (2006) concluded that Ellis ascribed a weak interface position to DeKeyser. If we misinterpreted Ellis, I would like to rectify things here. Having said this, R. Ellis (2005b: 144) clearly implies that in supporting the strong interface hypothesis, DeKeyser accepts that explicit knowledge becomes implicit. As I will discuss shortly, DeKeyser hedges his bets on whether or not implicit knowledge is identical to automatized explicit knowledge.

6 More than 20 years ago, Pica (1985) made a similar claim, arguing that instruction was most effective when it focused on linguistically simple rather than complex forms. Green and Hecht (1992) suggest that it may not be all that easy to determine which features of an L2 are simple, and therefore responsive to explicit instruction and which are complex and therefore less amenable to direct teaching. N. Ellis (1996: 131) cautions 'that explicit instruction can too simply result in students having explicit knowledge that is dissociated from, and which fails to affect, their fluent implicit performance ... what is needed next is to determine the conditions which optimize the interface'.

7 In addition to Negueruela's study, see Carpay (1974), Carpay and van Oers (1999) and Kabanova (1985) for other studies that implemented a systemic-theoretical approach to teaching foreign languages.

8 In this regard, following implementation of an extensive L1 language program based on systemic-theoretical instruction carried out with three thousand students in the Moscow school system, Markova (1979) reports that students were able to use their language in exceptionally creative ways, which often went well beyond grammatical and pragmatic norms.

9 It is interesting to note that in 1972 Bull co-authored a Spanish language textbook entitled *Communicating in Spanish*, which was notable for its inclusion of quite sophisticated explanations of grammatical concepts. The text was also notable for its lack of what today would be considered authentic communicative activities. Recently, cognitive linguists have turned their attention to the analysis of tense and aspect. (See Tyler and Evans 2001.) These may turn out to be more useful accounts than those of Bull and Bolinger and should be strongly considered for future concept-based instruction. In general, cognitive linguistics, because of its central concern with meaning, is a potentially powerful theoretical approach on which to base such instructional programs.

4

Task research and language teaching: reciprocal relationships

PETER SKEHAN

RESEARCH AND PEDAGOGY in language teaching have an uneasy relationship. To a certain extent this is inevitable. Researchers and pedagogues have different goals and these divergent goals create a fertile ground for misunderstanding. Researchers focus in ways that pedagogues find overly limiting and unrealistic. Pedagogues have to assimilate diverse and realistic contexts which frequently leave researchers, especially those of a quantitative persuasion, unable to accept claims of causality with any conviction. Nonetheless the two groups need to communicate and this communication also needs to be reciprocal. Clearly in this regard, the research–pedagogy direction for the relationship is reasonably familiar since research findings may have useful insights for classroom practitioners. But the pedagogy–research direction is no less vital. Pedagogues may reveal the importance of variables which researchers, very likely, either reject as irrelevant or as too difficult to research empirically, or as not central to a current theory which is being evaluated.

Following a consistent theme in Rod Ellis' work, this chapter explores how these two areas can mutually inform one another. Also following his work (R. Ellis 2003), the context for this exploration is task-based instruction, and the ways form can be brought into satisfactory acquisitional and pedagogic focus. In essence, it is argued that the two areas have a great deal to contribute to one another, in the one direction for interesting potential applications and in the other as the source of important research problems and hypotheses. Potential frameworks to enable mutual influence are described in later sections. They respond to a basic proposition: researchers have focused excessively on the immediate situation, but have done so in a controlled way. Pedagogues have necessarily been concerned with more extended learning, but have not sufficiently taken on board findings from the task-based instruction literature. By relating each of these domains to one another both can benefit.

What can be said about tasks

In this section I present a selective review of task research, emphasizing work of my own and that of research associates. The section starts with pre-task effects, then explores tasks themselves, and how they can be used, and concludes with the post-task stage. In principle, the first of these, the pre-task phase, could involve a great many things, as is shown in a later section. Such a range of pre-task activities is commonplace in pedagogy. But research, by its nature, focuses on one or at least a small number of things. And so, rather than investigating the wide range of possible pre-task activities, most research has focused on just one variable: planning. What has happened is that researchers, rather than finishing research on planning and going on to the next thing, have found planning more and more absorbing, and the conventional phrase at the end of research articles has proved extremely apposite: 'This research raises more questions than answers'. As a result, while researchers regard this approach as justified and necessary, practitioners may be impatient at the limited focus in what has been investigated.

Given such a qualification, one can still point to considerable progress. The seminal first article in this planning literature was R. Ellis (1987). R. Ellis reported that planned discourse generated greater accuracy, and that as planning opportunities decreased, emerging rule-based language was most influenced, negatively, while more lexical-based language was less affected. Crookes (1989), in another seminal early article, criticized R. Ellis (1987) for a modality confound, (i.e. comparing performance on written and spoken tasks) and himself used a pre-task planning condition of ten minutes, for only spoken interactive tasks. He then argued that planning is associated with greater language complexity and fluency, but not greater language accuracy. These two articles have shaped the nature of planning research ever since. Crookes defined planning as time available pre-task. R. Ellis, in contrast, was already associating planning with (a) time conditions at performance, and (b) the engagement of organized thought from previous performance. The article by Crookes has stimulated a wide range of planning studies, all of which use pre-task time given to learners to enable them to prepare for a task. The literature has suggested that such time is almost always beneficial, and, following Crookes, the findings have consistently shown this effect to involve complexity and fluency. The findings have been less consistent in the effects they have shown on accuracy. Some have reported such findings (Foster and Skehan 1996; Mehnert 1998) while others have not (Crookes 1989; Ortega 1999).

R. Ellis, in contrast, has taken a different approach to planning. Earlier, it was indicated that the 1987 study conceptualized planning as integrated previous activity and supportive time conditions. It is this second facet which has been the major basis for R. Ellis' research in this area, and he has formalized this through the construct of *on-line* planning. This concerns the second language speaker using time available during performance to regroup and to plan 'on the fly'. Practically, this is defined through the *amount* of time available for performance and the consequent level of time pressure, a variable which has been investigated in a series of studies (Yuan and Ellis 2003; Ellis and Yuan 2004, 2005), and which have broadly supported R. Ellis' prediction of a selective accuracy effect. Ellis and Yuan (2005) relate this to careful speech in unpressured conditions enabling the Formulator (from Levelt's 1989 model) to engage both lexical and syntactic encoding. When on-line planning cannot be drawn on, only lexical retrieval can be relied on. Most importantly R. Ellis' association of pre-task or strategic planning with complexity and fluency, and on-line planning with accuracy goes some way to resolving the disagreement within the literature which, as indicated earlier, associates strategic planning with non-existent or weaker accuracy effects.

We turn next to exploring the influence of tasks themselves. Subsequent to the R. Ellis (1987) and Crookes (1989) studies a wide range of tasks have been used, and many investigators have chosen to compare different task types. The choice now seems to be between genre-linked task types, such as personal, narrative, or decision-making (for example, Foster and Skehan 1996) and approaches which are more fine grained, and explore specific characteristics within tasks, so that particular genres may then be re-analysed as combinations of different task characteristics. Skehan (2001), for example, proposes that specific characteristics such as familiar information, number of transformations, degree of structure in the task, and the dialogic vs. monologic contrast are more salient and meaningful for categorizing tasks than the bundles of features that genres represent. More recently the feature of task structure has shown particular promise. Tasks containing structure seem to consistently favour accuracy and fluency (Skehan and Foster 1999; Tavakoli and Skehan 2005), as learners can exploit a larger macrostructure to channel attention to the formulation stage in speech production (Levelt 1989). In effect, task structure could be interpreted as facilitating on-line planning even when time conditions are quite demanding.

Research has also focused on the time conditions under which a task is done. There are two aspects to this: how long a task takes, and what the effect is of using more pressuring time constraints. Regarding the first, Skehan and Foster (2005) have shown that when learners are given ten minutes to do a task, and one compares the second five minutes of performance to the first five minutes, the level of performance, as measured by accuracy, drops off significantly, suggesting that learners find it difficult to maintain high levels of performance. Interestingly, learners who planned are not protected against this effect. In the first five-minute phase, planners produced superior performance. In the second five-minute phase, their performance deteriorated just as the non-planners performance did. This may be a sobering finding for task research applications—high level attention by learners may not be sustainable for longer than quite short periods. The other researched during-task area is the time-pressure variable, which we discussed above in relation to on-line planning. It only needs to be added here that the findings clearly indicate that research has clarified the functioning of another pedagogic option to promote form-focused instruction. It is clear that the conditions under which a task is done can have a significant effect on the areas of performance which are emphasized. The effect sizes for accuracy reported in Ellis and Yuan (2005), on speaking and writing tasks, were large, strongly supporting the classroom importance of this variable.

We turn next to the post-task stage. Here there has been relatively little research, although what there is is intriguing. Skehan and Foster (1997) demonstrated a selective accuracy effect for a decision-making (but not a narrative) task, with no effects on complexity or fluency when learners were required to engage in a public performance post-task involving repetition of the original task. (The accuracy effect was on the actual task, and so it seemed to be foreknowledge of the activity to come which led to less error in task performance.) In a later unpublished study, they (Skehan and Foster manuscript) replicated this effect, this time with learners required to transcribe some of their own performance. In this case the accuracy effect was with both decision making *and* narrative tasks, suggesting that different post-task conditions vary in strength: transcription seems more powerful than public performance. A different version of a post-task effect has been reported by Bygate (2001) but in his case, the focus is performance on a repetition of the task with this repetition coming not immediately but after a period of some days or weeks. Bygate reports interesting connections between the earlier task and the repeated task. First, even with an interval of several weeks, learners seem to recall a great deal of the actual language and exact wording that they produced on the first occasion. It is interesting that Sachs (1967), in one of the classic studies in psycholinguistics, reports that when listening, exact wording is very quickly forgotten, suggesting a clear contrast here between reception and production. In addition, repeated performances do show changes and these changes seem to reflect a greater syntactization of the same meanings expressed on the original occasion. Learners, that is, 'pack' ideas into more complex syntactic frames. Of course, temporally, here, the condition is one of a post-task. However, it may be more appropriate to view it in terms of planning, since, if the second performance is regarded as a task in its own right, it could be considered to have benefited from a different sort of pre-task activity, akin to planning. This could connect with the R. Ellis (1987) study, in which doing a task in written form was seen as the basis for claiming that subsequent oral performance was planned. In this case the planning seems to have focused particularly clearly on complexity.

Tasks, performance, and development

The review of task research so far has emphasized performance itself, and the differences in the language that learners produce with different tasks done under different conditions. If progress can be made in developing a general metric of difficulty for tasks, one can have greater confidence that the choice of a particular task for a particular group of learners will make appropriate demands on attentional resources. More selectively, and equally interesting, if knowledge is available that certain task characteristics or task conditions are associated with different performance areas, then this information, too, forms the basis for pedagogic decision making and more effective conditions to support form-focused instruction. We can take three examples to illustrate this. The examples are shown in Table 4.1, with desired pedagogic outcomes and the associated task characteristics and conditions that support them. The table shows the different combinations of the three performance areas focused on by task researchers. In each case, one can find a task characteristic, or task conditions, or a combination of

Desired outcome	Appropriate tasks and conditions
Complexity and fluency	Pre-task planning
Complexity and accuracy	Interactive tasks, especially with teacher-led planning
Accuracy and fluency	Structured tasks, possibly with planning Tasks based on familiar information

TABLE 4.1 *Examples of selective performance influences*

these, which produce the result that is desired. Pre-task planning enhances the two performance areas of complexity and fluency, but not reliably, as the literature indicates, language accuracy. In contrast, if one wants to enhance complexity and accuracy (but not fluency), then the best bet seems to be not a planning condition, but instead tasks which provoke effective interaction. Finally, it is interesting that other task characteristics, structured tasks or tasks based on familiar information, seem to support the remaining performance combination—accuracy and fluency. In addition, of course, individual performance areas can also be supported, for example, accuracy through on-line planning, or complexity with tasks that require a number of information transformations or linkages to be made.

Given that performance can be influenced by task characteristics and task conditions, one might well ask why it would be desirable to do this. And there are two answers, one that might be termed the weak form of a task-based approach to pedagogy, and the other, the strong form, and one to be developed later in this chapter. The weak form emphasizes that it is the goal of pedagogy to do more than inculcate language knowledge or competence, and that it is also necessary to ensure that performance is developed. This view would not assume that competence in the case of the second language learner will simply manifest itself, sooner or later, as performance, but that something positive needs to be done to achieve this. Since learners will not all be the same, it may well be that different learners may be better in some areas than others, and that, as a result, it is desirable for teachers to be able to choose more effectively, based on research, how to respond to the learners they have. Hence, if a particular group of learners incline towards fluency, but complexity and accuracy are unimpressive, then the table indicates the tasks and task conditions that are appropriate, i.e. interactive tasks. Similarly, if some learners can produce complex, advanced language, but prefer to do so slowly and in so doing, make errors, then structured tasks, and perhaps planning opportunities would be sensible. In this way, task research can be used to foster balanced language performance.

But the strong form of a task-based approach to pedagogy requires a linkage between tasks and development. In that respect, it has been proposed (Skehan 1998) that there is a desirable sequence of complexity > accuracy > fluency. In other words, complexity involves the use of more advanced and new language. It is assumed that initially this greater complexity would be associated with a greater likelihood of error and also a more halting dysfluent production. However, as the learner becomes more familiar with some new structure, this error-prone and slow performance is likely to give way to a performance which may still be slow, but is less likely to contain mistakes. Finally, when errors have been eliminated, (i.e. and complexity and accuracy have been achieved), then it is possible to automatize performance and achieve some reasonable degree of fluency. In other words, the three major areas that are used to measure performance in task-based research themselves have an acquisitional dynamic, and so the conditions that were earlier described in terms of performance only can also be related to a successful developmental path.

Understanding phases in task use

The previous section has indicated how task research can be applied to situations when the teacher has already decided that a task is going to be used. But the section has been superficial in its integration within general pedagogy. The key to understanding how task research can contribute to more effective form-focused instruction is a broader interpretation of the phases that may be used in task applications. There is a slight discrepancy here between the interpretation of phases by task researchers and the major interpretation offered by someone concerned with pedagogy (Willis 1996). The two approaches are juxtaposed in Table 4.2.

The approaches are interestingly similar and even more interestingly different. The similarities are clearest in that with each, there is an expectation that things can happen before the task and that things can happen afterwards, and that each of these are very important. In other words, simply to give learners tasks to do is not enough—there has to be something more which pushes learners not to simply concern themselves with getting the

	Task researchers	Willis
Pre-task phase	e.g. Planning	e.g. Planning Activation activities
Task phase	Task selection	Task selection
	Time conditions	*Task completion*
	Surprise elements	Task preparation
	Task completion	Task development/ repetition/extension
Post-task phase	Public performance	Analysis and FoF(s)
	Transcription of own performance	Consolidation
	Repetition of task	

TABLE 4.2 *Contrasting interpretations of task phases*

task done. Form or supportive conditions for a language focus need to be introduced somewhere.

Once we get to detail, though, it is the differences which stand out. This starts at the pre-task phase. Task researchers, as noted earlier, have focused on planning, while Willis broadens this phase to include many other things: input-based activities; activation activities; consciousness-raising activities, and also planning. The input-based activities, such as audio or video recordings of native speakers doing some sort of pre-task, could be used to increase the salience of certain ways language is used. (See R. Ellis 2003: Chapter 8 for review.) Alternatively, they could be used to stimulate ideas relevant to the task (in which case they could be considered a form of planning). Activation activities, for example, developing splash diagrams, similarly draw learners into organizing ideas which might then be more satisfying (and personal) to express. Consciousness-raising activities, which might also be input-based, are intended to push learners to notice forms, even if these are currently beyond their interlanguage level. The major point here is that a great many beneficial things can happen pre-task beyond simply opportunity to plan. Pedagogically, these are all very interesting, and serve simultaneously to foreground ideas and enrich the task, but also offer some opportunity for learners to think about relevant form, so that when they do the actual task they are less likely to think about meaning exclusively.

Differences are even more evident during the task phase itself. Researchers have identified tasks they want to explore, and perhaps tweaked the conditions under which the tasks are done. Then, the central *and only* activity here is the actual task and the performance which results. Researchers record this performance, take the recordings away, and code and analyse them. In contrast, Willis' task phase is more complex. The phase *starts* with a task which arises from the pre-task phase. But this, in fact, is far from the whole of the phase. The next thing is that learners engage in some preparation for what is really a second, but linked task which will end the wider task phase. During this period they will gather relevant material and input themselves, and also use the teacher as a resource. (In some ways, this phase of the methodology connects with project work, itself a model of extended task-based instruction.) In other words, the sequence of activities conforms nicely to Schmidt's (1990, 2001) ideas on noticing, except that here it is gaps in output (Swain 1995) that are actually the focus. The effect, though, is the same: the learner, equipped with noticing that hasn't occurred before, is in a better position to mobilize heightened attention directed at the new language. Then, the final phase of the task is that learners engage in a development of the original task. The development is necessary to give the new activity some degree of communicative authenticity. But it also serves to give learners the opportunity to re-use the language which has been made salient, to appreciate the forms of expression they have noticed and perhaps half-learnt, and even to take some ownership of them. In fact, this final within-task phase is quite close to the post-task phase used by task researchers, where typical activities might be task repetition, transcription, and public performance. For research investigations, manipulations such as transcription are intended to lead to different performance qualities during the task itself. For Willis, the second task within the task phase is intended to motivate the deeper work with the language which has been made salient, and then to start a process of consolidation.

So essentially, task researchers separate out Willis' task phase into two phases, one of these being the task, and the other what researchers call the post-task phase. In contrast, Willis includes researchers' post-task phase within the broader task stage and then adds a different set of activities for what is regarded as the post-task phase in her system. These activities are very interesting. The rationale for this phase is that the previous active communicative activity has prepared the ground for learners to reflect upon what they have done, and engage in analysis, reorganization of their language system, and consolidation of the progress they have made. In earlier stages, the emphasis is on doing, and getting the task completed. In Willis' post-task phase, in contrast, it is legitimate to make language itself the focus of activity, and to allow specific forms to come into focus. The major difference from more conventional methodologies is that at this stage the forms that are in focus are the forms *that learners have self-selected in the earlier task*. It is assumed, in other words, that we are very far away from a 'structure of the day' approach, and in contrast, learners are empowered to obtain feedback on the features of language that their personal approaches to doing a task have brought into prominence.

This third stage has no current counterpart in researchers' perspectives on tasks. Task researchers are more performance oriented. Cognitive approaches assume that creating beneficial performance conditions will lead to desirable performance changes, for example, an accuracy orientation, or a complexity orientation (Skehan 1998). Interactionists consider that the feedback moves which occur during well-designed conversations will provide all the support that is necessary for acquisition to proceed (Long and Robinson 1998). In neither case is there provision for explicit, sustained, and systematic concern for language. The Willis third stage, in contrast, does allow for some explicit language focus, and very much against the background that the language focus is with language *which is salient to the learner*. The focus can take many forms, such as review, consolidation, restructuring or integration with other features of language, connection with other more advanced language and general consciousness-raising, or simply greater analysis of what has been noticed because of the communicative demands which have arisen during the task. It is, after all, the teacher's decision here as to how to react to the language which has emerged. It is possible that task demands may have provoked learners to need language which they will find difficult to learn, given their current state of interlanguage development. In such cases, teachers may downplay the emphasis given to such forms during the post-task phase. On the other hand, if the forms which are in salience are also feasible, given learners' current developmental stage, then they will be worth more pedagogic attention. A teacher at this stage might well make decisions about what to emphasize at the post-task stage on the basis of his or her knowledge of developmental sequences.

Also striking here is the difference in assumptions about how difficult it is to make the transition from not knowing something to knowing it. Some task researchers, emphasizing interaction, view well-designed communication as sufficient (as it mostly is in the L1 case), implying that feedback, if given contingently to an error or a breakdown, and if it is attended to, may be incorporated into the learners' developing system. Other task researchers view helpful attentional conditions as sufficient. These imply a rather immediate form of learning, where one is only looking for the appropriate and timely language area-by-feedback juxtaposition or a well-timed FoF. In contrast, the Willis approach portrays development as more hard-won. First, it assumes that change does not take place simply through a judicious encounter, but instead requires sustained attention. The post-task phase provides the arena for this to happen, since there can be a wide range of activities, including even some opportunity to practise. There is certainly opportunity to think around the language area in question and to keep focusing upon it. As a result, the language area, initially apprehended within an exclusively communicative task, can now benefit from sustained attentional focus. But more than that, at this point the area of language, which may be quite specific, can be related to other areas of language. These may be related in a simple way (for example, some different tense forms), or they may be simpler ways of saying the same thing (for example, within the area of modality and probability), or they could even be wider, more complex systems within which the current area fits. In any case, the opportunity is present here for the learner to integrate what is new with material that is already established, to some degree, within interlanguage.

Acquisition and pedagogic tasks

The last section went some way to linking task-based instruction research and pedagogy. But I am still a little detached from general second language acquisition (SLA) processes. In this regard, I have proposed a sequence that is followed when language is being learnt (Skehan 2002). The sequence is shown in Table 4.3, together with the ways in which various aspects of task-based approaches can link with the different stages.

The table suggests that different acquisitional phases are best supported by different features of task-based instruction. The first stage, noticing, requires the learner to realize that there is some feature of the target language that is of interest. In some ways, this represents only limited progress, since, following Schmidt (1990, 2001), with noticing in input, or Swain (1995) with noticing in output, this only means that the learner is now aware of something, and so might direct implicit or explicit attention to this area later. Noticing does not mean development or change. But it is a precursor, and so the different activities which promote it are desirable. In this respect, perhaps the most obvious of these is Willis' suggestion that doing a task, as part of her task phase, will cause learners to realize that they lack formal resources to express some meaning that they wish to express. Their attention to this area is thereby heightened, and if the methodology works well, the next activity, preparation for the repeated/extended task, will address what has been noticed, in however embryonic a form, and even enable the next stage in the table, pattern identification (or even pattern restructuring) to also be embarked upon. But of course, there are other ways of promoting noticing. Pre-task activities, for example, consciousness-raising, or activation of relevant knowledge, or listening to input of, for example, native speakers doing the task, could also, in the context of the upcoming performance, lead to something new being noticed. So might the process of planning, where the learner tries to organize what is to be said, and in so doing, realizes that additional knowledge is required. Focused tasks (R. Ellis 2003) could also function in this way. Similarly, with interactive tasks at the task stage itself, learners might notice features of their interlocutor's speech which they realize may be useful. Their interlocutor, in other words, may be scaffolding them to a new level of performance, just as they may be scaffolding their interlocutor in turn. Finally, noticing can also be promoted at the post-task stage. The earlier task (and any pre-test activities) may well have created a language database, and even if these earlier stages have not led to noticing, it is possible that reflection and analysis at the post-task stage may enable the noticing that was not achieved

Acquisitional phase	task-related activity
Noticing	In Willis' approach, focus on needed forms between initial and repeated tasks within task phase itself Input based pre-task activities Strategic planning, and identification of need for new language Interactive tasks, scaffolded language, and useful recasting from partner Focused tasks Post-task activity (Willis)
Pattern identification	As above
Pattern restructuring	Repeated tasks Post-task phase (Willis)
Repertoire development	Strategic planning and mobilization of resources On-line planning Teacher mediation
Control and accuracy	On-line planning Supportive task characteristics and conditions Post-task phase (task research)
Integration and fluency	Strategic planning Supportive task characteristics and conditions

TABLE 4.3 *An acquisitional sequence, with associated task activities*

earlier. For example, as part of a learner exploring their own transcription they may realize belatedly that alternative methods of expression were possible. It would therefore be their own performance which becomes the vehicle for noticing, but after the task itself, provided that opportunity is given to look back on what has been done.

The above analysis also applies to the phase of pattern identification. The same activities and processes are involved. On this occasion, though, the contribution of the learner is more extensive and needs to be more impressive. It may not simply be the noticing of a particular form or expression, but the noticing of a language pattern or a generalization about the data. Once again this could occur through the activities of a learner in between the task and the repeated task in the Willis system; or through a range of non-planning pre-task activities, or any of the other options as well.

Focused tasks (R. Ellis 2003) could be particularly important here since they provide helpfully structured data to maximize the chances that learners will identify patterns. Also noteworthy in this regard is the post-task phase, because it is here that the teacher can draw attention to patterns in the language which has been used in preceding stages. The valency of this language will be particularly great since it will have been produced by learners themselves. It is also the case that the teacher can build upon individual examples to reveal a wider pattern that lies behind.

The notion of pattern restructuring is a more complex extension of pattern identification. There are times when a pattern has been identified which is only part of a more complex story. For example, in the simple past tense in English, the learner is faced with the problem of learning that a regular and an irregular form co-exist. The learner might make progress on one or both of these, as a pattern, without particularly relating them to one another. Then, a stage may come where the learner realizes the semantic unity of the different forms and reorganizes them into one system. Two particular phases of task work are highlighted here to achieve such restructuring. First, evidence from task repetition studies (for example, Bygate 2001) suggests that learners benefit when they can draw on previous language, and are able to transform it to achieve more advanced levels of syntactic complexity. The other area for restructuring, in a teacher-led context, would seem to be the post-task phase. At this point, when learners have possibly used related features of language and have the opportunity, with other students and with the teacher, to reflect on this fresh data, they may well be able to see deeper patterns and reorganize what have previously been separate language sub-systems (Samuda 2001).

The remaining phases to consider do not have the feature of working on new aspects of language, but rather are concerned with making better use of what has been learnt but may be avoided, or only used haltingly and incorrectly. In other words, if previous stages emphasize complexity, those which remain are closer to accuracy and fluency. The issue of avoidance and repertoire salience has not been extensively treated in SLA research (with Schachter 1974 as an interesting early exception). It requires that learners are able to access appropriate and native-like language when needed, and not resort to simpler forms which express the same meanings less well and in a less native-like manner, probably with some L1 connection. To change the language routinely used in production is a distinct instructional challenge. Here, it is proposed, strategic planning has a considerable role to play, as planning time is used to access material from long-term memory which would otherwise be less likely to be used (Skehan and Foster 2001). This would be consistent with the very regular complexity effects found with strategic planning. But it is likely that on-line planning will also have some importance, as learners exploit time availability to access more advanced material in the same way (Ellis and Yuan 2005). Pressured communication, as R. Ellis (1987) pointed out, may be more lexical and routine: communication when some time for regrouping is available will enable alternative means of expression to be accessed. In addition, Samuda (2001) has shown how judicious teacher intervention can also induce learners to use less readily available forms, showing how more complex expressions of modality can be encouraged, so that they come to replace simpler forms.

A major role for online planning, though, is with the development of control and accuracy. R. Ellis (2005b) has argued that error avoidance is associated with task conditions in which time is less pressured for learners. To put this another way, task conditions which do not provide much opportunity for learners to engage on-line processing processes may have more frequent errors. Similarly, effective task choice can also help learners to avoid errors, as fewer processing demands are put upon them while doing a task. Familiar information tasks, and tasks based on structured information exemplify this. In both cases, on-line planning and supportive task conditions, the key seems to be to provide the Formulator stage (Levelt 1989) with sufficient time in which to operate effectively and enable good processes of lexical *and* syntactic selection.

Finally, we come to a form of control which goes beyond simply avoiding error. It also involves being able to produce speech fluently. Here the existing research suggests a strong role for strategic planning, which has also been consistently associated with these performance areas in a wide range of studies. This is one of the most powerful generalizations to come out of the task literature. It appears that when learners are given time to plan, pre-task, they access material and even possibly chunk this material to enable them to cope with the real-time pressures of the task itself. In addition, supportive task characteristics come into play here as well. Once again, as with accuracy, familiar information and tasks based upon clearly structured information seem conducive to greater fluency. It is interesting that both these characteristics impact upon the Formulator, and so advantage both the performance areas concerned.

Conclusion

What we can conclude from this re-analysis of the findings in the task literature is that one can relate decisions regarding task conditions and task characteristics to different phases of acquisition. As a result, it is possible to argue that while task-based research is a long way from accounting for the whole story, there are findings which fit within a meaningful framework and which can make some contribution to effective instruction. The range of options is already considerable and will undoubtedly grow. So the chapter has argued that task-based research, through its already-established range of findings, has a lot to contribute to such a form-focused language pedagogy. But if anything, the claim has been made equally strongly that pedagogy has a lot to contribute to task research. In particular, the differences in preoccupations of pedagogues and researchers point up how researchers, using cross-sectional research designs, have tended to explore relatively limited timescale tasks. As a result, their view of learning tends to focus on immediacy. In contrast, pedagogues are more likely to assume that learning is complex and occurs over extended time periods. This is even apparent in the respective ways that tasks are used. It is axiomatic for pedagogy that involvement with a particular structure or form will be sustained, since change in the system, as well as the development of control, do not come easily. Much of pedagogy therefore is concerned with this slow process of nurturing what is new. It is clear that task-based instruction research designs will themselves need to respond to such influences, and devise research methods which investigate extended learning.

Part Two
Focus on form and classroom practices

5

The distributed nature of second language learning: Neil's perspective[1]

MERRILL SWAIN and SHARON LAPKIN

ROD ELLIS' writings exemplify the distributed nature of learning. He could not have written what he has without engaging with the minds of many others, and there are many of us who would not understand second language (L2) instruction and learning as we do without having engaged with Rod's writings and his mind. The knowledge constructed has been distributed over time and space, hundreds of minds, and thousands of pages of text, discussions, and lived experiences.

When we designed the study we will discuss in this chapter, one of our questions was whether students working together in pairs on a language-related task would perform better than those working alone. One of the students who worked alone was Neil. In analysing Neil's behavior as he participated in our study, it became clear to us that the question we were asking was too general. A different, more refined set of questions gradually took shape: Where does the learning that we researchers observe in our participants' language use come from? What mediates it? What does focusing on form and meaning look like?

Some theoretical underpinnings

In 1993, Salomon published his now well-known edited book on distributed cognitions. The book deals with concepts that cognitive psychology has theorized as being characteristics of an individual—characteristics such as thinking, cognition, memory, and intelligence—and offers alternative visions of them. Traditionally, these characteristics have been thought of as being situated in the heads of individuals. However, as Salomon (1993: xiii) states, 'People appear *to think in conjunction or partnership* with others and with the help of culturally provided tools and implements'. These other

73

people and artifacts 'not only are sources of stimulation and guidance but are actually *vehicles of thought* ... they become genuine *parts of the learning* that results from the cognitive partnership with them' (italics in original). In other words, our cognitions and memories may be distributed across the individual, artifacts, and people with whom the individual is interacting. In writing this chapter, we are not 'thinking-solo', but rather we are thinking (and remembering) with the help of each other and the myriad of written and visual resources surrounding us. Together our thinking is structured and created through talk. Wertsch, Tulviste, and Hagstrom (1993: 337) referred to cognition as 'extend[ing] beyond the skin', and argued strongly that the appropriate unit of analysis in psychology should not be the individual alone, but rather as an 'individual(s)-operating-with-mediational-means' (p. 342). (See also Wertsch 1985, 1991, 1998.) In a similar vein, Cole (1991) argued that the proper unit of analysis in psychology should be joint socially mediated activity.

One source of the idea that cognition is a distributed activity is Vygotsky's SCT. Vygotsky argued that higher mental functions (for example, cognition, voluntary memory) derive from interaction with social and cultural contexts. The social is primary, the individual is secondary. According to Vygotsky, 'the social dimension of consciousness is primary in time and in fact. The individual dimension of consciousness is derivative and secondary' (1979: 30).

> In order to explain the highly complex forms of human consciousness one must go beyond the human organism. One must seek the origins of conscious activity ... in the processes of social life, in the social and historical forms of human existence.
>
> (Vygotsky 1981: 25, as cited in Wertsch and Tulviste 1992)

In this chapter, we focus on L2 learning as a distributed process. We describe Neil's interactions with the persons and artifacts in his immediate, localized environment. By detailing them, we are able to see how they are 'sources of stimulation and guidance' and that they become, from 'cognitive partnership' with Neil, 'genuine parts of the learning process.' This is both stimulated by, and revealed through, Neil's languaging (Swain 2006).

The study

Participants

In the spring of 2000 we collected data from 12 grade 7 early immersion students, including Neil. The participants were drawn from a single class in a middle school in the greater Toronto area where most students come from middle-income families. Neil's teacher judged his proficiency in French to be 5 on a seven-point scale where 7 indicated a high level of French proficiency.

Neil is an outgoing 13-year-old who was surprisingly upbeat about being taken out of class and put in front of a video camera with three researchers in the same room. His family is Greek, and he speaks Greek and English at home. He wants to learn Spanish and Latin in high school. French has already been useful to him—when he visited his cousins in Quebec and then traveled around Quebec with his parents and sister (a grade 8 French immersion student). Neil thinks French will be useful to him in the future because, as he pointed out, he 'lives in a country where it's very bilingual. There's French, there's English'. And importantly, 'Like if you're watching something on TV and some dude is speaking French and they don't have the close captioning, you don't know what it means unless you know French. So, yeah, it's helpful to know [French]' (interview, turn 213).

Procedures

For each of the task sessions, the students (individually or in pairs) came to a small room in the school where tape- and video-recorders were set up. The data collection unfolded over a period of two school weeks in the stages/sessions shown in Figure 5.1.

The multitask activity began with the writing stage. In this stage, Neil viewed a videotaped mini-lesson about French reflexive verbs. The videotape also included a boy Neil's age modeling a similar writing task. After Neil watched the video, we gave him a set of pictures depicting a story based on a 'tricky alarm clock' (see Swain and Lapkin 1998) in which a sleeping girl is wakened by an alarm clock. When she ignores it and goes back to sleep, a

Week 1			Week 2	
Monday	Wednesday	Friday	Tuesday	Wednesday
Stage 1	Stage 2	Stage 3	Stage 4	Stage 5
Writing (pre-test)	Noticing	Stimulated recall	Post-tests	Interview
30 minutes, in French	10 minutes, in French	40 minutes, in English	15 minutes	15–20 minutes in English

FIGURE 5.1 *Data collection timetable*

mechanical arm comes out of the clock and tickles her foot, so that she is forced to get up and get ready for school. Working from the series of eight pictures, Neil wrote his story. His written story constitutes the pre-test. We then asked a French-speaking graduate student to reformulate Neil's pre-test by maintaining its content, correcting lexical and morphosyntactic errors, and generally writing it the way that a native speaker of French would. Levenston (1978), the first person to propose the notion of reformulation, pointed out that the reformulator needs to take into consideration not only lexical and grammatical correctness, but also conceptual clarity, organization, and stylistics. (See the discussion of this technique in Qi and Lapkin 2001.)

In stage 2 (noticing), Neil compared his story to the reformulated version, and noticed the differences between the two versions. This noticing session was videotaped and played back later as a stimulus in stage 3. During the stimulated recall, Neil talked about the changes he noticed and why he thought they had been made. In stage 4, he rewrote his original story, which served as a post-test. A subsequent interview allowed Neil to reflect on what he learnt and the usefulness of the activities.

Our multitask activity included focus on form (FoF) tasks. The mini-lesson was intended as explicit instruction of a grammatical point—the formation and use of pronominal (primarily reflexive) verbs in French. The series of pictures used to prompt the written story Neil created depicted actions (for example, getting out of bed) that entail the use of reflexive verbs. The reformulation provided implicit feedback, as does an oral recast, to Neil in that it included some vocabulary items and morphosyntactic forms that differed from those he had produced. It was in his verbalization of those differences in the noticing stage that Neil engaged cognitively with the reformulated items. These features of the activity are consistent with what Nassaji (1999) calls (FoF) 'through design', and 'reactive' FoF. Our multi-task activity was designed to focus on pronominal verbs during the meaningful creation of a story. We provided reactive feedback on form through the reformulation. The activity also falls into the category of 'focused communicative tasks' in that the 'production of the target feature is useful, natural, or essential to the performance of the task' (R. Ellis 2001a: 22).

Integral to the activity were multiple opportunities for noticing and focusing on form (for example, explicit instruction in the video). During the noticing and stimulated recall stages, Neil verbalized his identification of language-related 'problems' that were salient or of interest to him and his understandings of how French 'works'.

Findings

Learning

With respect to Neil's L2 learning, the reformulator made 24 changes to Neil's pre-test. In Neil's post-test, 12 responses matched the reformulation exactly, indicating that those were learned. In two other cases Neil used alternatives to the reformulation that were acceptable. Leaving three minor spelling errors aside, this means that Neil got 14 out of 21 responses correct (66 per cent), indicating that considerable L2 learning occurred.

Learning exemplified

In this section we present examples of Neil's pre- and post-test language use, along with the protocols of the noticing and stimulated recall sessions. These examples instantiate his interactions with many of the mediating tools available to him. During the multitask activity, Neil's learning environment included the videotaped mini-lesson on French reflexive verbs, the researchers, the pictures given to him, the story he wrote, the reformulation of his story, the video of the noticing session, and the self. In confronting and solving the language problems that arose during the multitask activity, Neil interacted with these cognitive resources. In some of the examples discussed below, Neil made greater use of particular cognitive affordances than others; however, in all cases, Neil used a variety of these resources to mediate his language learning.

As shown in Table 5.1, in the pre-test, Neil used the verb '*brosser*' ('to brush', as in 'I brush my cat', '*je brosse mon chat*'). French requires the pronominal form of the verb, however, when the action involves body parts. Thus, the reflexive verb '*se brosser*' is obligatory in such contexts as '*je me brosse les cheveux*' ('I comb my hair').

In the noticing session, Neil noticed that the reformulator had changed his version of the verb '*brosser*' to '*se brosser*': '*oh, oui, et c'est "se brosser" …* ' (see turn 12). Here, it is clear that Neil used the reformulation to mediate a cognitive act of comparison. The act of stating '*oh, oui, et c'est se brosser*' out loud focuses his attention on a particular instance of a reflexive verb of personal care.

In turn 76 of the stimulated recall session, when Neil was reflecting on what he had noticed earlier, he verbalized two important points. First, he stated that he had forgotten to apply what he had seen/learnt in the mini-lesson. He referred explicitly to the mini-lesson ('And I was thinking like I just saw this whole lesson on like the *verbe réfléchi* … '), one of the important cognitive resources available to Neil. Secondly, Neil used this occasion to repeat the correct form '*se brosser ... se*'. Furthermore, as Neil stated later in his interview, he got to see himself on the video, which he felt certain 'helped him to remember' the correct form to use in the post-test. As can be seen in the last column of Table 5.1, Neil used the correct form in his post-test.

In Example 1, then, Neil learned and consolidated his linguistic knowledge by interacting with a variety of resources in his environment—the mini-lesson, his own writing along with its reformulation, and the video of the noticing session. He also referenced his own thought processes.

Our second example (Table 5.2) is closely related to the previous example. In the first example, Neil's stimulated recall suggests that he was focusing on the use of the reflexive pronoun *se* in the reflexive verb of personal care '*se brosser*'. In Example 2, Neil placed the emphasis on '*les*' in '*les cheveux*', indicating his change of focus from the verb ('*[se] brosser*') to the article ('*[mes] les*'). (This emphasis is indicated by boldface type in Tables 5.1 and 5.2.) Furthermore, he verbalized the correct '*les cheveux*', contrasting it against what he initially wrote: '*j'ai écrit ses ...* ' (turn 12) ['I wrote *ses*']. The way that reflexive verbs of personal care function in French (Connors and Ouellette 1996) is that the semantic notion of possession (for example, 'her') is carried by the pronoun that precedes the verb ('*se*'); a literal translation of the French '*se brosser les cheveux*' is something like 'to

	Languaging	Translation
Stage 1 *Pre-test*	*... pour **brosser** ses dent et ses cheveux*	... to brush her teeth and her hair
Reformulation	*... pour se brosser les dents et les cheveux*	... to brush her teeth and her hair
Stage 2 *Noticing*	12: *... Okay, um, oh oui, et c'est se brosser ... les dents*	Okay, um, oh yes, and it's to brush ... her teeth
Stage 3 *Stimulated recall*	76: ... And I forgot to write, to put **se brosser**, *se. And I was thinking like I just saw this whole lesson on like the verbe réfléchi and I forgot to put it ...*	
Stage 4 *Post-test*	*... pour **se brosser** les dents et les cheveux*	... to brush her teeth and her hair

TABLE 5.1 *Neil's languaging related to* brosser/se brosser *from pre-test through post-test*

herself brush the hair'. The body part (hair) is marked by the definite article, in this case, '*les*', and not the possessive determiner '*ses*'.

In the stimulated recall session, right after Neil viewed himself pointing out that it should be '*les cheveux*' where he had written '*ses cheveux*', the researcher, in turn 79, asks him to explain why Neil thought '*ses*' had been changed to '*les*'. In response to her question, Neil draws on his own knowledge of the rule, using the metalinguistic term 'possessive', though he cannot quite articulate the rule that in a reflexive verb, the pre-verbal pronoun '*se*' carries the semantic information of 'possession'. Turn 82 indicates that he understands that in a literal sense, '*ses cheveux*' ('her hair') means the same as the alternative '*les cheveux* ('her hair') that is required[2] following a reflexive verb of personal care. Neil states (turn 82): 'Well *SES cheveux* is possessive and um, *LES cheveux* is just like the hair, it's like her hair. But I think they imply the same thing'.

	Languaging	Translation
Stage 1 *Pre-test*	... *pour brosser ses dent et* **ses cheveux**	... to brush her teeth and her hair
Reformulation	... *pour se brosser les dents et les cheveux*	... to brush her teeth and her hair
Stage 2 *Noticing*	12 ... *Et* **les cheveux**, *j'ai écrit ses ...*	... and her [definite article] hair, I wrote her [possessive]
Stage 3 *Stimulated recall*	R. 79: I did have one little question. Where it's changed from **ses cheveux** to **les cheveux** ... Why would that be? N. 80: Yeah. R. 81: Why would that be? N. 82: Well, **ses cheveux** is possessive and um, **les cheveux** is just like the hair, it's like her hair. But I think they, they imply the same thing.	
Stage 4 *Post-test*	... *pour se brosser les dents et* **les cheveux**	... to brush her teeth and her hair

TABLE 5.2 *Neil's languaging related to* ses/les cheveux *from pre-test through post-test*

Neil's post-test response was correct, as shown in the last column of Table 5.2. We attribute this to the fact that knowledge about the aspect of the TL he was concerned with here was distributed across multiple sources of information—the reformulated text, the mini-lesson, the video of the noticing session, the researcher with whom he interacted, and the self.

In the story told by the pictures, a girl hears her alarm clock ring, wakes up, but then goes back to sleep. When Neil wrote the story, he used the phrase 'elle continue à s'endormir', literally 'she continues to fall asleep'. The reformulator changed the verb to 'she goes back to sleep' ('elle se rendort'). In the

	Languaging	Translation
Stage 1 Pre-test	15: ... Elle continue à s'endormir ...	... She continues to fall asleep ...
Reformulation	Elle se rendort.	She goes back to sleep.
Stage 2 Noticing	10: [whispering] continue à s'endormir. [in a normal voice] Elle se rendort et elle continue à s'endormir.	Continues to fall asleep. She goes back to sleep and she continues to fall asleep.
Stage 3 Stimulated recall	R. 40: So what's the difference there? Elle se rendort. N. 41: Well, elle se rendort means she ... goes back to sleep. And I wrote she continues to sleep. R. 42: Um-hum N. 43: But that's not right because she was awake, so it doesn't really make much sense there. Yeah. R. 44: Um-hum. Se rendort make more sense. N. 45: Yeah, se rendort makes a lot more sense.	
Stage 4 Post-test	Elle se rendort.	She goes back to sleep.

TABLE 5.3 *Neil's languaging related to* continue à s'endormir/se rendort *from pre-test through post-test*

noticing session (turn 10), Neil read his structure quietly (an example of private speech: see Ohta 2001), and then read the two verbs (the reformulator's and his own) aloud. As we saw in the first example, the verbalization of the differences mediates the cognitive act of comparison and, along with the interactions in the stimulated recall stage, ensures his learning of the lexical verb '*se rendormir*'.

In the stimulated recall session, the researcher elicited an explanation from Neil. Having shown him the relevant excerpt from the videotaped noticing session, she asked him to explain the difference he noticed. Her initial question and subsequent agreement ('um-hum' in turns 42 and 44) encouraged Neil's reflection on the lexical verb, '*se rendort*'. In interaction with the researcher, Neil verbalized the meaning of the reformulated (and correct) verb (turn 41): 'Well, *elle se rendort* means she goes back to sleep. And I wrote she continues to sleep'. He explains why his original was logically inconsistent: the girl at this point in time was awake, so she could not be continuing to sleep. Thus, the original '*continue à s'endormir*', as he says in turn 43, is 'not right, because she was awake, so it doesn't really make much sense'. This 'talking it through' (see Swain and Lapkin 2002) with the researcher and the self helps Neil come to the realization that his original verb phrase conveyed an inaccurate meaning.

The researcher confirms that Neil's explanation is correct (turn 44) and Neil agrees in turn 45. He gets the item correct in his post-test. Again, his interaction with multiple cognitive resources distributed across his immediate environment are responsible for his use of the correct verb in the post-test.

In the example displayed in Table 5.4, we can infer (after examining all the transcripts) that Neil has searched his memory for the lexical item for 'washroom' ('*la salle de bains*'), failed to locate it, and settled for '*la baignoire*', which means 'bathtub'. In turn 15 of the writing stage, Neil hesitated as he wrote ' ... *et va au bain ... au baignoire*'. In stage 2, Neil noticed the lexical item '*salle de bains*' in the reformulation and realized laughingly that it meant washroom and that the item he used, '*baignoire*', was incorrect.

Prompted by the relevant segment of the noticing video (another cognitive resource), Neil verbalized this in turn 70 of the stimulated recall: 'I was thinking washroom. And all I could think of was ... bathtub'. The researcher asked (turn 71) if that is why he had laughed during the noticing session, and Neil confirmed her interpretation in turn 72: 'Cause I realized I did it wrong when [I compared my story to the reformulation]'. The excerpt from the stimulated recall protocol shows Neil's internal dialogue as he interacts with himself about the vocabulary 'mix-up'. Again, Neil gets the

	Languaging	Translation
Stage 1 *Pre-test*	15: ... *et va au bain* ... *au baignoire* ...	... and goes to the bathtub
Reformulation	... *et va à la salle de bains*	... and goes to the washroom
Stage 2 *Noticing*	12: *Elle va à la salle de bains,* *et pas la baignoire* [laughs]	She goes to the washroom, and not the bathtub.
Stage 3 *Stimulated recall*	70: Yeah, I wrote *baignoire* instead of *salle de bains*. I was thinking washroom. And all I could think of was *baignoire*, so uh bathtub, [laughing], so I just wrote that. R. 71: Is that why you were smiling when you ... ? N. 72: Yeah, I was kind of laughing 'cause I realized I did it wrong when I compared my story to the reformulation ...	
Stage 4 *Post-test*	*Et va au salle de bain* ...	And goes to the washroom [incorrect gender marking]

TABLE 5.4 *Neil's languaging related to* baignoire/salle de bains *from pre-test through post-test*

lexical item right in his post-test, although he assigns the wrong gender ('*salle de bains*' is feminine) and omits the (silent) 's' from the word '*bains*'.

This example highlights the importance of interaction with the self, and perhaps to a lesser extent, the written mediation of the reformulation, the video, and the researcher, in the learning that occurred. It also underscores the role of FoF and the opportunities that negotiation and reformulation provided the learners to help them notice the gap between the TL form and their original output.

In his final interview, Neil claimed that he learned 'a lot about verbs, and how to say bathtub, and other things' (interview, turn 7) from doing our multitask activity because he could recall the specifics of the activity. He said: 'I didn't actually try to remember. But I still remembered. I remembered them from when I was doing the activity' (interview, turn 135). Neil thus locates his learning within a highly specific setting. Neil also stated that he 'learned a lot about [verbs and stuff]' because he 'saw it twice' (interview, turn 79), once as a written reformulation of his own writing, and once during the stimulated recall session 'watching me do it again' (interview, turn 21). He also mentioned how he learned 'about the *verbe réfléchi* thing' from the initial mini-lesson. Thus, from Neil's perspective, his learning was distributed across a variety of resources present in his immediate environment.

Discussion and implications for teaching

We have demonstrated that Neil has learned something because he used language differently the second time that he wrote a story compared to the first time. And importantly, we have related this learning to Neil's interactions with specific aspects of his environment, each of which is mediated by language. In this chapter, our goal was to demonstrate ways in which Neil's L2 learning is distributed across his immediate physical and social setting. To put this another way, we have demonstrated that the cognitive processes that underlie L2 learning are 'situated and distributed' (Salomon 1993: xiv): situated in the particular ongoing activity and distributed across the cognitive resources found in that particular environment.

When Neil was asked to read and compare his own text to the reformulated one, he was pushed to attend to the target forms in his output. The activity created opportunities for 'noticing the gap' and FoF.

In answer to the original question 'Where does the learning that we researchers observe in our participants' language use come from?', we can say that it comes from the Neil/environment interactions. It comes from 'the set of interactions', ' the union of involvements', 'the sum and swarm of participations' (Perkins 1993: 107). Neil, in conjunction with the mini-lesson, the reformulation, and the research assistant, mediated his own learning. Primarily, Neil's learning is mediated by his own languaging. Languaging focused his attention, drew on and constructed new understandings, and consolidated existing knowledge.

In our study we withdrew Neil from his grade 7 immersion classroom on several occasions to participate in our multitask activity. Although we had asked our research assistant not to provide help with the task, she did play a 'teacher-like' role. She set up the activity and the recording equipment, played an instructional video, and structured the time Neil spent while he was engaged in the activity. She provided expert feedback via the reformulated text that was given to Neil in stage 2. This is typical of what teachers regularly do in classrooms.

The role of the teacher, then, is to shape the learning opportunities and provide resources for learning:

> Learning cannot be designed. Ultimately, it belongs to the realm of experience and practice. It follows the negotiation of meaning; it moves on its own terms. It slips through the cracks; it creates its own cracks. Learning happens, design or no design.
>
> And yet there are few more urgent tasks than to design infrastructures that foster learning.
>
> (Wenger 1998: 225)

The learner looks for help in the learning task to all the mediational means at his or her disposal; it is the teacher who must foresee the potential learning needs and structure the learning environment to ensure that learning can also take place without teaching (Wenger 1998: 266). In this chapter, we have seen evidence for Wenger's (1998: 267) assertion that 'Learning is an emergent, ongoing process, which may use teaching as one of its many structuring resources'.

One of the key resources in the multitask activity was the reformulation. It was the trigger for the noticing task and an authoritative model of the TL. We think that reformulation has received too little attention as a source of positive feedback to learners faced with seemingly endless forms to master. When learners compare their own written production to a reformulated version, they notice how their own writing differs from that of the TL speaker. Differences are salient because they are comparing two texts—one of them their own—and verbalizing the comparisons. This encourages them to identify language-related problems and talk them through, often with the self.

Although we exposed Neil to explicit instruction in the mini-lesson on pronominal verbs, it is clear that he attended to other aspects of the TL as well (for example, the lexical item '*salle de bains*'). Mantello (2002), a grade 8 late immersion teacher, reformulated her students' stories written in the past tense. She suggested that attention to multiple features of the TL might be characteristic of stronger students (like Neil), and found that with weaker students, focusing their attention on only one feature (in her case, the compound past tense in French) was productive.

Teachers may need to adapt the structure of some activities if they are to be done during class time (Lapkin 2003). For example, if teachers wanted to adapt our activity, students could work in small groups to construct a jointly written text—ideally, perhaps, a text linked to an aspect of the school syllabus. The teacher would then reformulate the groups' texts, and the following day, the groups would reconvene to compare their text with the reformulated version. This noticing activity would resemble what Neil did, and since it is impossible to incorporate stimulated recalls for multiple groups in one classroom, the students could then talk through the language problems that they identified in the noticing activity in their groups. Each group might then present the teacher with one or two salient language problems they had encountered, and the collected language problems (from all the groups) might inform one or more 'language lessons' in whole-class time.

In Canadian immersion classrooms, like most classrooms, there are dictionaries, wall charts, books of many sorts, writing samples displayed on bulletin boards, computers, and so on. What may be missing are the opportunities to interact with all these artifacts by verbalizing understandings that arise from such interactions. We placed Neil in a situation where it was 'natural' to do this. Past research in immersion classrooms (Allen, Swain, Harley, and Cummins 1990) suggests that opportunities for sustained languaging are few. Neil's learning of TL lexical items and forms is convincing evidence of the benefits of languaging (Swain 2006) as a mediational tool that brings together internal and external cognitive resources.

Appendix

Neil's pre-test

(his original piece of writing)

Le soleil monte, c'est le petit matin, Jeanette dort. C'est 6:00 le matin et il ne veut pas reveillé. Son alarme sonne et elle se reveille au mauvais côté du lit. Elle continue à s'endormir, ca lui fiche que l'alarme sonne, elle pèse une bouton avec son pied. Après une minute, elle est encore en lit. Elle va être en retard. Une main méchanicale sort de son horlage et la reveille en passant un plume le long de ses pieds. Jeanette sort de sa lit et va au baignoire pour brosser ses dent et ses cheveux. Elle se regarde dans le mirroir. Elle quitte la maison pour aller à l'école et elle voit Daniel qui marche à l'autre côté de la rue.

Reformulation

Le soleil se lève, c'est le petit matin, Jeanette dort. Il est 6 :00 du matin et elle ne veut pas se réveiller. Son réveil sonne et elle se réveille du mauvais côté du lit. Elle se rendort. Elle s'en fiche que le réveil sonne, elle appuie sur un bouton avec le pied. Une minute plus tard, elle est encore au lit. Elle va être en retard. Une main mécanique sort de son réveil et la réveille en passant une plume le long de ses pieds. Jeanette sort de son lit et va à la salle de bains pour se brosser les dents et les cheveux. Elle se regarde dans le miroir. Elle quitte la maison pour aller à l'école et elle voit Daniel qui marche de l'autre côté de la rue.

Notes

1 This research was made possible through a grant (#410–99–0269) from the Social Sciences and Humanities Research Council of Canada to Merrill Swain and Sharon Lapkin, for which we are grateful. Additionally we would like to thank members of our research team—Carole Bracco, Lindsay Brooks, and Agustina Tocalli-Beller—who helped in the collection, transcribing, and coding of data; and the principal, teachers, and students of the school where we gathered the data.

2 In some varieties of Canadian French, the use of possessive '*ses*' is permitted (R. Mougeon, personal communication, February 2005).

6

Recontextualizing focus on form

ROB BATSTONE

RECENT RESEARCH from a number of scholars working in second language acquisition (SLA) has suggested that focus on form (FoF) might be at its most effective when its pedagogic purpose is clear to the learner, and where it arises out of a prior 'negotiation of form' (NoF). The argument for NoF is intuitively plausible, and the data used to back it up suggest that there is a case to be made. But the kind of theorizing which underpins it still lacks explanatory power. The chapter begins with a discussion of the issue of explanatory power in SLA theorizing and with the suggestion that a discourse perspective is needed in order to help explain how an FoF may (or may not) arise in the first instance. Data from a study of FoF in the context of a private language school in Auckland, New Zealand (Ellis, Basturkmen, and Loewen 2001a) are re-examined in order to argue that negotiations of form are contingent upon how learners are primed to interpret the surrounding discourse, both in terms of the ways in which negotiations of form are 'framed', and in terms of the wider discourse context and the expectations generated therein. The chapter concludes with the suggestion that FoF is essentially a sociocognitive phenomenon, because it presumes that the cognitive mechanisms of attention are shaped and directed through learners' ongoing interpretation of classroom discourse.

FoF in the context of discourse: debates, differences, and divisions in SLA

Research into FoF has been subject to considerable criticism in recent years for deploying a research methodology which is overly quantitative and experimental, for its dependence on a communicative model of language use which provides a poor basis for the initial stages of language learning

(Batstone 2002, 2005) and for focusing on a narrow view of cognition at the expense of social context (Firth and Wagner 1997; Block 2003). But this is not to say that FoF is necessarily incompatible with insights from other fields. For instance, the notion of attention (such a central part of the cognitive tradition in SLA) has recently been revisited by a number of scholars who take what amounts to a more sociocognitive line (for example, Van Lier 1998), and it is this more sociocognitive perspective which is the basis for the argument proposed in this chapter.

The Negotiation of Form

The notion of FoF is contested not only from the outside but also from within, and never more so than in the ongoing debate over the kind of negotiation most likely to lead to a focused engagement with linguistic form. Some scholars (for example, Long 1996; Long and Robinson 1998) argue that learners can best attend to linguistic form through negotiating and clarifying uncertainties about meaning through so-called 'negotiation for meaning' (NfM).

Others argue that learners' ongoing preoccupation with meaning implicit in NfM makes it difficult for them to see that linguistic deviations in their talk are being implicitly corrected (Lyster and Ranta 1997). Scholars who take this view point to research in cognitive theory which suggests that learners may need to pay conscious attention to (or 'notice') linguistic form as such in the initial stages of learning (Schmidt 1990, 1992). Consequently, they propose that a different kind of engagement with language is called for—the Negotiation of Form (NoF). In NoF, the fact that a learner has made a linguistic error is made explicit, and the ensuing negotiation encourages learners not only to notice the error but to do something about it by self-correcting. A variety of interactive moves have been proposed to facilitate NoF, including repeating the learners' utterance but highlighting the error through phonological stress, and providing metalinguistic clues that an error has been made, for example by saying 'that's not how we say it in English' (Lyster and Ranta 1997; Lyster 1998b). Such moves explicitly encourage learners both to notice and to act upon their errors as they occur, and thus NoF 'serves a pedagogic function' (Lyster 2002: 382).

Decontextualizing FoF: statistics and the focus on the synchronic

When learners focus on form, they do so not in a vacuum but in the context of ongoing discourse. As a result, focusing on form presupposes interpreting form (or more precisely, interpreting discourse in ways which will make linguistic form relevant and noticeable in its own right). In mainstream SLA, though, there is a strong tendency to play down the role of discourse, and in a variety of ways.

Firstly, a key quality of discourse is the fact that it is ongoing. Learners (like any other language users) would find it difficult or impossible to understand what is being said 'now' without reference to what came before. In contrast, a great many studies of NfM and NoF are heavily synchronic, focusing largely on a small number of turns which constitute the immediate linguistic context, with little if any systematic attention to the kind of interactions or interpretations which preceded (and conceivably had a major role in shaping) the final FoF. A number of studies show a concern for somewhat longer stretches of discourse than this (for example, Williams 1999; Lyster 2002), but overall there is a very marked tendency towards minimalism.

Secondly, studies of FoF rely on the statistical representation of data which in most instances is entirely quantitative (for example, Williams and Evans 1998), with examples of the actual language used being provided primarily to illustrate coding procedures (for example, Leeman 2003). But once actual instances of negotiation are converted into abstract tokens they are decontextualized, making it difficult or impossible to gauge how particular features of the context might have influenced what was said or what was meant.

Decontextualizing FoF and problems of determinism

The foregrounding of statistical data has a number of advantages, not the least of which is that it enables the researcher to make generalizations across a wide range of instances, and without generalizations of one kind or another it would be impossible to theorize in any meaningful way about classroom interactions. If the processes for making and interpreting meaning in discourse were always self-evident and unvarying, then statistical data might well be able to stand alone. But discourse meaning is never self-evident. On the contrary, everything that is said in a classroom requires interpretation. This is where studies of NfM and NoF reach the limits of their explanatory power: they can point to patterns in classroom interaction which are potentially significant, but left to their own devices they cannot explain how the meanings which give such patterns their significance are brought into existence in the first place.

An illustration of this tendency is the following example of an NoF from a Canadian immersion grade four class where there is an ongoing interaction between teacher and students concerning what they did during the holiday (Lyster 2002: 383–4):

Example 1

1   s   Pis, eihm, *j'ai allé au mail ...
        um, I (*use of wrong auxiliary] went/gone to the mall ...

2   T   J'ai allé ca ne se dit pas
        '*I [use of wrong auxiliary] went/gone' we don't say that*

3   s   Je suis alle au mail de St-Benoit et j'ai ...
        I went to the St-Benoit mall and I... ... .

4   T   Tu as achete quelque chose?
        Did you buy anything?

5   s   Ma grande-mere a achete *du laine pour faire euh
        euh ... t'sais ... ...
        My grandmother bought wool [masculine: wrong gender] to make, um, you know

6   T   Du laine?
        Wool? [repeating the error in gender])

7   s   De la laine
        Wool [now correctly changed to feminine gender]

If we begin by focusing on lines 5–7, the teacher responds to the learner's error with the preposition by repeating the erroneous form: 'du laine?' This is a well-known technique within NoF to make learners' errors salient, and it is one which in this instance is successful, since it prompts the learner to self-repair, thereby completing a successful NoF episode.

From the discourse perspective, however, this kind of analysis is problematic. Taken at face value, the teacher's correctional cue is ambiguous: it could be a request for repetition; it could be an expression of disbelief; it could be a call for clarification; or it could be (and according to proponents of NoF it often is) an elicited self-correction.

The implication of Lyster's argument is that such ambiguity is resolved largely through the inherent explicitness of the cues offered by the teacher. NoF moves such as repetition and the provision of metalinguistic clues, says Lyster, '*return the floor to students* along with cues to draw on their own resources' and thus they 'serve a pedagogical function that *draws attention to form* and aims for accuracy in addition to mutual comprehension' (2002: 382 emphasis added).

One assumes that Lyster's intention here is to point to a significant statistical correlation between certain discourse moves and related learner responses (for example, 'on over 50% of occasions, teacher elicitation moves were followed by a response where the learner self-corrected'). But this way of framing the argument, commonplace in SLA, employs a level of generalization which can easily lead to misunderstandings. Specifically, it could be taken to imply that such moves possess inherent, almost magical powers: in and of themselves they 'return the floor to the students' and 'draw attention to form'. Taken to an extreme, such a deterministic view flies in the face of a basic tenet in discourse analysis: that meaning is arrived at through interpretation, rather than simply existing, self-contained, within single utterances. Undoubtedly the way that individual utterances are phrased has a role to play in shaping how particular interpretations are arrived at, but ultimately the explicitness of any utterance in discourse will always be relative to how participants are positioned to interpret it.

Attributing particular meanings to NoF moves in relative isolation is an example of the tendency in SLA noted earlier to focus on the immediate and to play down the significance of the wider discourse context which gives it meaning. Such generalizations are an important aspect of SLA theorizing, but when given too much prominence they obscure the complex interplay of cause and effect in classroom discourse, implying that NoF moves are themselves causative and playing down the notion that other factors (such as learners' interpretative predispositions) might have a critical role to play.

Patterns in discourse

The potential effectiveness of NoF is entirely contingent upon the kind of discourse which precedes it. In this sense, at least, mainstream SLA theorizing about FoF is limited in its explanatory power, because it severs the connection between the interpretation of individual utterances and its roots in what came before. In this regard, it may be instructive to look at what preceded the NoF in example 1, where the teacher's relatively implicit prompt in line 6 is almost immediately preceded by a more explicit indication that a linguistic error has been made (line 2). This earlier move might have had the effect of making the learner more alert to form. As a result, by the time the more implicit cue in example 1 is encountered, he is already primed to interpret the teacher's repetition in the way Lyster proposes. This idea, that learners' alignments to form are shaped by their engagements with prior discourse, forms the basis for the discussion which follows.

Frames, contextualization cues, and the creation of meaning in classroom discourse

It is often said that making sense in language use requires a capacity to perceive patterns or regularities between the kinds of discourse we are experiencing now, and similar patterns of one sort or another which we have experienced in the past. The generic term often used to talk about such regularities is 'frame' (Tannen 1993), although a variety of different terms have been used to discuss similar concepts, including 'schema' (Bartlett 1932) and 'script' (Shank and Abelson 1977).

For purposes of the present argument, the term 'frame' will be used to refer to regularities in the patterning of classroom discourse. Such regularities provide clues as to who can talk and when they can talk during turn taking between teacher and learners, as well as the kind of speech acts which might arise and their probable sequence (including pedagogic speech acts like elicitation), and the kind of pedagogic intent which lies behind what is said. Frames of this sort play a pivotal role in language pedagogy and in the analysis of classroom discourse (for example, Sinclair and Coulthard 1975; Cazden 2001).

An important question which arises here is how learners are able to recognize that particular frames are in play. One obvious source is the language used by teachers. We have just seen a relatively clear illustration of this in example 1, where the teacher's comment 'we don't say that' (line two) helps to orient the learner towards a focus on the NoF. Lyster implies that didactic cues of this sort are easily interpreted by learners, but frames are frequently signalled through a variety of quite subtle rhetorical devices which work in tandem and whose salience depends upon the ability of learners to take the appropriate interpretative bearings. In discourse analysis such devices are often referred to as contextualization cues (Gumperz 1982), understood as verbal and non-verbal signals which can help discourse participants to infer what the speaker intends on the basis of past experience with similar encounters (Gumperz 1992: 230). Such cues come from a variety of sources, including prosody and paralanguage (Gumperz 1992: 231–2).

It is interesting to speculate on the possible role of contextualization cueing in example 1. In line six, the teacher's repetition of the learner's incorrect utterance is a move which Lyster classifies as 'NoF', noting that although repetition can also be used simply to call for a clarification of meaning, 'teachers often use [this move] not because they did not understand, but rather to feign incomprehension and thereby draw attention to non-target forms' (1998b: 382). But the fact that teachers often use this device for didactic purposes does little in itself to explain how a learner is able to perceive it as such. Interpreting repetition as a call for NoF may require access to a variety of contextualization cues, and although one cannot be sure exactly what kind of cueing is operative in the case of Lyster's data, a number of possibilities suggest themselves. These include becoming cognizant of the co-occurrence of repetition with earlier metalinguistic cues (example 1, line 2), the systematic correlation between particular forms of teacher repetition and NoF discourses (rather than NfM), the subtle use by teachers of intonation to add a didactic emphasis to repeating a learner's error (as is argued in Lyster and Ranta 1997), and the frequent embedding of repetition within teacher interruptions of the learner's immediately preceding turn (interruptions themselves carry meaning in discourse: see Sacks, Schegloff, and Jefferson 1974). All these cues work in tandem, and if they co-occur with sufficient frequency and salience, then they provide learners with cues through which to take their interpretative bearings, whilst at the same time signalling that a frame for structuring the NoF may be underway.

Frames and contextual bearings: a case study from Ellis, Basturkmen, and Loewen (2001a)

Contextualizing the study

On the basis of a recent empirical study into the uses of FoF by teachers in a private language school in Auckland, New Zealand, R. Ellis and his colleagues have argued strongly that moving between a focus on meaning and an FoF is not only possible but occurs frequently in their data. As they put it, 'teachers and students appeared to be able to navigate in and out of focusing on aspects of the code while keeping the overall orientation to message intact' (Ellis, Basturkmen, and Loewen 2001a: 310). More specifically, they provide evidence that learners were able to focus on form both from a basis in meaning negotiation and (on other occasions) through the NoF. Such negotiations, they note, created plentiful opportunities for successful 'uptake', defined as the incorporation of a corrected feature by a learner, usually in response to an implicit cue from the teacher (2001a: 286).

These claims are on the basis of a study which is largely quantitative, but in the analysis which follows, additional transcribed data from the original study are examined in some detail[1] in order to provide further evidence for how the surrounding discourse shapes particular FFEs. On this basis, it is suggested that many of the successful shifts of attention from meaning to form may emerge out of a prior orientation to form, an orientation which is facilitated both through learners' recognition of frames, and through their capacity to anticipate FFEs by taking interpretative bearings on the wider discourse context.

Shifts of emphasis

Amongst the 12 hours of data used to inform the R. Ellis study, there are identifiably distinct stages, stages within which a variety of activities constellate around particular themes (including predictions, national holidays, and a murder mystery). One such stage is based around the theme of alibis. It is a lengthy segment, taking up over 45 minutes in all, and it is based on the premise that there has been a robbery for which everyone in the class is a suspect; hence much of the time is taken up with the learners discussing what their alibis might be.

The teacher begins by explaining the theme to the class and eliciting possible alibis with no attention to the linguistic errors which ensue. Minutes later, the focus on meaning is even more pronounced, as the learners (now divided into pairs) set about discussing their alibis. Yet in between these two activities there is a period of relative calm, during which there is considerable NoF between the teacher and individual learners. These negotiations include learner-initiated queries about spelling, a learner-initiated and quite lengthy negotiation about linguistic conventions for telling the time (example 2), and a teacher-initiated elicitation of the past tense (example 3).

Example 2

 T Okay, you've got five minutes (.) together with your partner,
  (3.0) are you discussing what you're doing this evening
  (.) McDonalds (said to two students who are still talking.)
 S twelve am
 T twelve=
 S =this is not their lunch time.
 T no no
 S it's midnight.
 T it's midnight yes
 S when is lunchtime?
 T lunchtime is twelve pm
 T this is usually when I get hungry (.) after break yeah
 S this is pm,
 T yeah sometimes it's confusing but think (.) twelve am midnight (.)
  twelve pm
  (T writes '12 a.m. = midnight 12 p.m. = midday')
 T midday (.) okay?

Example 3

> T Remember, H., this is last night so I:?
> (2.0)
> S I went
> T I went, that's right, I went to the cinema

Each of these examples shows evidence of frames at work. Example 3, for instance, is based on a form of IRF (initiation—response—feedback) common to many classrooms (Sinclair and Coulthard 1975). The teacher elicits, the learner responds by self-correcting, then the teacher rounds off the episode by providing some reinforcing feedback. But this doesn't answer the wider question of why there should be a sudden, relatively intense period of NoF activity, surrounded on either side by what appear to be prolonged periods of meaning-focused activity with no recorded instances of NfM.

FoF and pragmatic bearings on the wider context

Part of the answer has to do with the wider discourse context. This constellation of individual episodes of NoF all occur within a sub-section of the lesson which is characterized (amongst other things) by a very noticeable reduction in talk amongst the learners, and a sense that the teacher is re-asserting her authority as the person who will define the parameters of the activity in progress. Both these characteristics are in marked contrast to the rest of the activity, where there is a high level of overlapping talk and laughter amongst the students, and where the teacher adopts a very low profile.

The teacher signals this new phase in the lesson through a variety of linguistic and non-linguistic cues. In part this cueing has to do with the introduction of the written modality. After eliciting ideas for possible alibis, the teacher gives the class instructions to work on agreeing and then writing down their alibis in pairs. As she does this, she is also writing up on the whiteboard the times between which the robbery occurred: '4.00 p.m., 5.00 p.m.' and so on up to 12.00 a.m. The shift in modality from oral to written form formalizes things. This is partly down to the teacher moving out of her role as a general elicitor of ideas, and into a more regulatory role as she indicates more precisely what the learners need to do in their pairwork. In part, too, a stronger sense of formality is evoked by the written form, both by the teacher on the whiteboard, and by the learners in their pairs. The change of focus has an immediate effect. Even before the teacher has finished setting up the pairwork activity, one of the students raises a question about the format for writing down times of the day (example 2), something which leads to a lengthy interaction involving two learners as well as the teacher. Once the pairwork commences, the teacher begins to monitor the activity, moving from pair to pair and commenting briefly before moving on. This, too, is an event full of potential meaning. From the learners' perspective, it may well signal that this activity has a formal edge, and that a concern with linguistic form is 'in the air'. Example 3, in which the teacher elicits a past tense self-repair from the learner, takes place during this monitoring phase.

It seems, then, as if a variety of cues are being used to move the lesson into a more formal stage, a stage in which matters of linguistic precision and negotiations of form are seen as appropriate. Temporarily, at least, the context has shifted: the roles of teacher and learners have moved, with the teacher adopting a more formal 'front of the class' role as the learners quieten down and take note of the teacher's instructions.

Participation, predispositions, and the co-construction of focus on form

The shift is neither dramatic nor long-lasting, as within minutes the group work begins in earnest with a renewed sense that meaning and not form is the priority, at least for those learners whose voices are discernible. But it is nonetheless of potential significance, since it enables the learners both to anticipate and subsequently to participate more fully in the kinds of NoF noted in examples 2 and 3.

It needs to be emphasized, too, that this kind of learner involvement and participation reflects the nature of FoF in discourse as being *co-con-structed*. Rather than simply arriving ready-made at the appropriate moment in discourse, frames often emerge through active meaning making by all parties involved in the discourse (Kramsch 1986). In example 2, the learner appears to be taking the initiative from the outset, initiating the FoF episode with an implicit query ('twelve am') without trying to signal the relevance of this to the teacher's preceding turn, and persisting with his queries until he gets a satisfactory response. In this episode, at least, one gets a real sense of shared agency and negotiation (Jacoby and Ochs 1995: 177).

So whilst frames facilitate an FoF in reference to patterns of turn taking in the immediate context, taking bearings on the wider context creates a general *predisposition* towards form. The latter helps set the scene for the former, with the two acting in concert in ways which are surely facilitative (and may in some contexts be necessary) for effective FoF to occur.

This is an argument which may have relevance well beyond the specific data under discussion here. We might, for instance, speculate on whether learners actually have the kinds of discourse predispositions which particular kinds of lesson, or particular stages within a lesson, presuppose, and upon which their success may depend.

Synthesis: explaining the movement between meaning and form

How does this position sit with the argument proposed by R. Ellis and his colleagues? Their claim, as noted earlier, is that 'teachers and students appeared to be able to navigate in and out of focusing on aspects of the code while keeping the overall orientation to message intact' (Ellis, Basturkmen, and Loewen 2001a: 310).

There seems to be evidence in their data to substantiate this assertion. Example 3, for instance, is both preceded and immediately followed by what appears to be very meaning-focused discussion and debate between the learner and her partner as they continue working together on their alibis. Example 2 follows immediately on from (and indeed overlaps with) the teacher's clarifications about time, and is quickly followed by a resumption of more meaning-focused activity in the form of the paired discussions.

Ellis *et al.*'s notion of 'navigating' between meaning and form could, perhaps, be elaborated in a way which takes account of the discourse from which is arises. The argument made here is *not* that learners can glide freely between form and meaning, but that their negotiations of form are facilitated by their capacity to co-construct commensurate frames, and (more generally) through a discourse-motivated predisposition to engage with form.

Socio-cognition: the interdependence of attention and interpretation

Implicitly, at least, much of the preceding discussion has been about attention, and about ways in which learners are able more easily to focus their attention when they anticipate how the discourse might progress. Much is made of attention by those who have an interest in applying findings in cognitive psychology to language teaching (for example, VanPatten 1990; Skehan 1998). But just as with research into FoF, there is a noticeable neglect of the wider discourse out of which attention emerges. As a result, the idea that attentional choices are an expression of how one *interprets* discourse tends to get sidelined. The argument proposed here is that attention is framed in discourse: attention, in other words, is shaped by a learner's sense of where the discourse is heading. In this regard, the link between attention, frames, and predispositions is a very close one.

In cognitive psychology it has long been understood that attention is a limited resource, so that learners may be unable to attend both to meaning and form if both require focal attention (Schmidt 1990). As a means of lightening the processing load, it is argued that learners need to anticipate when and how attention to form may be called for, thereby helping them marshal their attentional resources in advance (for example, Leow 1998).

Various types and degrees of anticipation are discussed in the literature, including the distinction between attention as orientation, and attention as alertness (Posner and Peterson 1990). Orientation has to do with channelling one's attentional resources in a particular direction, largely to the exclusion of other potential directions, with reference to features of the immediate context. Alertness is a much broader concept, suggesting 'an overall, general readiness to deal with incoming stimuli or data' (Tomlin and Villa 1994).

Parallels between frames/predispositions and alertness/orientation

There is a striking parallel here between frames and predispositions on the one hand, and alertness and orientation on the other. Both pairings have to do with expectation, and both speak to the same general issue in language pedagogy: how to bridge the potentially unmanageable gap between a focus on meaning, and an FoF.

The learner in example 3, for instance, appears able to interpret with some precision what the teacher means ('check your past tense') on the basis of familiarity with an underlying frame. At the same time, it is the frame which helps orient the learner's attention to what is happening now and what is coming next.

Similar points could also be made with respect to alertness in relation to learner predispositions. Like predispositions, alertness has a relatively broad scope, and both alertness and predispositions reflect a general preparedness to encounter a particular kind of discourse (such as a discourse where NoF seems likely to occur). The learner in example 3, then, may already be predisposed to engage with linguistic form on account of the teachers' various contextualizing cues (like the move from spoken to written forms and the beginning of monitored group work), cues which serve to realign the learner's attentional alertness.

Attentional mechanisms and discourse frames as complementary and interrelated

There are at least two senses, then, in which discourse frames play a vital enabling role in the creation of FoF in L2 classrooms. On the one hand, they act as a resource for interpreting classroom events in terms of discourse pragmatics. On the other hand, they simultaneously serve to make such interpretations feasible in real time in terms of attentional capacity. The first perspective allows us to view discourse as a sociolinguistic event, whilst the latter says something more about discourse in its psycholinguistic context. More generally, this kind of theorizing can be said to be *sociocognitive*, in the sense that it seeks to discover ways in which the cognitive mechanisms of attention are interdependent with (and ultimately, inseparable from) matters of interpretation and meaning making in discourse.

Conclusion

Explaining how and why language learners pay attention to linguistic form demands that we theorize beyond what statistics can tell us, and beyond the immediate context of an FoF which looms so large in mainstream SLA research. Focusing on form is at once both a psycholinguistic and a socio-linguistic phenomenon. As a result, a more refined understanding of how it works will require a way of theorizing which acknowledges how the cognitive and the social interrelate, and which is therefore sociocognitive.

Undoubtedly the argument put forward in this chapter raises many more questions than it answers, and leaves much out of account. Amongst other things, little if anything has been said about identity, or about social relationships and socio-histories, or about the ways in which an FoF might emerge through the creation of mutual understanding and intersubjectivity. The relevance of this last point seems particularly germane in light of what has been said here about frames and predispositions, since it raises questions about whether such frames are actually available or mutually accessible to those who participate in classroom discourse. There would seem to be fertile ground, then, for continued research into the situating of cognition.

Notes

1 I am grateful to the authors for allowing me access to the original tape recordings and transcripts from this study.

7

The prior and subsequent use of forms targeted in incidental focus on form

SHAWN LOEWEN

FOCUS ON FORM (FoF) has received considerable attention recently (see Chapter 1) as SLA theorists and teachers attempt to find means of integrating meaning-focused instruction and form-focused instruction (FFI) (Hulstijn 1995; Skehan 1998; R. Ellis 2001a). In FoF, learners' attention is drawn to linguistic items only as the need arises and not in predetermined ways (Long 1991; Spada 1997); however, recent studies have investigated both planned and incidental FoF (R. Ellis 2001a). Both combine attention to linguistic items within the context of meaning-focused activities. With planned FoF, however, there is prior intention to intervene with regards to specific linguistic structures. Because the target structures are known ahead of time, it is possible to employ quasi-experimental procedures (for example, the use of pre-tests and post-tests) to measure effectiveness. However, incidental FoF occurs without prior planning, in response to whichever linguistic structures arise during meaning-focused activities; as a result, it is not possible to pre-test the linguistic items (Swain 2001a; Loewen 2005). Therefore, in order to investigate the effectiveness of incidental FoF, something other than the conventional pre-test/post-test method must be used to explore what happens both before and after the attention to form is given. The present study addresses this issue by examining learners' use of linguistic forms targeted in form-focused episodes (FFEs) both before and after the occurrence of the FFEs.

Although planned and incidental FoF may both be beneficial for learners (Doughty and Williams 1998a), their impact may vary. Planned FoF has the advantage of providing intensive coverage of (generally) one specific linguistic item, and its effectiveness has been investigated in various contexts (Doughty and Varela 1998; Mackey and Philp 1998; Lyster 2004; Ellis, Loewen, and Erlam 2006). In contrast, incidental FoF provides extens-

LIVERPOOL JOHN
LEARNING SERVICES

ive coverage, targeting a wide variety of linguistic items, often only once. A growing number of studies have begun to describe the occurrence of incidental FoF in various contexts and to consider its effectiveness (Lyster and Ranta 1997; Lyster 1998a, 1998b; Williams 1999, 2001; Ellis, Basturkmen, and Loewen 2001a, 2001b; Loewen 2003, 2004, 2005; Sheen 2004).

Measuring the effectiveness of incidental FoF

While incidental FoF may be beneficial for L2 development, it is important to be able to measure its effectiveness. One method for describing the utility of incidental FoF has been to investigate uptake, that is, what learners do with the feedback they are provided (Lyster and Ranta 1997). Several studies have argued that learners' responses to the provision of feedback can give an indication of the feedback's effectiveness (Chaudron 1977; Lyster and Ranta 1997; Lyster 1998a; Ellis, Basturkmen, and Loewen 2001a; Loewen 2004). However, these studies have cautioned that while uptake may be indicative of noticing and facilitative of acquisition, it does not in itself constitute evidence of acquisition; furthermore, some studies have found evidence of learning without the production of uptake (Mackey and Philp 1998).

Another measure of the effectiveness of incidental FoF consists of individualized testing, in which the specific linguistic items raised spontaneously in classroom discourse are tested. However, since the testing can be done only *after* the incidental FoF has occurred, it is not possible to investigate the learner's prior knowledge of the linguistic item, and it may be that the error is a performance error. Nevertheless, the fact that an error in production has occurred or a question about a linguistic item has been raised indicates learner difficulty with that item (Ellis, Basturkmen, and Loewen 2001a) and that further consolidation of learning may be needed (Swain 2001a). Thus, learning can be operationalized as an increase in the accurate use of the targeted forms in subsequently elicited situations (Williams 2001). Several recent studies (La Pierre 1994; Nabei and Swain 2001; Williams 2001; Loewen 2005) have begun to employ individualized testing and have shown generally encouraging rates of accuracy; however, the results have been interpreted cautiously due to the limitations of such testing, particularly the lack of pre-testing.

One final concern regarding individualized post-testing is the construct validity of the tests, that is to say, what the tests are measuring (Douglas 2001). Many tests used in SLA research may be better measures of learners' explicit L2 knowledge, rather than their implicit knowledge. Explicit knowledge can be briefly defined as 'knowledge that learners are consciously aware of and that is typically only available through controlled processing' while implicit knowledge is 'knowledge that learners are only intuitively aware of and that is easily accessible through automatic processing' (Ellis, Loewen, and Erlam 2006). Recent work by R. Ellis (2004a, 2005b) suggests that tests that have a clear focus on linguistic form, allow unlimited response time, and in which learners can apply metalinguistic knowledge are better measures of explicit knowledge, whereas tests which generally involve spontaneous, on-line production, or allow limited response time are better measures of implicit knowledge. In the previous studies of individualized testing, the tests have perhaps been better measures of explicit L2 knowledge since they generally focus explicitly on L2 forms and allowed learners unlimited response time.

Possibly the best measure of the effectiveness of incidental FoF, particularly in regards to learners' implicit L2 knowledge, would be learners' subsequent spontaneous production of the targeted linguistic forms, particularly when compared to any previous production; however, such data is often difficult to capture, especially in naturalistic classroom settings (Williams 2001). Such subsequent production differs from uptake, which has usually been defined as learners' immediate response to feedback, occurring either one, or sometimes two, turns after the feedback. Very few studies have examined learners' subsequent use of targeted linguistic forms; however, Williams (2001), in a study of eight L2 learners, found that only about 10 per cent of items focused on in language related episodes were subsequently used again. Because of this low occurrence of subsequent use, Williams did not investigate those instances further; nevertheless, accuracy scores on individualized tests for all targeted linguistic items ranged from 45 to 94 per cent, increasing with the proficiency level of the learners.

The present study addresses the issue of both prior and subsequent use of linguistic forms targeted in FFEs. This study is uniquely placed to examine prior and subsequent use and to relate it to other methods used in the investigation of the effectiveness of incidental FoF since this data set has already been examined for uptake (Loewen 2004) and individualized test scores (Loewen 2005). Therefore, the study seeks to answer the following research questions:

1 Do learners use the targeted linguistic items prior to the FFEs? If so, how accurately do they use the linguistic items?
2 Do learners use the targeted linguistic items subsequent to the FFEs? If so, how accurately do they use the linguistic items?
3 What is the relationship, if any, between correct subsequent use and successful uptake?
4 What is the relationship, if any, between correct subsequent use and individualized test scores?

Method

The present study involves an analysis of a subset of the data from Loewen (2002, 2004, 2005). As such, minimal information is provided about the participants and context, and the reader is referred to the previous studies for more information. It should be noted that the present analysis is based on a subset of the total data.

Participants

The study was conducted at a private language school in Auckland, New Zealand. A total of three classes, each with a different teacher, were observed. There were 33 students in these classes, with class sizes ranging from seven to 14. The teachers (one female and two male) were native speakers of English, and the students came from China (fifteen), Korea (seven), Japan (four), Switzerland (four), France (one), Thailand (one), and Vietnam (one).

Procedures

Two meaning-focused lessons were observed for each class. The activities observed included two information/opinion gap tasks, a picture narration/drawing task and a discussion question activity. These activities were conducted in a variety of classroom configurations, including whole class, small groups, and pairs. A total of four and a half hours (275 minutes) of classroom interaction constituted the data for the present study. For recording, a wireless cassette recorder with a clip-on microphone attached to the teacher was used. This arrangement recorded all student–teacher interaction; however, it did not capture any student-student interaction when the teacher was not present.

FFEs, which were defined as all the discourse related to the targeted linguistic form (Ellis, Basturkmen, and Loewen 2001a), were identified in the interaction. A total of 121 FFEs served as the data set for the current study. Although the FFEs had been identified and transcribed from the previous study (Loewen 2002, 2004), the lessons had not always been transcribed in their entirety. Thus, for the present study, the audio-recordings were revisited in order to check the original transcriptions and to amend any incomplete sections. (See the appendix for the transcription key.) After the transcriptions were complete, each FFE was analysed to identify a) the learner who instigated that FFE, and b) the specific linguistic structure targeted in the FFE. After this identification process, the transcripts were loaded into *MonoConc Pro 2.2*, a corpus analysis software program, and a search of the relevant transcripts was conducted. Since the purpose of the search was to find prior and subsequent production by the student who was originally involved in the FFE, the transcripts from each class were searched separately. Both the erroneous item(s) and the correct item(s) were entered as search terms. For example, in episode 843 below, both the incorrect form *don't* and the correct form *doesn't* were searched for.

Episode 843

c she don't have children so they don't have
t she doesn't
c she doesn't
t have
c have have help from the children

The search was confined as much as possible to the context of the original FFE. Thus, in the case of bound morphemes such as plural -*s*, or third person -*s*, only the original word from the FFE was searched for. It is acknowledged that the form may have been used on other nouns or verbs; however, given the exploratory nature of the analysis, a more conservative approach was adopted. Again it is important to note that prior and subsequent use was only counted for the student involved in the FFE.

While every effort was made to include all FFEs in the analysis, it was necessary to exclude some FFEs from the data set. Spelling FFEs (n = 14) were excluded since they often elicited written, rather than verbal, responses which were not captured by the audio-recording. Another set of FFEs regarding pronoun gender (n = 11) were excluded due to the difficulty of determining the obligatory contexts for masculine and feminine pronouns during the tasks. Finally, if a linguistic item was the target of more than one FFE, this was not counted as prior/subsequent use. Instead, the FFE was counted only once, but it was noted that more than one FFE targeted that item. Three linguistic items had more than one FFE for the same student. One student was corrected twice on his incorrect use of the plural form 'childrens', one student was corrected twice on her failure to mark plurality on 'window', and another student was corrected three times for the subject verb agreement 'she don't'. Each of these forms was only counted once in the analysis.

Once the search terms were identified, all tokens occurring outside of the FFEs were counted. Then a target-like use analysis was conducted (Pica 1983; Ellis and Barkhuizen 2005) in which the number of correct tokens, including self-corrections, was counted as well as the number of incorrect tokens and any oversuppliance. The result was expressed as a percentage accuracy score. This analysis was conducted separately for tokens occurring prior and subsequent to each FFE.

In addition to coding for prior and subsequent use, the coding of successful uptake from Loewen (2002, 2004) was used, with uptake being categorized as either successful—the learner incorporates the linguistic information provided in the feedback into his or her own production, or unsuccessful—the learner responds to the feedback but does not incorporate the linguistic information into his or her own production.

Finally, the individualized test items from Loewen (2005) were used. The test items were constructed directly from the transcribed FFEs, and based on a template, involving either correction, suppliance, or pronunciation. Learners' responses to the test items were coded as correct, incorrect, and partially correct; however, partially correct responses were excluded from this analysis. Only learners who were involved in the FFEs were tested on those items. Tests were administered either two days or two weeks after the FFEs. The tests were conducted one-on-one and were audio-recorded.

Analysis

Raw frequencies and percentages were calculated for the targeted linguistic items used prior and subsequent to the FFEs. Mean scores were calculated for the number of correct and incorrect tokens used. Percentage accuracy scores were also calculated, using target-like use analysis. To determine if there was any relationship between correct subsequent use and a) successful uptake and b) correct test scores, a Fisher's Exact chi-square analysis was performed. An alpha level of $p < .05$ was set for all chi-squares. All statistics were performed using the *Statistical Package for the Social Sciences* (SPSS) 12.1. Finally, several extracts of data, showing prior use, the FFE, subsequent use and test performance were included to illustrate the trends in the data.

Results

The first research question concerns the frequency of prior use of the linguistic items targeted in the FFEs. Table 7.1 shows that only 15 (just over 12 per cent) of the linguistic items targeted in FFEs occurred in prior use, with just three each in two of the classes and nine in the third class.

The first research question also addresses the level of accuracy in the prior use of the targeted forms. Table 7.2 shows the mean number of tokens used correctly and incorrectly. The number of tokens used correctly ranged

Class	C8	C9	C12	Total
Not used				
n	31	45	30	106
%	77.5	93.8	90.9	87.6
Used				
n	9	3	3	15
%	22.5	6.3	9.1	12.4

TABLE 7.1 *Number of targeted linguistic items used prior to the FFE*

Class	C8	C9	C12	Total
Correct				
Mean	1.4	.3	.7	1.1
Sd	1.51	.58	.58	1.28
Minimum	0	0	0	0
Maximum	4	1	1	4
Incorrect				
Mean	.4	1.3	2.3	1
Sd	.53	1.15	.58	1.00
Minimum	0	0	2	0
Maximum	1	2	3	3

TABLE 7.2 *Number of tokens used correctly and incorrectly prior to FFE*

among the three classes from .3 to 1.4, with an average of 1.1. For the number of tokens used incorrectly, the average was 1.0, with a range from .4 to 2.3. Finally, the percentage accuracy of these tokens, shown in Table 7.3, averaged 47 per cent, again with a considerable range among the three classes from 19 per cent to 61 per cent. Thus, all of these tables show that C8 had a higher rate of accurate use of the linguistic items prior to the FFEs; however, given the small sample size, it was not possible to determine if this was a significant difference. Also note that the maximum accuracy score of 100 per cent for both C8 and C9 indicates that both classes had at least one linguistic item each that was used completely accurately prior to the FFE.

Research question 2 asks about frequency and accuracy of subsequent use of the targeted linguistic items. Table 7.4 shows that learners used 24 of the targeted linguistic forms after the FFEs, for an average of almost 20 per cent.

Class	C8	C9	C12	Total
Mean	61.1	33.3	19.4	47.2
Sd	48.6	57.7	17.3	46.8
Median	100	0	25	33.3
Minimum	0	0	0	0
Maximum	100	100	33.3	100

TABLE 7.3 *Percentage accuracy of prior use*

Class	C8	C9	C12	Total
Not used				
n	30	40	27	97
%	75.0	83.3	81.8	80.2
Used				
n	10	8	6	24
%	25.0	16.7	18.2	19.8

TABLE 7.4 *Number of targeted linguistic items used subsequent to the FFE*

As for the accuracy of subsequent use, Table 7.5 reveals that the average number of tokens used correctly was 1.3. The average number of tokens used incorrectly was .6. Table 7.6 shows that the average percentage accuracy in subsequent use was almost 75 per cent. The minimum score of zero, however, indicates that some linguistic items were not used accurately at all following the FFE.

The previous tables have demonstrated the frequency and accuracy of either prior or subsequent use; however, the tables have not paired prior and subsequent use for the same FFEs. Further analysis revealed that only three of the 121 FFEs were accompanied by both prior and subsequent use. The prepositions 'behind' and 'below' were used partially correctly before the FFE and correctly after the FFE. The word 'children' was correctly marked for plural before the FFE but incorrectly after, and the pronunciation of 'woman' (shown in extract 4 below) was partially correct before the FFE and correct after.

The third research question addresses the relationship between subsequent use and successful uptake. Table 7.7 shows that more FFEs with successful uptake also had correct subsequent use (79 per cent) but also that FFEs with unsuccessful uptake had more correct subsequent use (67 per

Class	C8	C9	C12	Total
Correct				
Mean	1.5	.9	1.5	1.3
Sd	1.08	.99	1.2	1.08
Minimum	0	0	0	0
Maximum	4	3	3	4
Incorrect				
Mean	.1	.9	1.2	.6
Sd	.32	1.36	2.04	1.31
Minimum	0	0	0	0
Maximum	1	4	5	5

TABLE 7.5 *Number of tokens used correctly and incorrectly subsequent to the FFE*

Class	C8	C9	C12	Total
Mean	90.0	56.2	72.9	74.5
Sd	31.6	49.6	43.6	42.1
Median	100	75	100	100
Minimum	0	0	0	0
Maximum	100	100	100	100

TABLE 7.6 *Percentage accuracy of subsequent use*

cent). The Fisher's exact test did not reveal any significant differences among the data, (n = 22, p = 1.0, two-sided).

The fourth research question addressed the relationship between correct subsequent use and test scores. Table 7.8 reveals that more FFEs with correct test scores also had correct subsequent use (73 per cent), but that FFEs with incorrect test scores also had more correct subsequent use (67 per cent) Again, the Fisher's exact test did not reveal any significant differences among the data, (n = 18. p = 1.0, two-sided).

While the numbers provide an overall picture of prior and subsequent use, it is worthwhile to illustrate prior and subsequent use from the data. In extract 1, the teacher and two students are involved in an information/ opinion gap task in which the object is to decide which prisoner will receive early parole. The teacher asks about the personality of the candidate belonging to J and E. Both J and E provide an answer, but then E asks if what she has said is right, thereby instigating an FFE. The teacher provides a more

| Uptake | Subsequent use | | | |
| | Incorrect | | Correct | |
	n	%	n	%
Successful	4	21.1	15	78.9
Unsuccessful	1	33.3	2	66.7

TABLE 7.7 *Subsequent use and successful uptake*

| Test score | Subsequent use | | | |
| | Incorrect | | Correct | |
	n	%	n	%
Correct	4	26.7	11	73.3
Incorrect	1	33.3	2	66.7

TABLE 7.8 *Subsequent use and test scores*

Extract 1

FFE

T   what sort of personality has she got
J   uh she's hardworking
T   mhm, yeah, okay
E   /13:50/ she's =
J   = outlook positive
T   yeah
E   yeah positive thinking can you say she's positive thinking
T   um you can say she has a positive attitude
J   oh
T   she (.) you could th- (.) if you wanted to use think um you could say she thinks positively (.) but she has a (.) I think norm- a more natural saying would be to say she has a positive attitude
E   mhm
T   or a positive outlook /14:10/
J   mm

7:30 minutes after FFE
E   /21:42/ and she's also positive and she's got a positive attitude

Test two weeks after FFE
R   she's positive thinking
E   she's a positive thinking person

'natural' way of saying it, and E acknowledges the teacher's response; however, she does not incorporate the new form into her own production. Subsequently, seven and a half minutes later, E successfully uses the phrase 'positive attitude' in describing her candidate to another group. However, two weeks later when E was tested on this item, her response did not include 'attitude' but was a modification of her original question.

In extract 2, the students are discussing which one of four candidates should receive a heart transplant. In discussing why her candidate should not get the heart, F makes an error in the use of the present perfect. The teacher repeats the error and a discussion follows in which the teacher attempts to elicit the correct form from F. In the end, F successfully comes up with the correct form. Then 18 minutes later, F uses the correct phrase in her discussion with another student. On the immediate test, two days after the FFE, she also provided the correct form.

Extract 2

FFE

F	/14:00/ he is long long time smokert (.) and he is never think about diet (.) he's still going \<macdonald\>
T	He's he's he's never think?
F	he never think or
T	he's never think is what you said so can you change that
F	I said
T	he
	(laughter)
F	he () I \<could\> use never
T	yeah you could use never
F	he never
T	but rather than think (.) he's never thi- you said he is never think (.) he
F	has ah has ah he ha- he has never (.) thought of giving up smoking
Z	mm
F	good?
T	that's a better way of doing it yeah
F	/14:44/ thank you

18:04 minutes after FFE

F	/32:48/ has never thought about his diet (.) and it takes (.) it took him for a long to time to giving (.) give up smoking

Test two days after FFE

R	He is never think about his diet.
F	He has never thought about his diet.

While the previous two examples have shown successful subsequent use of the form targeted in the FFE, the next example does not. The extract comes from the same 'heart' task as the previous extract. One way in which this teacher focused on form was to save up errors that he observed during the discussion and review them at the end of the task. In this extract, he writes down an error involving third person subject verb agreement. He then nominates C to correct the error. She does so, and the teacher provides

Extract 3

FFE

(As students finish their discussion, T writes on board 'She have a big business'. Along with 6 other incorrect sentences)

T /58:23/ how bout that one () C (.) that look familiar?

C oh

   (laughter)

C she have be-

T what's wrong

C she has

T yeah

C she has

T yeah and you you C this is something you do a lot

C yeah

T you say she has (.) she have (.) you say she do (.) she don't instead of she does she doesn't (.) a couple of times I heard you stop and change to the correct one

C yeah

T so part of you you knows that it's not right but you keep falling into the same pattern so I don't know what we can do about that ( ) electric shock collar (zzt)

   (laughter)

T it- I think it's just something to try and remember because you you do this a lot you don't you don't um conjugate the verb and you need to do that yeah /59:17/

Lesson two days after FFE

C /15:20/ because they want to know what she have in her head for control her

C /47:10/ and uh because she have spent yet five years in jail

C /48:39/ and she have to find something else

Test two days after FFE

R She have a big business

C She has a big business

---

more discussion about this item. Although the audio-recording did not capture C making this error prior to the FFE, the teacher's remarks nevertheless indicate that this error is something C does 'a lot'. Although the FFE occurred at the end of the lesson, two days later the learners were involved in another information/opinion gap task, and in this lesson C used the form, albeit incorrectly, on three separate occasions. On the test, which took place two days after the FFE, she was able to provide the correct form, which would support the teacher's assessment that 'part of you knows that it's not right'; however, she did not appear able to use that knowledge in spontaneous communication.

The final extract shows an instance where both prior and subsequent use were recorded. In the first lesson, ER pronounces 'woman' correctly at almost six minutes into the lesson. Then, 11 minutes later, ER mispronounces 'woman' by adding a final [d]. Two days later, ER produces the same error, which is this time recast by the teacher. Fourteen and a half minutes after the FFE, ER again uses 'woman', and this time pronounces it correctly. In ER's test, two weeks later, he also provides the correct pronunciation.

Extract 4

Lesson two days prior to FFE	
ER	/5:40/ he have a very busy job (.) full time and <he/she> must pay for woman to take care of <this/his> children
ER	/16:40/ um my uh my case is a (.) is a girl (.) is a womand (.) uh his name is Sandy

FFE	
ER	/6:30/ she's a kind womand
T	she's a kind woman
ER	yeah you know and because

14:30 minutes after FFE	
ER	/21:00/ I think she's a kind woman too

Test two weeks after FFE	
ER	She is a kind woman

Discussion

The answer to research questions one and two is that there was some use of the targeted linguistic structures both prior and subsequent to the FFEs. Around 12 per cent (n = 15) of the linguistic forms occurred prior, while 20 per cent (n = 24) occurred subsequently. Although these figures are not particularly high, the rate of subsequent use is higher than the 10 per cent found in Williams (2001). However, even when the targeted structures were used, they were not necessarily used frequently. Some items occurred only once in subsequent production, while the highest number of tokens for a structure was four. Such small numbers suggest that caution is needed when conducting a target-like use analysis since such small figures can distort the percentages (Ellis and Barkhuizen 2005). Even so, both prior and subsequent use can provide some insight into learners' ability to produce the targeted forms in spontaneous communication. Additionally, it should be noted that a lack of use of the targeted forms does not necessarily indicate an inability to use those forms; it may simply be that learners had no occasion to use them.

Having discussed the occurrence of the targeted forms, it is important to examine the accuracy of use. Since one of the problems of individualized post-testing is the lack of a pre-test (Swain 2001a; Loewen 2005), it would be desirable to have some evidence that the linguistic items being focused on in the FFEs are demonstrably problematic for the learners, rather than just performance errors. The data indicate that learners were on average less accurate before the FFEs than after (47 per cent and 74 per cent respectively); however, for prior use, there was a range of accuracy levels for the three classes, from 19 per cent to 61 per cent. This variation suggests that the teachers might be 'correcting' some non-existent errors as well as real ones. Nevertheless, the prior-use accuracy levels for most of the targeted structures were relatively low, and it is encouraging that the average percentage accuracy was higher for subsequent use. Given the lack of similar studies, it is difficult to compare these figures; however, the results provide some evidence that incidental FoF may have an immediate effect on learners' ability to produce the forms accurately in subsequent interaction.

Regarding the final two research questions, the results indicate that there is no relationship between correct subsequent use and either successful uptake or correct test scores. Thus, learners are no more likely to use the form again correctly if they produce successful uptake or not. While Swain's (1995, 2000) Output Hypothesis argues for the benefits of uptake, these findings suggest that studies of uptake should continue to be cautious in interpreting its significance (Lyster and Ranta 1997; Ellis, Basturkmen, and Loewen 2001a; Loewen 2004). However, it should be noted that the lack of a significant relationship between correct subsequent use and successful uptake could be due to the small sample size. Similarly for the individualized testing, the correct subsequent use of the targeted form did not have any relationship to correct test scores. Again, the small sample size may account for the results; however, it is also important to consider the construct validity of the two measures (Douglas 2001; R. Ellis 2004a, 2005b). The individualized tests were relatively decontextualized, the primary focus was on linguistic form, and learners had unlimited response time—all conditions that R. Ellis argues encourage the use of explicit L2 knowledge. By contrast, in subsequent use, learners were processing language online for communicative purposes, and thus were more likely drawing on their implicit L2 knowledge. This point is illustrated in extract 3 where C used the correct subject verb agreement on two occasions—when her attention was drawn to it during the FFE and when she had time to think about it during the test. However, in her spontaneous production, she failed to produce the correct form on three different occasions. These results illustrate the importance of measuring learners' L2 knowledge in a variety of ways.

While the study has provided some insights regarding incidental FoF in classroom interaction, it is necessary to consider some of its limitations. As has been previously mentioned, one limitation is the small sample size, both in the amount of observed classroom interaction and in the number of tokens found. Related to this limitation is the fact that learners were recorded only when interacting with the teacher; however, all activities involved some amount of group/pair work, with learners working on their own and potentially producing targeted forms, which were not recorded. While this recording arrangement limited the amount of data, it also suggests that use of the targeted forms may have been more prevalent than this study has found. Consequently, recording all student interaction, even when the teacher is not present, is important.

Another limitation regards the length of time observed. Many studies have found effects for corrective feedback on delayed rather than immediate tests (Mackey 1999; Ellis, Loewen, and Erlam 2006). However, the subsequent use captured here occurred either within the same lesson, or at most two days later. While the results suggest that subsequent use in the short term is generally accurate, they do not provide information about long term use. Extract 1 illustrates this point, with E using the targeted form 'positive attitude' seven and a half minutes after the FFE but failing to provide it two weeks later on the test. Although only one example, it demonstrates the importance of examining both short and long term effects.

In spite of these limitations, the data provide insights into the relationship between incidental FoF and learners' prior and subsequent use of targeted items. FFEs do, on average, target forms that learners have had prior difficulty with, and learner production after FFEs is often accurate. None the less, the study suggests that while prior and subsequent use can be informative, such measures provide a limited picture, due in large part to the small number of exemplars. Therefore, analysis of spontaneous production is perhaps best combined with other measures, such as individualized tests. In addition, future research would do well to incorporate methods which would maximize the recording of targeted forms to provide greater evidence regarding the effects of incidental FoF.

Appendix

Transcription conventions

Symbol	Meaning
S or any initial except T or R	Student
T	Teacher
R	Researcher
(laugh)	Extra information
◇	Inaudible
(.)	Micropause
=	Linked speech
?	Rising intonation
-	Interrupted speech
//	Time index marking

8

Reactive focus on form through negotiation on learners' written errors[1]

HOSSEIN NASSAJI

THE ROLE of negotiation and its effects on the development of inter-language have recently received considerable theoretical attention in the field SLA (for example, Pica 1994; Long 1996; Lyster and Ranta 1997; Van den Branden 1997; McDonough and Mackey 2000; Nassaji and Swain 2000; Oliver and Mackey 2003). However, most of the research in this area has focused on oral errors. This study examined the occurrence and role of negotiation in response to learners' written errors in an adult ESL classroom. Using videotaped data of student–teacher interaction, the research first documented such reactive FoF feedback in the classroom, and then addressed the question as to whether students benefited more from the feedback that involved negotiation than feedback that involved no negotiation. The study also examined whether the effectiveness of feedback depended on the degree of negotiation within feedback.

There is a growing body of evidence regarding the positive role of corrective feedback and FoF in L2 learning (see Chapter 1 for a review). However, there is not yet a universal agreement among SLA researchers that FoF has any direct impact on L2 accuracy. One topic that has been most controversial is the effectiveness of form-focused feedback on L2 learners' written errors. This controversy is represented in the current debate among several L2 researchers on the role of error correction in L2 writing (Truscott 1996, 1999; Ferris 1999, 2002; Chandler 2003, 2004). Truscott (1996), for example, agued that corrective feedback is not only unhelpful but also detrimental. He believed that most of the arguments that are made in support of error correction in L2 writing have no merits. Reviewing the literature in this area, he noted that 'Substantial research shows it to be ineffective and none shows it to be helpful in any interesting sense' (ibid.: 327), and hence concluded that 'grammar correction has no place in writing courses and should be abandoned' (ibid.: 328).

Certainly, Truscott's position is a very strong one, and therefore several researchers have reacted to what he had stated, expressing their disagreement with his arguments (for example, Ferris 1999, 2002; Lyster, Lightbown, and Spada 1999; Chandler 2003, 2004). However, the above controversy suggests that corrective feedback is a much more complex issue than it appears. Thus, Ferris (1999), in response to Truscott, pointed out that 'If nothing else, reading Truscott's essay and reviewing the primary sources he cites has highlighted for me the urgent need for new research efforts which utilize a variety of paradigms to examine a range of questions that arise around this important topic' (Ferris 1999: 2). Ferris argued that 'despite the published debate and several decades of research activity in this area, we are virtually at Square One, as the existing research base is incomplete and inconsistent, and it would certainly be premature to formulate any conclusions about this topic' (Ferris 2004: 49).

Despite the current debate, dealing with learners' errors is an important aspect of L2 teaching. Therefore, a growing body of research has focused on addressing this issue in L2 classrooms. Although some of this research has produced evidence that does not fully endorse the effectiveness of such feedback, most of the evidence points to the usefulness of error correction versus no error correction (see Russell and Spada 2006 for a meta-analysis of these studies). Moreover, research involving written errors seems to suggest that if corrective feedback is provided appropriately it has important impacts on the learners' writing accuracy (for example, Lalande 1982; Ferris 1999; Ferris and Roberts 2001). Given such overall support, the real question for many L2 researchers has become not so much as to whether corrective feedback or FoF has any effects but what kind of feedback is more effective and how it should be incorporated into L2 instruction (for example, Fotos 1991, 1994; Fotos and Ellis 1991; Spada 1997; Doughty and Williams 1998a; Lightbown 2000; Mitchell 2000; VanPatten 2002; see also Chapter 1).

The role of negotiation in corrective feedback

In recent years, in keeping with current interests in FoF, on the one hand, and the importance attributed to the role of communicative interaction in L2 learning, on the other, the role of negotiation has attracted much theoretical and empirical attention (Pica 1994b, 1996; Long 1996; Lyster and Ranta 1997; Van den Branden 1997; McDonough and Mackey 2000; Nassaji and Swain 2000; Oliver and Mackey 2003; Nassaji and Fotos 2004). Within the interactionl perspectives on L2 learning, negotiation has been defined as the back and forth interactional strategies used to reach a solution to a problem in the course of communication (Pica 1994), and has been suggested as a means of providing learners with both positive and negative feedback (Long 1996).[2] Two types of negotiation have been distinguished: form negotiation and meaning negotiation. Meaning negotiation refers to the side sequences to the conversational interaction in order to deal with communication problems and to make input more comprehensible (Pica 1988, 1994; Van den Branden 1997). This is usually achieved through various interactional strategies such as asking for clarification or reformulating the learner error in the course of meaningful interaction to deal with comprehension diffi- culties. Form negotiation, on the other hand, is triggered by an attention to form (Lyster 2001) and occurs when 'one interlocutor tries to "push" the other towards producing a formally more correct and/or appropriate utter- ance' (Van den Branden 1997: 592). What was examined in this study was a kind of form negotiation, for it happened for the purpose of correcting the learners' output.

Arguments for the role of negotiation also come from the Vygotskian sociocultural theories of L2 learning, which place particular emphasis on the role of student–teacher interaction and collaboration when solving linguis- tics problems. In the sociocultural view, language learning is essentially a socially mediated process and one which is highly 'dependent on face to face interaction and shared processes, such as joint problem solving and discus- sion' (Mitchell and Myles 2004: 195). In this view, learning takes place mainly through dialogic interaction and negotiation of what learners want to do rather than what they are asked to do (Nassaji and Wells 2000). Within this framework, a few recent studies have revealed significant bene- fits for feedback that involves interaction and negotiation between the teacher and the learner (Aljaafreh and Lantolf 1994; Nassaji and Cumming 2000; Nassaji and Swain 2000; Haneda 2004). However, most of the current research in this area is in the context of oral errors.

In the present study, I examined the potential role of negotiation in an ESL classroom and in the context of addressing written errors. I first documented the occurrence of such processes and then explored whether students benefited more from feedback that involved negotiation than feed- back that involved little or no negotiation. In view of what occurred in the classroom, I formulated the following three research questions for the purpose of the study.

1 How frequently was corrective feedback provided through negotiation?
2 Were students more likely to benefit from feedback that involved negotia- tion than feedback without negotiation?

3 Did the success of the feedback provided depend on the amount of negotiation given?

Methods

Research setting

This study is part of a large scale classroom-based research project that investigates the nature and usefulness of interactive FoF in adult ESL classrooms. Data for this study come from one high-intermediate adult ESL classroom in an intensive ESL program in a university context. An important feature of this class was that L2 written errors were treated orally and through form-focused discussion and interaction. The FoF feedback took place in the context of a routine classroom activity in which students wrote weekly journals on topics that they liked. The teacher reviewed the journals, identified samples of the erroneous utterances that included common errors and then conducted follow-up feedback sessions in response to those utterances. These reactive FoF practices were documented and then analysed for the purpose of this study.

Participants

The class originally consisted of 14 students. Three students dropped out in the middle of the semester and one towards the end, reducing the total number of students in the course to 10. The remaining students were of different nationalities: 2 Chinese, 3 Japanese, 1 Spanish, 1 Thai, 1 Korean, 1 Portuguese, and 1 Taiwanese. Their age ranged from 21 to 37. At the beginning of the semester, they had been living in Canada for an average length of 5.5 months. The teacher was a male native speaker of English with 16 years of ESL and EFL teaching experience. He had been teaching in that program for about 10 years. The teacher's method of instruction was primarily communicative. His method of error correction included a combination of both form-focused explanation and meaningful interaction and discussion.

Data collection, transcription, and coding

Data were collected through classroom observation, audio and video-taping of the student–teacher interaction, a final student-specific error identification/correction test, and an interview with the teacher prior to the start of the classroom observation. The class was observed, audio-, and videotaped for nine times during a 12 week semester, producing a total of 12 hours of video-taped data. Five of these classroom meetings included corrective FoF feedback on students' written errors. Each feedback session lasted about 30 minutes, hence producing about 150 minutes of data.

Recording, transcription, and coding of the data were conducted by a trained graduate student of applied linguistics. After recording the lessons, the tapes were transcribed by the research assistant using normal orthography. To code the data, initially all the transcribed data were examined in order to identify what was called 'reactive focus on form episodes (RFFE)'. A RFFE was defined as an episode in which a particular erroneous form in the journal was identified, reacted to, and resolved. The boundaries of an episode were marked by attention to the erroneous form, which was called a 'trigger', and the correction of the form, which was called the 'resolution'.

All RFFEs were first coded in terms of the presence or absence of negotiation, and then in terms of the degree of negotiation. RFFEs that involved no negotiation were those in which the error was resolved by the teacher unidirectionally and without any interaction or negotiation. This kind of feedback represented a one-way FoF in which the teacher was the single provider of the feedback and the learner the single receiver. RFFEs that involved negotiation were those in which the error was resolved interactionally through elicitation-response sequences. This kind of FoF represented a kind of reactive FoF that involved form negotiation similar, in many ways, to that shown in classroom conversation (for example, Lyster and Ranta 1997; Ellis, Basturkmen, and Loewen 2001a) with the difference that the FoF occurred in response to written output produced prior to the interaction.

RFFEs involving negotiation were further coded in terms of the degree of negotiation. The degree of negotiation was determined based on the number of elicitation-response sequences within feedback (see, for example, Braidi 2002; Pica 1998). Accordingly, two types of negotiation opportunities were distinguished in each RFFE: limited negotiation and extended negotiation opportunities. RFFEs with limited negotiation were those that involved only one elicitation-response sequence. Elicitations were typically initiated by the teacher and the response was provided by the student(s). RFFEs with extended negotiation involved more than one elicitation-response sequence. (See the following section for examples.) Thus, altogether three types of RFFEs were identified and compared: RFFE with no negotiation, RFFE with limited negotiation, and RFFE with extended negotiation.

Each RFFE usually ended with a teacher's follow-up move, in which the teacher either verified or elaborated in some way on the student response. In RFFE with limited negotiation, if the student's initial response was successful, the teacher usually provided a verification of the correct form in the final move by either repeating, acknowledging, or elaborating on the learner's response. If the learner's initial response was not successful, the teacher usually resolved the error by providing the correct form himself. In RFFEs with extended negotiation, if the student's initial response was not successful, the teacher pushed and guided the learner further towards identifying and correcting the error, hence, allowing for more opportunities for negotiation and resolving the error.

In the last step of coding the data, the student responses in negotiated RFFEs were coded in terms of the degree of success in correcting their erroneous output. Responses were coded as successful, partially successful, or unsuccessful. Successful responses were those in which students successfully corrected or reformulated the erroneous output following the teacher's elicitation, for example

Partially successful responses were those that included only partial correc-

Trigger	Every country have
T	Every country have? Is that right?
S	has.

tion or reformulation of the error, for example:

Unsuccessful responses were those that included an incorrect response, an

Trigger	I want to know what different between Victoria and Vancouver.
T	Can you fix it, Dany?
S	I want to know what difference ...

irrelevant response, or no response, for example:

In cases where there were more than one elicitation-response sequence in

Trigger	My first time when I went to night club in Victoria ...
T	Did you find a mistake?
S	No.

the RFFE, always the final response was coded for the degree of success. As for the reliability of the coding, initially, I discussed the coding scheme with the research assistant and also coded some examples of the feedback episodes together. Then the research assistant continued coding the rest of data. Finally, I selected a random sample of 10 per cent of the data and coded that again. The inter-rater agreement obtained for both the feedback and response categories in the sample data was 93 per cent.

Student-specific error identification/correction test

Since the interactive FoF took place in a classroom context, the interaction was not always dyadic and the response to the error was not always from the same student who had made the error. Therefore, successful correction of the error did not necessarily indicate that the same student who had made the error succeeded in correcting the error. Thus, in order to determine whether students who had made the error were able to correct their own error, students participated in a final student-specific error identification/correction test. To this end, we collected each student's erroneous sentences which had received both negotiated and non-negotiated feedback and then administered those sentences to the same students after the feedback sessions. The students were asked to go over their own original sentences and identify their errors and make any corrections needed. The difference between the original performance and the test performance was used to show the extent to which the students had learned from the feedback. None of the students knew in advance that they would receive such a test.

Examples of types of focus of form feedback

Examples of the feedback types are presented in Tables 8.1 to 8.3. Table 8.1 illustrates an example of non-negotiated feedback. The feedback is triggered in response to the incorrect use of 'city' for 'cities' in the utterance, 'Victoria, one of the most beautiful city in Canada, … '. In this episode, upon noticing the error, the teacher provides the correct form immediately with no interaction or negotiation.

In the example in Table 8.2, the feedback is triggered in response to the problematic use of the word 'Canadian'. Unlike the episode in Table 8.1, in which the teacher resolved the error immediately with no negotiation, in this one the teacher starts by eliciting the correct form from the learner. Keil, the learner, responds to the teacher's elicitation but her response fails to correct the error. Following the student's unsuccessful response, the teacher provides the correct answer by alerting the learner that the 's' has been used

Trigger	Victoria, one of the most beautiful city in Canada, …
Teacher	Ah, city becomes cities, one of the most beautiful cities in Canada. OK?
Feedback type	Non-negotiated

TABLE 8.1 *Example of non-negotiated feedback*

Trigger	It's cheaper than Canadian's one.
1 Teacher	It's cheaper than Canadian's one?
2 Keil	Canadians
3 Teacher	The Canadian. The S is in the wrong place.
	A pack of cigarettes is cheaper than Canadian ones.
Feedback type	Negotiated
Response	Unsuccessful
Negotiation	Limited

TABLE 8.2 *Example of feedback involving limited negotiation (all names are pseudonyms)*

Trigger	Teachers in class like our friend …
1 Teacher	So who can make a correction? Who's got an idea to correct this? Mitny what would you do to correct this? Any idea?
2 Mitny	I don't know. I don't know.
3 Teacher	Just try. Just try. Just try your best.
4 Mitny	Okay, okay. Their
5 Teacher	OK so there is 'their'?
6 Mitny	Their teachers?
7 Teacher	How about I'll help here. How about 'our teachers'?
8 Mitny	Our teachers?
9 Teacher	Can you start with that?
10 Mitny	Our teachers?
11 Teacher	Yeah.
12 Mitny	Hm. Hm. They are?
13 Teacher	OK. So we have 'teachers', so we don't need 'their'. We just need 'teachers are.'
Feedback type	Negotiated
Response	Partially successful
Negotiation	Extended

TABLE 8.3 *Example of feedback involving extended negotiation*

wrongly and that the correct word in this context is 'Canadian'. The teacher then reformulates the whole utterance.

In the above episode, the teacher begins by eliciting the correct form from the learner, so it gives the learner some negotiation opportunity, but the teacher stops pushing the learner any further after the learner's initial attempt. Thus, the episode was coded as involving feedback with limited negotiation.

Table 8.3 illustrates an example of feedback involving extended nego-tiation. The feedback is triggered in response to the problem arising from the need for the plural verb 'are' in 'Teachers in class like our friend … '. The teacher begins the feedback by asking if anyone knows how to make a correction. He then asks Mitny. Mitny responds that she does not know the correct form. The teacher asks her again and wants her to try her best. The learner responds by suggesting the word 'their', thinking that what is miss-ing is the possessive adjective 'their'. The teacher asks for clarification, and the learner responds by elaborating on her answer. The teacher still does not provide the correct form but tries to help the learner by suggesting 'our teachers' instead of 'their teachers'. The negotiation continues until even-tually the learner produces the phrase 'they are', which could be a partial solution. But she still does not fully correct the sentence. The teacher then conveys to the learner that what the sentence needs is just the word 'are'. Referring to the learner's previous production of 'their', the teacher empha-sizes that when we have 'teachers', there is no need for 'their'.

As can be seen, there is more negotiation going on in this episode than in the previous one. As with the episode in Table 8.2, the teacher starts the exchange by eliciting the correct form from the learner, but, unlike that episode, upon the learner's initial failure, the teacher pushes the learner further in her output, providing the learner with ample opportunities for negotiation and scaffolding. Therefore, the episode was coded as involving feedback with extended negotiation.

Analyses and results

Analyses involved calculating the total number of FFEs, their types, success in repairing the error in the course of interaction, and success in identifying and correcting the error in the final student-specific error identification/correction test. Tables 8.4, 8.5, and 8.6 display the results of these analyses. Table 8.4 presents and compares the frequency of the different feedback types. Section A shows the frequency of the total feedback types as well as those involving negotiation and no negotiation. Section B shows the fre-quency of the feedback types involving limited and extended negotiation. The total number of feedback episodes identified were 134, out of which 83 (62 per cent) involved negotiation, and 51 (38 per cent) involved no negotia-tion. The chi-square test showed a significant difference between the fre-quency of these two feedback types: χ^2 (1, $N = 134$) $= 7.64$, $p < .01$, suggesting that feedback with negotiation occurred significantly more often than feed-back without negotiation in the classroom. Out of 83 negotiated feedback episodes, 53 (64 per cent) involved limited negotiation and 30 (36 per cent)

Types of feedback	Frequency	Per cent
A Negotiated	83	62%
Non-negotiated	51	38%
Total	134	100%
B Negotiated-limited	53	64%
Negotiated-extended	30	36%
Total	83	100%

TABLE 8.4 *The frequency and percentages of feedback types*

	Unsuccessful	Partially successful	Successful	Total
Limited negotiation	17 (32%)	5 (9%)	31 (59%)	**53 (100%)**
Extended negotiation	3 (10%)	7 (23%)	20 (67%)	**30 (100%)**
Total	20 (24%)	12 (15%)	51 (61%)	**83 (100%)**

TABLE 8.5 *Response success in feedback with limited and extended negotiation*

involved extended negotiation. Chi-square showed a significant difference between the frequency of these two feedback types: χ^2 (1, $N = 83$) = 6.37, $p < .05$, suggesting that feedback involving extended negotiation occurred significantly more often than feedback involving limited negotiation.

Table 8.5 presents the students' success in correcting the erroneous output during feedback with limited and extended negotiation. Results showed that feedback that involved extended negotiation resulted in more successful and partially successful correction of the erroneous forms than feedback with limited negotiation by the learner and their peers. Feedback with extended negotiation resulted in 67 per cent successful and 23 per cent partially successful correction of the targeted errors whereas feedback with limited negotiation resulted in 59 per cent successful and 9 per cent partially successful correction. A two-way chi-square revealed a significant relationship between success rate and type of feedback: χ^2 (2, $N = 83$) = 6.64, $p < .05$.

		Correct	Incorrect	Partially correct	Total
A	Negotiated	21 (60%)	12 (34%)	2 (6%)	35 (100%)
	Non-negotiated	3 (23%)	10 (77%)	0 (0%)	13 (100%)
	Total	24 (50%)	22 (46%)	2 (4%)	48 (100%)
B	Negotiated-limited	11 (55%)	7 (35%)	2 (10%)	20 (100%)
	Negotiated-extended	10 (67%)	5 (33%)	0 (0%)	15 (100%)
	Total	21 (60%)	12 (34%)	2 (6%)	35 (100%)

TABLE 8.6 *Response success in the final error identification/correction test*

Table 8.6 shows the students' performance on the final student-specific error identification/correction test. The results showed that students corrected more of their own errors when they obtained feedback that involved negotiation than feedback without negotiation (60 per cent and 23 per cent, respectively). A two way chi-square analysis revealed a significant relationship between the degree of success and feedback type: $\chi^2 (2, N = 48) = 7.09$, $p < .05$. The results also showed that feedback with extended negotiation resulted in more correction of the same errors than feedback with limited negotiated (67 per cent and 55 per cent, respectively), but this difference was not statistically significant.

Discussion

In his review of literature on FoF, R. Ellis (2001a) pointed out that although much theoretical discussion exists on how to FoF in SLA, much less attention has been paid to the way it actually occurs in L2 classrooms. This small scale study documented and examined the efficacy of such reactive FoF practices, with particular focus on interactional negotiation in an adult ESL classroom. The findings provided important insights into the nature and role of these processes.

The results showed that much of the FoF feedback that occurred in the classroom involved some kind of negotiation and discussion. They also showed important differences among the different types of feedback involving different degrees of negotiation. A comparison between the two types of negotiated feedback revealed that feedback with extended negotiation resulted in more successful repair of the errors by the learners and their peers during interaction than feedback with limited negotiation. Also, feedback with negotiation resulted in more correction of the errors on the final error correction test by the same student who had made the error than feedback with no negotiation. These findings highlight the importance of negotiation and hence support the argument that the effectiveness of feedback depends to a large extent on the degree of the 'meaningful transactions between the learner and the teacher' (Nassaji and Swain 2000: 35).

There are many theoretical reasons why negotiation is helpful. From the input-output perspective, negotiation provides opportunities for comprehensible input and pushed output, which has been shown to improve L2 accuracy (Swain 1985, 1995, 2000; Swain and Lapkin 2001; Fotos and Hinkel: Chapter 9 of this volume). From a sociocultural perspective, the dialogic characteristics of negotiated feedback are pedagogically powerful features of the feedback (Nassaji and Wells 2000) as these characteristics provide opportunities for scaffolding, that is, the supportive conditions created through social interaction (Donato 1994). In addition, negotiation provides the learner with more time to attend to the error and process the feedback. This increased processing time can enhance the effectiveness of the feedback and hence improve L2 acquisition. Finally, during negotiation learners have opportunities to find out and self-correct their own errors. This provides a discovery-based approach to error correction (see Tomlinson: Chapter 12 of this volume), which has been described as not only motivating but also helping learners 'to make inferences and formulate concepts about the TL, and to help them to fix this information in their long term memories' (Hendrickson 1978: 393).

In conclusion, this study suggests that unidirectional feedback may not be very effective in promoting L2 accuracy in learners' written work in comparison to negotiated feedback and that the effectiveness of feedback increases when learners participate and become engaged in the feedback process. (See Swain and Lapkin: Chapter 5 of this volume.) However, it is important to note that the results reported here are based on data from one adult ESL classroom. Therefore, the merits of the findings should be interpreted within the limits of the contexts in which the study took place. Moreover, in view of the uncertainties about the role of error correction in L2 learning, it is important to examine not only whether corrective feedback has any effects on L2 learning, but also the various factors that influence its effectiveness. Previous research, for example, has shown that learners respond differently to corrective feedback depending on their level of language proficiency. In particular, it has shown that learners with higher level of language proficiency are more likely to benefit from negotiated feedback than those with lower level of language proficiency (Mackey and Philp 1998; Williams 1999; Iwashita 2001). Therefore, future research can examine the effects of negotiated feedback on written errors with learners with different language proficiency levels. Future research can also address these questions more systematically in experimental research that selects and manipulates different feedback types and the different discourse contexts in which they occur.

Notes

1 The study was supported by a research grant from the Social Sciences and Humanities Research Council of Canada (410-2004-0923). I would like to thank the teacher and the students who participated in this study as well as my research assistant, Kyoko Kaneko, who helped with collecting, transcribing, and coding the data.
2 Positive evidence refers to information about what is possible in a language, and is received from exposure to target-like language input. Negative evidence refers to the information about what is not possible in a language, and is obtained from explicit or implicit corrective feedback on erroneous output.

9

Form-focused instruction and output for second language writing gains[1]

SANDRA FOTOS and ELI HINKEL

SECOND LANGUAGE educators generally agree that the combination of some type of grammar instruction and the provision of opportunities to receive meaningful input and to produce meaningful output constitutes an optimal approach to L2 instruction (for example, see Swain 1985, 1995, 2000; Swain and Lapkin 1995, 2001; R. Ellis 1997a, 2001a, 2001c, 2002a, 2004a, 2004b; Long and Robinson 1998; Nassaji 1999; Hinkel 2004; Nassaji and Fotos 2004). Most current pedagogy now includes both meaning-focused instruction and FFI, the first referring to purely communicative activities, and the second to activities promoting learner awareness of target grammar forms in input and production of the forms in output. (See Chapter 1 for a detailed treatment.)[2]

This chapter considers the role of FFI and output in assisting L2 writers to achieve fluency, accuracy, and complexity, three components of L2 proficiency (Ellis and Yuan 2004; Skehan 1996a). Based on the findings of current research, it will be suggested that FFI and the provision of output opportunities are essential for L2 writing development regardless of the learners' level of TL proficiency. As an example of a curriculum option, an email writing project for English as a foreign language (EFL) learners will be presented illustrating an output-based, reactive FFI approach incorporating corrective feedback and revision, components suggested to be essential for the development of L2 writing skills.

FFI and output for L2 acquisition

As discussed in Chapter 1, researchers have concluded that meaningful input alone, even enhanced input, does not promote the development of target-like L2 accuracy. Both grammar instruction and opportunities for output are now seen as additional requirements. The necessity for grammar instruction is further supported by the results of an extensive meta-analysis (Norris and Ortega 2000, 2001) of research indicating that FFI of any type is more productive, both in the short and long term, than purely communicative exposure to the L2. Significant L2 proficiency gains made from FFI were found to be durable over time, and learners exposed to FFI significantly and consistently outperformed those who were not instructed. Additional studies examining whether learners process TL input for meaning prior to processing for form (for example, VanPatten 1990; Leow 2001a; Lightbown 1998) indicate that, although learners generally allocate most of their attention to meaning, if the target form is important for decoding meaning, it is often noticed as well. In particular, learners who received FFI appeared to be able to focus their attention on the target forms while they were processing the meaning of the input (Doughty and Williams 1998a; Leow 2001a; Lightbown 1998).

In addition to FFI, many researchers also suggest that learner output is essential, particularly output eliciting the production of instructed forms so that learners can encounter them within communicative contexts. (See activities in Fotos and Ellis 1991; Fotos 1993, 1994, 1998, 2002; Doughty and Varela 1998; Doughty and Williams 1998a; Nassaji 1999; Ellis, Basturkmen, and Loewen 2001b; R. Ellis 2001a, 2003.) As explained in Chapter 1, noticing target forms is generally regarded as a precondition for their acquisition, and production of target forms is suggested to promote noticing. In a recent overview of the need for output in SLA, Swain (2005) observes that the cognitive requirements for output production are distinct from those involved in input processing, and identifies three unique functions for output (Swain 2005; originally in Swain 1995): (1) the noticing/triggering function, (2) the hypothesis-testing function, and (3) the metalinguistic or reflective function. These functions will be discussed below.

The noticing/triggering function refers to situations where learners produce the TL and then notice a 'gap' between what they wish to say and what they are able to say, or become aware of what they do not know in the TL, this is termed a 'hole'.[3] Such noticing is suggested to trigger cognitive processes generating new linguistic knowledge or consolidating existing knowledge, both essential for L2 learning (Swain 1985, 1995, 2000, 2005; Schmidt 1990, 1993, 2001; Swain and Lapkin 1995, 2001a and b; Robinson 2003).

The hypothesis testing function refers to situations where learners produce output and then receive feedback on its correctness, often modifying subsequent output so that it becomes more accurate. Extensive research on L2 learner interaction (summarized in R. Ellis 1997a, 2003; Nassaji 1999;

Nassaji and Swain, 2000; Gass 2003; Russell and Spada 2006) indicates that learners particularly modify their output in response to clarification requests and other negotiations of meaning. Such findings have been interpreted to indicate that internal hypothesis testing has taken place within the learner's interlanguage system (Gass 2003; Robinson 2003) as a result of output and subsequent feedback.

The metalinguistic or reflective function refers to learners' use of output to reflect on TL use, particularly during collaborative learning. There is considerable research analyzing learner dialogue during performance of interactive communicative tasks (for example, see Lantolf 2000a, Chapter 3 of this volume; Swain and Lapkin 2001a and b, Chapter 5 of this volume; R. Ellis 2003) indicating that learners often improve their understanding of the TL when they discuss it with others, thereby becoming aware of gaps in their linguistic knowledge, linking form, function and meaning, and receiving feedback (Kowal and Swain 1994), processes which often result in accuracy gains in the structures that were the task content. (See the review in R. Ellis 2003.) Swain therefore suggests that, when learners produce the TL, they

> move from the semantic, open-ended, strategic processing
> prevalent in comprehension to the complete grammatical
> processing needed for accurate production.
>
> (Swain 2000: 99)

Although the linguistic focus of an FFI output-based activity may not always be obvious, noticing of the target form is promoted since the form must be processed to perform the activity. From this perspective, TL output is suggested to perform the following important functions: (1) it consolidates previous instruction, (2) it encourages noticing of instructed forms in subsequent input, and (3) it facilitates L2 processing and acquisition.

Output thus bridges meaning and form, allowing learners to repeatedly encounter instructed forms within meaningful contexts, thereby facilitating noticing and eventual acquisition. The following section links these considerations to the L2 writing classroom.

Reading is not enough: FFI and output for L2 writing gains

During the past several decades, studies of the development of L2 writing proficiency have addressed the issue of whether exposure to the L2 through meaning-focused activities alone (for example, by reading writing samples) enables L2 writers to acquire the skills needed to produce fluent, accurate, and complex written output (Celce-Murcia 1991; Celce-Murcia and Hilles 1988; Doughty and Varela 1998; R. Ellis 1997a, 2002a, 2002b, 2003; Ferris and Hedgcock 2005; Hinkel 2002, 2003; Murunoi 2000; Swain 1985, 1991; Radwan 2005), and the results have not been positive. Hinkel's (2002) large scale empirical analysis of learners' written text indicates that despite years of experience with, and exposure to, the L2 in English-speaking countries, including completion of college-level education, most L2 writers' text continues to differ significantly from that of novice L1 writers in regard to linguistic and rhetorical features. Even advanced and highly L2 trained writers continue to have a limited lexical and syntactic repertoire that enables them to produce only simple text restricted to common language features encountered predominantly in conversational discourse (Hinkel 2003), rather than the formal text appropriate for the academic register.

Additional studies of ESL writers instructed only through input-based approaches (summarized in Hinkel 2002) have found that even highly productive writers seldom reach TL levels of accuracy and complexity, especially in academic writing, but continue to produce very simple text, similar to TL native speaker elementary students (Hinkel 2003). Consequently, when teaching L2 academic writing, comprehensible input alone—through presenting learners with TL academic texts to read—is not sufficient to develop the skills needed to produce acceptable formal writing. The majority of experts on L2 writing now postulate that without both FFI and intensive and extensive output learners are unable to develop the range of advanced grammar features required to generate formal written prose. (See R. Ellis 1994a; Hammerly 1991; Shaw and Liu 1998; Ferris and Hedgcock 2005.)

Considering this problem, R. Ellis (1990: 121) has suggested that 'formal classroom teaching with its emphasis on linguistic accuracy will engage the learner in planned (spoken or written) discourse and develop the corresponding type of competence'. Other experts in teacher training and L2 pedagogy (see reviews in R. Ellis 2003; Ellis and Yuan 2004; Hinkel 2002; Williams 2005a, 2005b) have similarly noted that both FFI and writing output opportunities are essential if L2 learners are to attain the component skills requisite for production of TL written output.

To this end, FFI is now seen to be foundational in the teaching of L2 writing as long as two conditions are fulfilled: (1) appropriate and accurate use of explicitly or implicitly instructed target forms should take place in meaningful contexts so that learners can notice their use, and (2) learners should be given numerous opportunities to practice the target structures through written output, subsequent feedback and the requirement for revision.

FFI-based writing instruction

Addressing shortfalls in the teaching of L2 academic writing, Frodesen (2001: 234) observes that 'the wholesale adoption of L1 composition theories and practices for L2 writing classes seems misguided in light of the many differences between first and L2 writers, processes, and products'. Frodesen also comments on the absence of FFI prevalent in many US writing curricula, where teachers continue to believe that comprehensible input alone is sufficient to achieve TL writing proficiency. Other specialists, such as Birch (2005) and Byrd (2005), suggest that L2 curricula must include attention to a range of grammar features to enable writers to produce superior written output.

Thus, recommended L2 writing pedagogy now includes use of a FFI approach based on the provision of ample practice opportunities and incorporating the following four steps: (1) pre-writing planning, (2) guided output, (3) corrective feedback (Ferris and Roberts 2001; Ferris and Hedgcock 2005), and (4) learner revision.

Regarding these recommendations, R. Ellis has emphasized that FFI may not necessarily take the form of explicit rule teaching, and that a variety of communicative methodological options are available to achieve some form of explicit instruction. The key is to identify pedagogical options that are cognitively valid and are matched with the needs of the L2 learners. According to R. Ellis (2001a, 2002c; Ellis and Yuan 2004), a FFI methodological approach should lead to writing activities that promote effective communication through the application of grammar rules in meaningful discourse as opposed to, for example, merely learning about lexical and grammar rules without subsequent opportunities to produce guided output containing the instructed forms.

In light of these considerations, it is clear that learners who seek to improve their L2 skills for vocational or academic purposes require FFI rather than deductive instruction alone. For this reason grammar and advanced lexis should be taught thoroughly and intensively, and incorporated into written tasks. As Frodesen (2001) has noted, the lack of thorough and consistent instruction in grammar in current L2 writing pedagogy does learners a disservice because it limits their vocational, academic, and professional options. (Also see Celce-Murcia 2001; Christie 1998.) Since recent research has demonstrated that explicit instruction, even on complex grammar features, leads to significant and durable grammar gains that produce improvements in L2 writing quality (Radwan 2005; Williams 2005b), it is essential to make it a part of classroom practice.

Task-based FFI for academic writing

Within communicative and task-based approaches to teaching, various methodological modifications in L2 pedagogy have been proposed that permit integration of the fluency and accuracy foci (for example, Fotos 2002; Nassaji: Chapter 8 in this volume; Pica: Chapter 11 of this volume; Skehan: Chapter 4 of this volume) and impact favorably on writing production. According to R. Ellis (2003), task-based teaching provides built-in opportunities for the type of planning that result in more accurate and complex uses of the TL. R. Ellis explains that carefully designed tasks foster the development of various aspects of L2 production. For example, narratives and descriptions can be effective in fluency-focused teaching, while problem-solving tasks can promote increased grammatical and lexical complexity in learner language use.

Another advantage of using tasks in L2 writing instruction is that rehearsal (or task repetition) affords learners an opportunity to accommodate competing cognitive demands. Advanced planning of content and formulation (for example, planning what to say/write and how to say/write it) leads to substantial improvements in the amount of TL output, and enhanced grammatical and lexical accuracy (R. Ellis 2001a, 2003). In content and task-based instruction, contextualized uses of specific grammar structures and vocabulary can be emphasized to connect the subject matter and language learning activities.

Thus, much current L2 writing pedagogy incorporates task-based grammar teaching and task planning activities. For example, a study by Ellis and Yuan (2004) addressing the development of fluency, complexity, and accuracy in the writing of EFL students in a Chinese university indicates that pre-task planning enabled learners to produce more fluent text than that produced by learners who did not engage in planning. The planners also included significantly more complex and varied language in terms of both syntactic and lexical constructions in their writing. Ellis and Yuan found that verb tenses, the passive voice, and complex sentences represented important foci of the learners' attention during the writing process. These constructions occurred more frequently in the writing of learners who received prior FFI and the opportunity to plan their writing than in the writing of those without FFI or planning opportunities.

In his overview of the effectiveness of FFI, R. Ellis (2002b: 231) observed that 'FFI can have a significant effect on the accuracy of use of grammatical structures, although ... these gains are ... are contingent on a number of factors'.

In the context of L2 writing instruction, therefore, effective grammar pedagogy centers on cumulative curricula that move forward from the structures that learners already know or from those that are less complex to more advanced constructions (R. Ellis 2002b). At low and intermediate levels of learner TL proficiency, FFI can begin with noticing and analyzing the grammatical and lexical features in authentic (and possibly simplified) written discourse. At this level of FFI, the curricular objective is to heighten the learners' awareness of prevalent grammar constructions in written text. During the subsequent stages of L2 development, the contextualized uses of grammar and lexis can become a focus of practice writing activities and enriched input in content-based writing instruction (R. Ellis 1990, 1994a, 1997a, 2002b).

At the high intermediate and/or advanced levels of TL proficiency, grammar teaching for writing development can focus on the more advanced lexicogrammatical features of written output such as the distinctions between the historical present tense and the past tense as well as complex noun phrases, subordinate constructions, and the passive voice (Hinkel 2005a).

Noticing and error correction

Noticing how language constructions are employed in formal written prose, combined with a formal explanation, is particularly put forward as a way of assisting L2 writers to improve their skills. Three general requirements (Schmidt 2001) for using FFI to promote the noticing of TL grammar structures are: (1) learner awareness of the particular constructions they should notice, (2) explicit instruction or more indirect forms of FFI on the specific characteristics of these constructions that require focused attention, and (3) increased learner awareness of the structure of complete sentences in written academic discourse (as opposed to fragments or isolated sentences), as well as the distinctions between the spoken and written register, particularly the formal register of academic language.

According to R. Ellis (1990) and others (Schmidt 1990, 1993, 2001; Robinson 1995, 1996, 2003), attention and awareness are important for the development of accuracy and self-correction skills in L2 writing. Noticing the occurrences of incorrect constructions and subsequent self-editing require learners to analyze grammar use in context. This activity, which is essential in refining L2 writing skills, begins with noticing (James 1998), with a clear role for explicit instruction rather than implicit FFI.

Regarding this point, Radwan (2005) emphasizes that directly explaining regularities in the use of L2 syntactic constructions is far more efficient than implicit teaching that is often slow and laborious. It may be unreasonable to expect L2 learners to be able to tease out, on their own, the complex rules that govern, for example, sentence boundaries or article use in English. Thus, a more direct and explicit version of FFI is suggested to be of special usefulness in the promotion of L2 academic writing skills.

The following section discusses output and reactive FFI in an L2 writing class where computer-assisted language learning (CALL) is used in the FL context and considers possible TL gains resulting from this type of activity. The description is not intended to be a research report but is rather an example of the classroom application of the pedagogy recommended above.

Email exchange: output, reactive FFI, and revision for FL writing gains

It is extremely difficult for most FL learners to receive large amounts of TL input and even more problematic to have opportunities to produce authentic TL output. This section describes an EFL writing course consisting of email exchange and home page construction, activities suggested to provide learners with authentic meaning-focused input and the requirement to produce accurate written output through FFI, feedback on errors, and learner revision (Shetzer and Warschauer 2001). Research on TL email exchange programs is also discussed to indicate how such CALL-based activities have successfully produce TL writing gains.

L2 writing gains through computer use

As CALL becomes increasingly significant in L2 teaching and learning, a number of surveys on its use to promote different TL skills have appeared. (See reviews in Levy 1997; Egbert and Hanson-Smith 1999; Chapelle 2001; Warschauer and Kern 2001; Fotos and Browne 2004; Egbert 2005.) An overview of research on ESL/EFL learners writing with computers (Pennington 2003) suggests that the use of word processors results in longer texts and enhanced revisions compared with pen-and-paper writing. Other studies indicate that EFL learners make more meaning-level revisions than pen-and-paper comparison groups. Research with Asian EFL learners (Brock and Pennington 1999) observed that learners who used computers and then received peer feedback made significantly more grammatical and content revisions than a comparison group who did not use computers. Thus, research on computer-based FL writing has found positive effects for

L2 writers in general and for ESL/EFL writers in particular, in terms of (a) attitudes and (b) length of texts, along with more modest positive effects in terms of (c) overall writing quality and (d) quantity of revision; there are also suggestive findings in a positive direction for (e) quality of revision. The word processor may help these writers to compensate for their lack of full proficiency in the L2 and to develop a more effective and efficient writing process.

(Pennington 2003: 78–9)

There has been considerable investigation of one type of computer-based writing, email exchange, and the results indicate extremely favorable learning outcomes. Email activities have been shown to motivate learners, increase self-esteem and critical thinking skills, develop knowledge about the target culture, and promote L2 writing proficiency (Kern 1995; Warschauer 1995, 1996; Beauvois 1998a, 1998b; Gaer 1999; Holliday 1999; Skinner and Austin 1999; Pellettieri 2000; Sotillo 2000; Blake and Zyzik 2003; Greenfield 2003; O'Dowd 2003; Stockwell and Harrington 2003; Fotos 2004; Egbert 2005). Although the participants in many email exchange programs are L2 learners paired with TL native speakers, it has been observed that even when L2 learners exchange email with each other, their text is often 'grammatical, targetlike input displaying a range of language features similar to those used by L1 speakers' (Holliday 1999: 187).

Similar positive results have been obtained for a series of Japanese university EFL learner email-based writing classes (Fotos 2004). As noted, R. Ellis suggests (2003) that well-designed tasks supply learners with TL input that is rich in communicative usages of instructed grammar forms, and that task performance can provide opportunities for students to produce the TL and to receive feedback on their production. Following these considerations, the various EFL email classes employed combinations of the following real-life tasks: (1) writing and answering email from English native speakers, the instructor, and other class members, (2) writing a personal introduction and other information and making multiple revisions following corrective feedback and FFI, and (3) constructing a TL web page using the personal introduction. Thus, there was an authentic purpose for the TL activities, and accuracy was important at each stage, particularly when writing the web page contents.

Email output, FFI and revision

Research on three semester-long EFL classes performing email exchange activities with TL native speakers indicates that TL proficiency gains

(Fotos 2004) were consistently achieved. Although it must be acknow-ledged that proficiency gains tend to occur over time regardless of the instructional treatment, other studies of email exchanges have reported similar gains in L2 proficiency (for example, Warschauer 1995, 1996; Stockwell and Harrington 2003). It is suggested that TL proficiency gains through participation in email exchange programs can be fostered by the requirement for regular authentic output, feedback on errors, reactive FFI, and learner scaffolding on embedded email text as a strategy to facilitate increasingly target-like output (Fotos 2004).

Reactive FFI occurs when the teacher reacts to learner errors through provision of explicit instruction on problematic forms. For example, in a series of year-long email exchange and web page construction classes, the researcher/instructor gave weekly instruction on common TL grammar errors, inaccurate lexical items, and pragmatic errors that appeared in the previous week's email. This was followed by an instructor-initiated Internet search for communicative usages of the instructed forms (performed by entering the target form in the window of a search engine), the results of which were displayed on the learners' monitors. Learners could therefore encounter communicative usages of the problematic form immediately after FFI.

In addition, the instructor corrected multiple drafts of the web page contents often by indirect correction methods indicating only the location or type of error, a technique suggested to have a more positive effect on accuracy gains than direct correction (Ferris and Hedgcock 2005). Corrections were then input by the learners. As mentioned, writing research (Ferris and Hedgcock 2005; Ferris 2001; Pennington 2003; Russell and Spada 2006) indicates that L2 writers must revise their text to achieve accuracy gains.

Scaffolding on embedded email text

A second factor suggested to promote TL gains is the fact that the EFL learners often scaffolded[4] on their interlocutor's embedded email text. (See Fotos 2004 for examples.) Scaffolding has been defined (R. Ellis 2003: 180–1) as 'a dialogic process by which one speaker assists another in performing a function that he or she cannot perform alone'. Studies of email exchange and network-based communication (Kern 1995; Trenchs 1996; Pellettieri 2000; Egbert 2005) report multiple instances of L2 learner scaffolding on embedded email text, and it has been observed that such learners exhibit increased TL production as well as TL accuracy and complexity gains through use of the embedded email text to construct their own text. An investigation (Pellettieri 2000) analyzing synchronous electronic communication (chat) for negotiations and responses to negotiations found that L2 learners incorporated 70 per cent of the explicit feedback they received from their teacher and other learners, often through scaffolding techniques, and 75 per cent of the implicit target feedback (mainly recasts), resulting in more target-like output.

Additional research has reported this phenomenon for L2 writing in general (Swain 2000). One study (Nassaji and Cumming 2000) found that scaffolding enabled an ESL learner writing a dialogic journal to develop improved accuracy by adopting the instructors' syntax, thus becoming aware of the correct usage of problematic forms. Additional research (Swain and Lapkin 2001; Swain, Brooks, and Tocalli-Beller 2002; Blake and Zyzik 2003; also see Swain and Lapkin: Chapter 5 in this volume) suggests that collaborative rather than individual L2 writing promotes improved grammatical accuracy even when the interlocutors are L2 learners rather than learner-TL native speaker pairs (Holliday 1999), due to the requirement for output and the subsequent attention to linguistic form that results.

Gains in writing fluency, as measured by increased lexical production and increased numbers of T-units[5] has also been promoted by the regular provision of TL production opportunities through email exchange (Van Handle and Corol 1998; Sotillo 2000; Pennington 2003).

It can therefore be suggested that within the FL context CALL-based activities can provide FL writers with abundant opportunities to receive authentic TL input and produce meaning-focused TL output. Learners can receive explicit FFI on output errors and make repeated revisions, thus facilitating noticing of instructed TL forms, and can also use embedded email text as a scaffold to extend their output capability and to further promote noticing of key target forms.

Conclusion

This chapter has addressed the development of proficiency in L2 writing and has noted that input alone is insufficient. Research has shown that numerous factors confound the development of fluency, accuracy, and complexity in L2 writing, and most (if not all) have to do with shortfalls in the L2 writers' language proficiency. L2 writing is an advanced skill, and even highly educated learners have been shown to require years of training to attain the level of TL proficiency necessary to create effective written prose. In this context, the importance of FFI to develop learners' writing skills cannot be overestimated.

Following these insights from research and our own classroom experience, we recommend a writing curriculum based on planning opportunities, explicit FFI, the provision of ample output opportunities, followed by corrective feedback from the instructor, reactive FFI, and multiple revisions by the authors, and, when feasible, the provision of scaffolding. FFI combined with teaching pedagogy addressing discourse and the conventions of writing have much to contribute to the development of L2 writing skills.

Notes

1 Some portions of S. Fotos' contribution to the chapter appeared as an in-house working paper at the author's university in 2005. See S. Fotos. 'Output-based activities for enhancing second language acquisition' in *Seventh LL Workshop Proceedings: Practical Issues in Foreign Language Education*. Institute of Language Education, Senshu University: 25–30.

2 In his review of research on FFI and the development of implicit knowledge, R. Ellis (2002a: 224) cautions that the cognitive requirements for processing time and frequency of exposure make it unlikely that a few incidents of FFI will develop implicit knowledge, although the ability of FFI to impact on explicit knowledge has been shown repeatedly (R. Ellis 1997a, 2002a). Since explicit knowledge can lead to implicit knowledge gains when the learner becomes aware of the target form, R. Ellis therefore suggests that it may not be necessary to develop implicit knowledge directly.

3 A distinction in the noticing and output literature (Doughty and Williams 1998a; Swain 1998) has been made between two types of noticing: (1) when learners notice a *gap* between what they want to express in the TL and the ability of their current interlanguage to do so, and (2) when learners notice a *hole* in their interlanguage, this defined as the lack of ability to express themselves because of the absence of the required form (Swain 1998). It has been suggested (Williams 2005a) that, although cognitively more difficult, noticing a gap may result in improved accuracy since the learner's interlanguage must be restructured, whereas activities promoting noticing a hole (a lexical item, for example), although easier to construct, are less cognitively demanding since comparison with the learner's current interlanguage is not required.

4 R. Ellis (2003: 82) notes that the terms 'scaffold' or 'scaffolding,' expressions indicating that people supply part of an utterance for their interlocutors who then use it to build their own utterances, are being replaced by 'collaborative dialogue' in many reports. Swain (2000: 102), for

example, uses 'collaborative dialogue', defining it as 'dialogue in which speakers are engaged in problem solving and knowledge building'.

5 A T-unit is defined (Hunt 1970) as the main clause of a sentence plus any attached subordinate clauses and non-clausal structures.

Part Three
Focus on form and teacher education

10

Materials development and research: towards a form-focused perspective[1]

JACK C. RICHARDS

WITHIN APPLIED LINGUISTICS, the activities of those involved in developing instructional materials and those working in second language (L2) learning research and theory are often seen to have little connection. Traditionally there has been relatively little crossover between those working in either domain, as seen in the very different issues written about in journals such as *ELT Journal* as compared to journals such as *Applied Linguistics*. Practitioners in one domain seldom work in the other, although people like Rod Ellis, David Nunan, and myself might be considered exceptions. In this chapter I want to explore the kinds of interaction that are possible between research/theory and materials design, and illustrate such connections from my own experience as a materials developer who is also interested in research and theory. Particular reference is made to the implications of the theory of form-focused instruction (FFI) for materials development and curriculum design.

Effective instructional materials in language teaching are shaped by consideration of a number of factors, including teacher, learner, and contextual variables. Teacher factors include the teacher's language proficiency, training and experience, cultural background, and preferred teaching style. Learner factors include learners' learning-style preferences, their language learning needs, interests, and motivations. Contextual factors include the school culture, classroom conditions, class size, and availability of teaching resources. In planning a new textbook or course book series, the publisher will normally provide the writer with a profile of the target teachers, learners, and teaching context to enable the writer to tailor the materials to the target audience. In curriculum planning this phase is part of situational analysis.

Two other factors play a crucial role in determining what the appearance of materials is and how they will function. One is the theory of language and language use reflected in the materials, and the other is the theory of language learning on which the materials are based. These two sources of input provide the necessary links between theory and pedagogy. But how is this actually reflected in practice? The following sections will explore this question.

Theories of language and language use

In developing materials for any aspect of language learning, whether it be a skill-based course in listening, speaking, reading, or writing, or an integrated-skills basic series, the writer's understanding of the target language (TL) and language use will have a major impact on material design by determining the goals set for the materials, the focus of the materials, and the activities contained within them. I will refer to this level of conceptualization as the writer's theory of language and language use. In planning materials for the teaching of writing, for example, the materials developer could start from any of a number of views of the nature of writing or of texts. He or she could start from a view of written language that focuses on *writing modes,* i.e. the organizational modes underlying paragraphs and essays, such as definition, comparison-contrast, classification, or cause-effect. Alternatively the materials developer might start from a genre or text-based view of written language in which texts such as news reports, business letters, or academic articles are seen to reflect L2 use within particular contexts. Alternatively, the writer could begin from a process perspective in which written texts are seen to reflect the cognitive and composing processes that go into their creation, such as pre-writing, planning, drafting, composing, reviewing, revising, and editing. If the materials developer were preparing a listening course, it would be necessary to clarify his or her understanding of the nature of listening. Is it viewed largely as a process of decoding input? Is it viewed in terms of the mastery of discrete listening skills and sub-skills? Or is it seen as a blend of top-down and bottom-up processing? For a speaking course, again, a starting point would be the selection of an appropriate theory or model of the nature of oral interaction. Is it based on a model of communicative competence and does it seek to address grammatical competence, sociolinguistic competence, discourse competence and strategic competence? Or is oral communication viewed more in terms of speech act theory, focusing on utterances as functional units in communication and dependent upon the performance of speech acts?

While the preparation of instructional materials might appear to be an essentially practical activity, the materials will inevitably reflect a theory of the nature of language, communication, and language use. As my former colleague Ted Plaister used to say, 'There's nothing so practical as a good theory'!

Theories of language learning

In addition to selecting a theory of language and language use to support the approach the materials writer will take, it is also necessary to consider the complementary question of the theory of language learning underlying the materials, since this will determine how the syllabus is implemented in the form of exercises, tasks, activities, and learning experiences. Particular language models are often linked to particular views of learning. For example a text-based approach to the teaching of writing is often linked to a Vygotskian view of learning based on the notion of scaffolding. (See Lantolf 2000a.) The teacher and the learners are viewed as engaged in collaborative problem-solving activity, with the teacher providing demonstrations, support, guidance and input, and gradually withdrawing these as the learner becomes increasingly independent. Models of good writing are employed and writing (or more correctly, text construction) is taught through a process of deconstruction, modeling, and joint elaboration and reconstruction as students create their own texts.

The theory of learning underlying approaches to the teaching of conversation might be based on a somewhat different view of learning. It could reflect an interactionist view of language acquisition based on the hypothesis that language acquisition requires or greatly benefits from interaction, communication, and especially negotiation of meaning, which happens when interlocutors attempt to overcome problems in conveying their meaning, resulting in both additional input and useful feedback on the learners' own production. For example, R. Ellis's task-based model of instruction (R. Ellis 2003) has been formulated using an interactionist view of learning drawing on the concept of FFI. This refers to activities designed to promote learner awareness of target forms in input and production of these forms in output. FFI has been described (R. Ellis 2001a: 1–2) as, 'any planned or incidental instructional activity that is intended to induce learners to pay attention to linguistic form', and has become a significant approach combining a communicative orientation with some type of grammar instruction.

Regarding FFI, L2 learning theory has been a ripe field for speculation in the last 20 years. Consequently the materials developer has a rich source of theories to draw from in deciding on a learning model to adopt. The changing state of theory and understanding in relation to language and language use is responsible for paradigm shifts in language teaching and for the ongoing need to review what the current assumptions are and sometimes to rethink how to develop materials. In particular, the current shift from a purely meaning-focused curriculum to one that suggests the need for integration of FFI and meaning-focused activities has had a profound impact on materials development (Doughty and Varela 1998; Doughty and Williams 1998a; R. Ellis 2001a, 2001b, 2002b, 2005a). Traditionally, much L2 material tended to be almost exclusively either meaning-focused or form-focused. In recent years in particular, language teaching courses and materials seem to focus more on meaning and real communication than on linguistic forms, with the stated goals being the development of students' communicative competence. However, neither a focus on meaning nor an FoF, by itself, promotes the design of balanced language materials.

Let us consider an example from materials development for L2 listening. One approach to the teaching of listening sees *listening comprehension* as the focus of listening materials. The assumptions underlying this approach are: (1) listening serves the goal of extracting meaning from messages, (2) in order to do this, learners must be taught how to use both bottom-up and top-down processes to arrive at an understanding of messages, (3) the language of utterances, i.e. the precise words, syntax, and expressions used by speakers, represents temporary carriers of meaning, and finally, (4) once meaning has been identified, there is no further need to attend to the form of messages. In the development of classroom materials a variety of techniques has been employed based on a view of listening as this type of comprehension. These include: (1) predicting the meaning of messages, (2) identifying key words and ignoring others while listening, and (3) using background knowledge to facilitate selective listening.

These assumptions and practices have served me well in developing successful listening texts in the past. However, as a result of changing theoretical perspectives on the nature of listening in language learning, I have recently been exploring the implications of a different but complementary view of listening, one that examines the role of listening in facilitating language acquisition. Schmidt (1990) and others (see R. Ellis 2001a, 2002b, 2005a) have drawn attention to the role of consciousness in language learning, and in particular to the role of *noticing*. The argument is that learners cannot successfully process TL forms from input unless they notice the form that encodes the input. Consciousness of language forms in the input can serve as a trigger activating the first stage in the process of incorporating new linguistic features into one's language competence.

Schmidt (2001) distinguishes between input (what the learner hears) and intake (that part of the input that the learner notices). In order for listening to lead to *language acquisition* and not simply to *comprehension,* it is argued that learners need to both *notice* the formal features of the input as well as have opportunities to try to incorporate new language items in their linguistic repertoire (Schmidt 2001; R. Ellis 2001a, 2002b). This involves processes variously referred to as restructuring, complexification, and producing stretched output. (See Swain 2005.)

This view of noticing has important implications for teaching listening and for materials development. We can distinguish between purely meaning-based approaches where comprehension alone is the instructional goal, and FFI, where both meaning comprehension and acquisition of language form are the focus. Examples of the former would be situations where listening in order to extract information is the primary focus, such as listening to lectures, listening to announcements, sales presentations, and service encounters such as checking into a hotel. In other cases, however, a listening course may be part of a general English course or be linked to a speaking course. In these situations both listening as comprehension and listening as acquisition is the focus. Listening texts and materials can then be exploited, first as the basis for comprehension, and second as the basis for acquisition.

This suggests a two-part cycle of activities in listening lessons and materials, a comprehension phase and an acquisition phase. The comprehension phase would focus on extracting meaning, as described above. The acquisition phase would include form-focused noticing activities and restructuring activities. Form-focused noticing activities involve returning to a listening text that has served as the basis for comprehension and then using it as the basis for FFI to develop language awareness (R. Ellis 2002b, 2005a). For example students could listen to a recording again in order to: (1) identify differences between what they hear and a printed version of the text, (2) complete a cloze version of the text, (3) complete sentence stems taken from the text, or (4) using a list, check off expressions that have occurred.

Restructuring activities are oral or written tasks that involve productive use of selected items from the listening text. Such activities could include: (1) pair reading of the tape scripts of a conversational text, (2) written sentence-completion tasks requiring use of expressions and other linguistic items that occurred in the text, (3) dialog practice based on dialogs that incorporate items from the text, and (4) role-plays in which students are required to use TL forms from the text.

Thus, anyone who sets out to write instructional materials for language teaching will start out with either some type of implicit or better still, explicit understanding of the issues discussed above, namely the theory of language and of language learning that the materials will be based on. Here the writer's familiarity with current trends and theory in language teaching, applied linguistics, and L2 learning will be helpful. However, in order to make use of this knowledge, it has to be operationalized in the form of *a syllabus* and a set of *instructional principles* must be extrapolated which will inform the pedagogical strategies used in the materials.

Developing a syllabus

One of the first applications of the theory of language that the materials designer has selected is determining the type of syllabus the materials will be based on. To re-visit some of the examples already cited, a writing course might be built around a functional syllabus, a text-based syllabus, or a process syllabus. A listening course might be built around a skills syllabus, a text-based syllabus, or a topical syllabus. A conversation course might be built around a functional syllabus, a task-based syllabus, or a skills syllabus. These different syllabus types may also be combined in different ways.

Syllabus design is an activity that can draw on a considerable body of relevant research. Since the field of *language description* (for example, as seen in register analysis, discourse analysis, corpus studies) is well established, there is a substantial research base that a materials developer can consult in order to make decisions about the linguistic content of instructional materials. In the case of reading materials, for example, there are a large number of corpus studies that can provide relevant information.

In developing the three-level reading series *Strategic Reading* (Richards and Eckstut-Didier 2003), one important issue was the vocabulary level of the reading texts. Particularly for the advanced level in the series, my co-author and I were able to consult not only standard word lists but also research on the most frequently occurring words in academic reading. (See Coxhead 2000.) Likewise the syllabuses I have developed for listening comprehension texts have been based to a large extent on research on listening skills and the sub-skills that are assumed to contribute to fluent listening. In a listening-skills project I am currently working on, one of the first tasks at the planning stage was to develop an updated taxonomy of listening skills to be referred to while developing the scope and sequence plan for the materials and activity types. In the area of conversation texts, sources such as *Threshold Level English* (Van Ek and Alexander 1980) can be consulted to identify a syllabus of basic functions. Whether *Threshold Level*

English can be regarded as research based, of course, is a matter of opinion. In *Person to Person* (Richards and Bycina 1984), for example, the functional syllabus underlying the syllabus is based largely on *Threshold Level English*, supplemented by other sources on essential functions and speech acts. In another series, *Springboard* (Richards 1999), a topical syllabus is used, the topics being derived from research on students' interests and preferences.

The grammatical syllabi in my course books used the Cobuild corpus-based grammar (Collins 1990) as a source for items to include in the syllabus, although other factors also played a role. These are the factors referred to earlier: *Contextual factors* (the kinds of grammatical items specified in national syllabuses in countries where the courses were to be marketed), as well as *teacher factors* (information from teachers and consultants on grammatical items they would expect to see included at different levels).

Today corpus research is providing invaluable information that can serve as a source for items in course syllabi, although corpus data which is based on native speaker usage is not necessarily the only relevant source in many cases. Why is this the case? Perhaps an example from the field of lexicography will serve to clarify here.

The definitions in the many L2 learner dictionaries on the market, such as the Oxford, Longman, or Cambridge learner dictionaries, are not based on native-speaker usage. Rather, these definitions have been written within a specially determined defining vocabulary, a 2000-word corpus of words that have been selected according to their definition power. For example, let us consider a word such as 'container'. Although this might not be a high frequency word, it is a word that is used to define many other words. A 'vase' is a 'container' for holding flowers, a 'bucket' is a 'container' for carrying water, and so on. Thus, the definition vocabularies used in learner dictionaries have been developed pragmatically by lexicographers who have identified the minimum number of words with the maximum capacity for definition. The syllabus underlying a basic materials series can be constructed according to similar principles.

This principle was well stated by Jeffery, who, in the preface to West's *General Service List* (1953: v), suggested:

> To find the minimum number of words that could operate together in constructions capable of entering into the greatest variety of contexts has therefore been the chief aim of those trying to simplify English for the learner.

A similar principle has recently been proposed by Jennifer Jenkins in her book *The Phonology of English as an International Language* (2001), in which she argues that, in teaching English in Europe, the traditional native-speaker based RP-referenced (Received Pronunciation—the type of British standard English pronunciation which has traditionally been considered the prestige variety of British English) phonological syllabus is not necessarily a suitable target for FL instruction. She proposes a simplified phonological syllabus as a basis for EFL instruction.

Identifying instructional principles

The relevance of research and applied linguistics theory to syllabus design is fairly easy to establish. However its relevance to the notion of *instructional principles* is less straightforward. Before the writer can make decisions on the specific exercises, tasks, and activities to be employed in materials, an overall instructional framework has to be agreed on. What is the rationale for the activities employed and their sequencing within the materials? What does research have to offer here? A naÿve view of the role of research would be to assume that researchers agree on what the implications of research are for language teaching and that one can derive from research findings validated activities for use in teaching materials. This view has often been supported by researchers themselves. Some of the literature on language teaching for example, gives the impression that the role of teachers and materials developers is to apply the findings of SLA research. (See Beglar and Hunt 2002.) Indeed, there is a fairly long tradition of researchers or theoreticians offering prescriptions to teachers and materials writers on what to teach and how to teach it. After all, currently discredited method-ologies such as audiolingualism or the cognitive code approach once had widespread support from researchers and theoreticians.

At present, however, researchers are more cautious about the kinds of advice they give. The most one can extrapolate from research are sets of principles that can be used to support particular pedagogical approaches. Kanda and Beglar (2004: 107) observe:

> Because SLA pedagogy cannot yet be based on a well-accepted,
> detailed theory, and many current proposals for task-based
> instruction are still in an early stage of development, we believe
> that one fruitful alternative is for researchers and teachers to
> utilize instructional principles to guide their work.

This has been my own approach in materials development. The first task I must solve in planning a set of materials is to identify an acceptable set of principles to support the instructional design process. In some cases these principles can be derived from the methodology of the day. The overarching principles of communicative language teaching as it was elaborated in the 1980s, for example, can be summarized as: (1) make real communication the focus of language learning, (2) provide opportunities for learners to experiment and try out what they know, (3) be tolerant of learners' errors as they indicate that the learner is building up communicative competence, (4) provide opportunities for learners to develop both accuracy, and fluency, (5) link the different skills such as speaking, reading, and listening, together, since they usually occur together in the real world, and (6) let students induce or discover grammar rules.

These are the principles underlying many of the mainstream communicative course books that were published in the 1980s and 1990s, including my own. The difficulty with principles, however, is that they mean different things to different people. That great philosopher Groucho Marx summed up this existential dilemma in the following words:

> 'Of course I have principles. And if you don't like these ones,
> I have others.'

Examination of contemporary versions of communicative language teaching that integrate FFI within a communicative framework might lead to the following underlying principles:

1 L2 learning is facilitated when learners are engaged in interaction and meaningful communication.

2 Effective classroom learning tasks and exercises provide opportunities for students to negotiate meaning, expand their language resources, notice how target forms are used, and take part in meaningful interpersonal exchange.

3 Meaningful communication results from students processing content that is relevant, purposeful, interesting, and engaging.

4 Communication is a holistic process that often calls upon the use of several language skills or modalities.

5 Language learning is facilitated both by activities that involve inductive or discovery learning of underlying rules of language use and organization, as well as by those involving language analysis and reflection.

6 Language learning is a gradual process that involves creative use of language and trial and error. Although errors are a normal product of learning the ultimate goal of learning is to be able to use the new language both accurately and fluently.

7 Learners develop their own routes to language learning, progress at different rates, and have different needs and motivations for language learning.

8 Successful language learning involves the use of effective learning and communication strategies.

9 The role of the teacher in the language classroom is that of a facilitator, who creates a classroom climate conducive to language learning and provides opportunities for students to use and practise the language and to reflect on language use and language learning.

10 The classroom is a community where learners learn through collaboration and sharing.

FoF principles in materials development

Kanda and Beglar (2004: 107) present four principles that support the use of FFI in communicative materials development: (1) teach form-function relations, (2) compare related forms, (3) promote learner autonomy, and (4) provide opportunities for generative use. The challenge for materials writers is to turn these principles into lesson plans and teaching materials. At the same time it must be recognized that any set of working principles must be compatible with the local context. Principles derived entirely from research and theory might not always fit well with the school teaching and learning culture. Here situation analysis (see Richards 2001) is needed to identify constraining factors that might hinder the application of theory-driven principles. Both top-down and bottom-up sources of information are needed, or in publishing terms what can be called product-driven as well as market-driven factors.

A useful exercise for teachers doing courses on materials development involves examining classroom texts and teacher's manuals to try to identify assumptions about language and language learning underlying materials and how these lead to particular decisions about syllabuses and exercise types in classroom materials.

The myth of authenticity

One issue in materials design that has aroused substantial debate over time is the role of authentic materials. Some have argued that classroom materials should as far as possible mirror the real world and use real world or 'authentic sources' as the basis for classroom learning. But is this always advisable? In the real world, people have already learnt to read and may read for a variety of purposes—to get information, to relax, to be entertained and so forth. In the language learning context, however, students may be reading in order to develop their reading and language skills in the L2, as well as for more general purposes. Thus, the two situations are not comparable. While in the former, the intention is to learn meaning, in the latter, it is to learn both meaning and form.

An extreme example of the authenticity fallacy is cited by Allwright (1981: 173), who described a language course at a British university in which one of the guiding principles was, 'Use no materials, published or unpublished, actually conceived or designed as materials for language teaching'. However, I would argue that the use of authentic materials (or more accurately, authentic source materials, since some degree of selection and arrangement of such materials is always required) in teaching materials is not always necessary or realistic. In some cases (for example, designing reading materials), authentic source texts are relatively easy to locate and are likely to have more interesting content than specially written author-generated texts. Nonetheless such texts still require modification to remove low frequency lexical items and obscure syntax or idioms and to accommodate the length of the text to the requirements of a lesson or page format. It is especially difficult to find authentic texts suitable for use in materials for beginner or low proficiency college-age readers. Authentic texts at an appropriate level of difficulty would typically be found in magazines or on the Internet, but are intended for very young learners. Hence the content would not generally be appropriate for older learners. In addition, since real world readers are assumed to have a reasonably high level of reading ability and a fairly substantial recognition vocabulary, authentic texts even for college-age learners, will generally be too complex for use without substantial adaptation.

In the case of speaking materials, other issues arise. For example, in providing oral texts that present new language forms model speaking tasks, or in providing content to initiate discussion, several design criteria must be met. There may be constraints in terms of sentence length, exchange length, and grammar that are essential to the design of a task chain within a unit. Chunks of authentic discourse, however obtained, would not meet these criteria, and as anyone who has examined samples of authentic conversational discourse can attest, such data has virtually no value pedagogically. Brown and Yule (1983: 11) point out that in the real world, informal conversation often serves the purpose of maintaining social relationships and that the primary purpose of 'chat' is not to convey information but to be nice to the person one is speaking too. Typically in such discourse, the speakers:

> ... tend to conduct a type of talk where one person offers a topic for comment by the other person, responds to the other person if his [sic] topic is successful, and, if it is not, proffers another topic of conversation. Such primarily interactional chats are frequently characterized

by constantly shifting topics and a great deal of
agreement on them.

(Brown and Yule 1983: 11)

Brown and Yule also point out that in authentic exchanges there is a lack of
clarity and specificity. Thus listeners must skim the message for gist rather
than detail. The discourse has an immediate function in terms of the speakers present at the time—it functions as interactional bonding—but has little
relevance to anyone else. Such discourse differs substantially from textbook
language since it serves a very different function from a dialog in a textbook.
Consequently, in attempting to illustrate the use of a target form, textbook
dialog often presents a parody of an authentic conversational exchange,
modeling a conversation that no one would have in real life.

Therefore, materials writers should aim to develop form-focused dialogs that both provide an opportunity to contextualize a target grammar
point as well as preparing students to understand and use English. The
important point about textbook dialogs is not that they model 'authentic'
conversational interaction but rather that they provide a springboard for
follow-up activities generating student interaction through simple adaptation or personalization. However, this does not mean that they need be
contrived or unnatural. Here is where the art and craft of the materials
writer comes into play.

Does this mean that the vast body of research generated by practitioners in the field of discourse analysis and conversational analysis is not
relevant to those developing language teaching materials? Sadly, much of it
is not, or at least not in preparing materials for L2 instruction. However, if
materials are being prepared for a very specific situation and involve
learners interacting intensively with native speakers in very specific situations, (for example, doctor–patient interviews), data on the nature of such
interactions in the real world is obviously relevant and usable. For most L2
learners, however, interaction is with their teachers and with other students
in the classroom, and what is important is that they acquire the tools needed
to make such interaction possible—i.e. a repertoire of essential vocabulary,
grammar, functions, and communication strategies.

Similar issues arise with the development of listening materials. In
the real world L2 learners are often surrounded by authentic examples of
listening texts such as overheard conversations, announcements, or radio
broadcasts. However, these are usually largely unusable for a variety of
reasons, including the logistical problems involved in recording genuine
interactions, as well as copyright and ethical issues that arise when one
wants to use data obtained from such sources. In addition, few texts so

obtained can be used in materials design without substantial modification. The alternative is to use simulated texts as a source for listening activities. In a series such as *Passages* (Richards and Sandy 1998), for example, listening texts were based on recordings of people improvising from cue cards, or in the case of interviews, recorded interviews with people. Scripts were then adapted from these sources, adjusted for length, difficulty, interest level, and redundancy, and then recorded by professional actors.

Others (for example, Widdowson 1987) have argued that it is not important for classroom materials to be derived from authentic texts and sources as long as the learning processes they activate are authentic. In other words, authenticity of process is more important than authenticity of product. However since the advent of communicative language teaching and the current emphasis on FFI, textbooks and other teaching materials have taken on a much more 'authentic' look: reading passages are designed to look like magazine articles (if they are not in fact adapted from magazine articles) and textbooks are based on the same standards of production as real world sources such as popular magazines.

The myth of native speaker usage

An assumption that is often made in language teaching is that the goal of language learning is to acquire a native-like mastery of the language, even if this is not a practical reality for most learners. Learner language is evaluated in terms of how closely it approximates native speaker norms, and native speaker usage as evidenced in corpus studies of native speaker discourse is used as a source for syllabus items. However it must be recognized that for many learners native-speaker usage is not necessarily the target for learning and is not necessarily relevant as the source for learning items. The concept of English as an international language recognizes the fact that localized norms for language use are becoming increasingly recognized as legitimate targets for language learning, and that FL varieties of English such as 'Mexican English' or 'Japanese English' marked both by phonological features from the mother tongue as well as characteristic patterns of lexical and syntactic choice are perfectly acceptable targets for many learners. As mentioned, Jenkins (2001) proposes a non-native phonological syllabus as a target for EFL learners in Europe.

Thus, in determining learning varieties for classroom use, it is worth considering again the implications of the quote cited earlier from Jeffrey, in which the goal of syllabus design is 'to find the minimum number of words that could operate together in constructions capable of entering into the greatest variety of contexts'. If this principle still holds true, and I would argue strongly that it does, then what is important in writing materials for EFL learners is not necessarily native speaker usage, but rather, what will provide the means of successful communication both within and outside the classroom. This means providing learners with a repertoire of well-selected vocabulary, sentence patterns, and grammar, as well as a stock of communication strategies.

Conclusion

I have argued here that the primary relevance of language and language learning research to materials development is through its application to syllabus design issues and as a source for instructional principles that can inform the design of instructional materials. The route from research to application however is by no means direct, since language teaching materials are also shaped by many other factors and constraints, and the success of teaching materials is not dependent upon the extent to which they are informed by research. It is not difficult to find examples of widely used teaching materials that succeed despite their archaic methodology because they suit the contexts in which they are used. Perhaps teachers and students like them because they are easy to use, they match the exam requirements, or they reflect teachers' and learners' intuitions about language learning. On the other hand, research-based teaching materials have sometimes not succeeded because they failed to consider the role of situational constraints.

Hopefully publishers and materials writers will seek to produce materials that are educationally sound and which also appeal to teachers and learners. Educational publication is after all, a business, and the challenge for materials writers is to meet educational objectives and standards while at the same time addressing market requirements.

Note

1   This is a revised version of a paper presented at the TESOL Convention, San Antonio, March 2005, and published in *RELC Journal* 37/1, 2006.

11

Time, teachers, and tasks in focus on form instruction

TERESA PICA

As a long-time classroom teacher who went on to become a classroom researcher, I find that my longevity in the field of education is both an outgrowth of my development as a language educator and a reflection of what I have learned from the work of others. Among them, Rod Ellis, has been a major source of information and inspiration. He has given teachers and researchers a model for bridging theory and practice, by posing research questions that originate in classroom concerns, resonate with theoretical issues, and lend themselves to empirical investigation. This approach is evident across a broad range of his many studies. He has asked about the impact of instruction on developmental sequences (R. Ellis 1984, 1989), the effects of students' planning on their production accuracy (R. Ellis 1987; Ellis and Yuan 2004), and the relationship between their metalinguistic discussion and grammar knowledge (Fotos and Ellis 1991). These and other publications reflect his ability to articulate classroom concerns as research questions on teaching practices and learning activities.

The questions, practices, and activities that appear in this chapter have classroom origins as well. Centered on factors of time, and on the use of tasks in focus on form (FoF) instruction, they stem from my professional experience as a language teacher and classroom researcher, and my collaborative work with other teachers and researchers. (See Pica 2005 for an overview.) My curiosity and commitment continue to be sustained by my interactions with teachers, especially those at work in classrooms of today. Many of them have been educated in research-oriented programs. Others, whose training occurred in earlier times, keep up with advances in the field through workshop and conference attendance and memberships in professional organizations. The long standing call for second language acquisition (SLA) research that has practical and immediate relevance to teaching remains evident (for example, Ortega 2005). However, it has been tempered by responses from researchers, whose classroom-related publications have increased in number and accessibility. (See, for example, R. Ellis 1994a; Pica 1994a, 1997; Lightbown and Spada 1999; Lightbown 2000; also see Chapter 1.)

Teachers and researchers have also come to see a good deal of expansion in their mutual interests and concerns. Some of the most critical questions of teachers also top researchers' agendas. Foremost among them are questions that ask about the relationship between language learning and content learning (for example, Wesche and Skehan 2002; Pica 2002, 2005; Stoller 2004). These questions have been made especially urgent as, world wide, teachers are being asked to expand their roles from teachers of language to teachers of language learners, in order to work more broadly across the academic disciplines. They find themselves responsible for teaching students content and skills in science, technology, and other subject areas, and for doing so in a language that the students are struggling to learn.

Within this context, teachers and researchers want to know how they can best help students whose academic achievement and career progression require them to be proficient in both subject content and the language in which that content is available. Earlier prerogatives to first teach the students their new language and then teach them content in that language have been overshadowed by the demand for activities and approaches that promote parallel instruction and ongoing integration of language and content.

The urgency of teaching content and language together, and doing so efficiently and effectively, can feel overwhelming at times. Fortunately, information and insight from SLA research, classroom observation, and L2 curriculum design, have begun to offset the tension and inform instructional practice. As numerous studies have revealed, subject content can provide a good resource for language comprehension and spoken expression. (See, for example, Swain 1985, 1991; Harley 1989, 1993; Swain and Lapkin: Chapter 5 of this volume.) Through content reading, writing, and oral production, learners can acquire many of the lexical items and grammatical forms needed for content communication and learning. Progress can be on L2 features that are abundant and functionally transparent in content texts and lessons. However, challenges abound for acquiring L2 forms that appear infrequently in classroom input, lack perceptual prominence or communicative significance, or are too complex in function or operation to be mastered independently (Harley 1993; Long 1996). For learners of English, such forms include articles and determiners, pronouns, verb particles, endings, and modals. Woven on to connected discourse, they seldom carry much semantic importance. However, their abundance in subject content makes mastery of such forms and their multiple functions a critical component of spoken and written competence.

Many professional resources provide approaches that integrate L2 skills, strategies, and literacy across the subject content curriculum. (See, for example, Cantoni-Harvey 1987; Brinton, Snow, and Wesche 1989; Chamot and O'Malley 1994; Palley 2000.) These volumes serve as a foundation for learners to access subject content and acquire a good deal of the L2. The tackling of linguistic forms with limited salience in the content, however, has required further precision and sensitivity. Such forms need to be highlighted in ways that are likely to gain students' attention but do not interrupt their understanding of content meaning. Successful approaches have been shown to engage students in transactions with content texts in which needed forms are made more abundant and visually identifiable (for example, Day and Shapson 1991) and in content-focused exchanges in which errors of form are recast (for example, Doughty and Varela 1998; Mackey and Philp 1998; Iwashita 2003), negotiated (Lyster and Ranta 1997; Mackey 1999; Mackey and MacDonough 2000), or subject to collaboration (Ellis, Basturkmen, and Loewen 2001a; Swain and Lapkin 2001, Chapter 5 of this volume).

These form-focused approaches are highly compatible with content teaching concerns, as they offer teachers a sense of anticipation that any number of difficult to learn L2 forms can be incorporated on to communicative activities and implemented on to a content focused classroom. So far, however, these approaches have emphasized the attention processes associated with 'focus', and the perceptual and grammatical features brought to bear by 'form'. Much less acknowledgment has been given to characteristics that center on 'time'. This chapter will turn, therefore, to time as a factor in FoF instruction, and describe the role of teachers and tasks in its classroom application.

Time is addressed as a factor in three areas: (1) decisions about the timing of when and how to re-direct classroom communication from a content focus to a form focus; (2) selection of forms that are timely for students to notice in light of their level of L2 development; and (3) implementation of form-focused activities in order to promote form retention over time.

Factors of time are especially relevant to the learning of L2 forms in content classrooms. The emphasis on content mastery puts teachers in a position in which they must teach L2 forms implicitly. Designing and implementing activities can be highly time consuming. Waiting for results can be long and protracted (DeKeyser and Juffs 2005). Unlike other meaning-focused classrooms in which conversation games and problem solving activities can be used to draw students' attention to L2 form, while communication is repaired, current topics are continued, or new ones advanced, there are fewer options in content classrooms. If letter grades are given for content learning, but not L2 learning, or if preparation for native speaker dominant content classes is the primary objective, it is content learning, more so than communication repair or topic switching, that administrators, parents and sponsors, and even the students themselves, want to have emphasized. Implicit approaches to L2 teaching and learning are a must, not an option, under these circumstances. This chapter will therefore address ways in which form-focused interventions can be timed during classroom discourse, extended throughout L2 development, and sustained over time.

Timing of FoF during classroom discourse

Cognitive approaches have emphasized the importance of form-focused feedback to learner errors in promoting self-correction in the short term (for example, Herron 1991), as well as language development over time (Mackey 1999). In SLA theory and research, a good deal of attention has been given to the linguistic information or evidence that such feedback supplies. As revealed in numerous studies, feedback to learners' imprecisions in message comprehensibility is particularly fruitful in supplying them with negative evidence about what is lacking in their own production compared to the L2 they are attempting to acquire. Support has been extensive and long standing (for example, Schmidt and Frota 1986; Mackey 1999; Mackey and Oliver 2002; Iwashita 2003; McDonough 2005).

Increasingly, favorable results have also been found for feedback in which recasts recode erroneous utterances with target-like forms, but leave message meaning unaltered. As such, recasts provide learners with not only negative evidence, but also positive evidence on forms in the L2 grammar they are trying to master (Doughty and Varela 1998; Leeman 2003). This latter characteristic has challenged researchers and educators as they strive to account for the effectiveness of recasts in SLA. As noted above, positive L2 evidence, which is abundant in content classrooms, may not be a sufficient resource for learners in drawing their attention to L2 features of limited salience.

What is it about recasts then, that makes them effective? Results of recast studies (reviewed in Doughty 2001) suggest that it is their immediacy that is also crucial to their success. Thus, in studies where positive evidence did not make a difference for the learner, the evidence was supplied in the form of enhanced texts, pre-modified on the basis of interlocutor judgments about the learner's abilities and needs. (See R. Ellis 1999a, for review.) In studies where positive evidence did make a difference, the evidence was supplied through immediate interlocutor responses, recast from the learner's very own message. This form of adjusted input was far more direct and individualized than its pre-modified counterpart. (See, for example, Long, Inagaki, and Ortega 1998; Mackey and Philp 1998; Han 2002; Leeman 2003; Philp 2003.)

This explanation not only reveals ways in which the impact of positive L2 evidence on SLA can be broadened in scope, it also underscores the importance of timing of form-focused interventions for L2 learning. Findings suggest that teachers can enhance their inventory of specially prepared materials by adjusting their input and tailoring their feedback in ways that are highly individualized for their students. Guided by an FoF perspective, teachers of content can feel more confident that when an activity reaches an unanticipated impasse in communication, even brief and immediate digressions to FFI and feedback will help students not only to repair the impasse, but to promote their L2 learning as well (Long 1991; Long and Robinson 1998).

Of course, it is not always easy for teachers to react to errors of form if they are deeply engaged in content instruction. Nor should their concern be directed to all forms, but rather, to those forms that learners are ready to acquire. With this in mind, we now turn to another factor of time, i.e. the timeliness of FoF in L2 development.

Timeliness of FoF in L2 development

As scholars and researchers have long emphasized, learners must be developmentally ready to benefit from a form-focused intervention in order to acquire a specific form or to move to a higher level in its development. Even in his early work, which aimed to describe effective input for SLA, Krashen (for example, Krashen 1981), looked to the importance of the learner's readiness. He noted that input needed to be comprehensible and its encoding slightly beyond students' current level of language development if it were to assist the acquisition process.

Pienemann (1989) described readiness in the context of his research on developmental stages. His findings revealed that learners could not skip any stages in their sequence of L2 development, but that appropriately timed instruction could help them go through intermediate steps more quickly than they would if left on their own. Thus, Pienemann (1989) and R. Ellis (1989) were able to show that learners at the 'particle' stage in their German L2 development benefited from instruction on 'inversion', which guided them to move verb particles within sentence internal positions. Learners at stages below 'particle', who could only move elements from sentence final to initial positions, but not move them internally, did not reveal such benefits from 'inversion' instruction. Developmental sequences have been noted throughout German (for example, Meisel, Clahsen, and Pienemann 1981; Pienemann 1985, 1989). They have also been identified for English, particularly with respect to formation of negative verb phrases and questions. (For reviews, see R. Ellis 1994a; Spada and Lightbown 1999.)

Lightbown (1998) has considered the learner's readiness to FoF within a classroom perspective. Acknowledging the wide range of readiness among learners in most classrooms, she has argued that form-focused L2 input tailored to the needs of advanced students can have a positive impact on classmates who are at earlier stages of acquisition. Supportive findings from Spada and Lightbown (1999) have shown that for question formation, even low level students can begin to display knowledge of advanced features, albeit not as consistently as peers who are closer to the stage where these features might next be anticipated. R. Ellis (1994a), who has also looked at stages of L2 development as important indicators of learner readiness, suggests that there is enough variation within the stages for learners to benefit from focused interventions encoded with forms beyond their current level.

Many researchers, in addressing questions on SLA within a cognitive perspective, have emphasized the connections between the cognitive process of noticing and the learner's readiness to notice. They argue that L2 learners are more likely to notice forms that they are ready to learn and internalize than those that are beyond their current level. Their research findings have offered considerable support to this view. (See, for example, Mackey and Philp 1998; Williams and Evans 1998; Han 2002; Izumi 2002.) Researchers have also turned to developmental readiness to explain results that differ from predicted outcomes. Oliver (1995), for example, attributed her participants' limited use of recast forms to the possibility that the recasts, which had emanated from spontaneous, conversational interaction, were of L2 features and structures that were beyond the developmental level of the students, and therefore went unnoticed.

Despite the elegance of developmental sequences in providing a basis for the timing of FoF intervention, they account for only a portion of the L2 forms that learners need to know and use in a language. Many L2 forms are variational, subject to learner orientations toward functional or formal accuracy, their age, and access to input. Grammatical inflections for verb tense and noun number, and functors such as copula, for example, neither align with developmental sequences, nor fall on to a predictable order of acquisition. Because these forms have very low perceptual salience or communicative value for learners, their learning trajectory is less predictable, and their mastery is often less likely than is the case for forms acquired in a developmental sequence. Interventions that draw the learner's attention to such forms might therefore begin early during the acquisition process, when form omission and mis-formation are apparent, and sustained throughout the course of L2 development, to allow for the attention and follow-up time needed for mastery.

The extent of time needed for form-focused interventions to advance acquisition of low salience forms calls for activities and materials that will promote and sustain the learner's interest as they promote their attention to form and meaning. When used in the content classroom, such interventions will need to fit on to content lessons and discussions, sustaining content meaning, as they direct attention to form. The interventions presented in the next section have been designed to respond to this call.

FoF over time

In many studies where a FoF intervention did not yield anticipated results, explanations have also turned to matters of time. In these studies, it was the duration of the treatment that was crucial for learning, rather than its timing during classroom discourse or its timeliness for the developmental readiness of the learner. Chen (1996), for example, found that the impact of explicit feedback on acquisition of Chinese quantifiers and measure words, observed in immediate post-testing, decreased after this treatment was removed. He speculated that the extent of the treatment was not sufficient to stabilize these items for the learner. Findings from other studies offer additional reasons why the effects of a form-focusing treatment might not hold up over time. For example, the form might not be available in subsequent input (L. White 1991); the treatment-group students might regress or their controls catch up (Harley 1989); or the treatment effects might be overtaken by processes of natural development (White 1998).

Occasionally, it is not the disappearance of treatment effects that is of concern, but the time they take to appear that matters. As Mackey (1999) discovered, the impact of recasts on her subjects' question formation was not seen until delayed post-testing, which was carried out well after the treatment was over. Muranoi (2000) found similar results for English articles, as did Van den Branden (1997) for developmental complexity and verbosity.

These findings reveal that form-focused treatments are helpful in the immediate term, even for difficult-to-learn L2 features such as measure words, questions, and articles. However, the findings also suggest that to have a lasting effect on L2 acquisition, the treatments need to be implemented on a regular basis, and sustained over time. The classroom provides a stable and accessible environment for such implementation. What is also needed, however, is a treatment that is authentic for students and can be implemented efficiently, without disrupting classroom life. The activities presented in this chapter have been designed with these considerations in mind.

These activities, which can also be referred to as tasks, originated in a theme-based course entitled 'Language through film'. Housed in a university level, English language program, this course emphasizes academic English language, literacy, and communication skills, and contemporary American culture. Students engage in film viewing, review, summary, and script reading, and teacher-fronted and small-group discussion. The tasks have been used, as well as recycled, with new and different content, during several sessions of the course, and at a local community center, where the course was also offered on a short term basis. Versions of the tasks have also been implemented in practice sessions at elementary and high school levels in the US, Europe, and Asia. Based on teacher interviews and classroom observations, we have found that the tasks respond to the linguistic needs of the students who have used them in content classrooms, and are consistent with the broader issues and challenges that confront any classroom where content in another language is taught to learners of that language. (See Pica 2002, 2005.)

Our project consists of multiple goals in research and pedagogy. Our initial goals have been to produce tasks that are effective for SLA, authentic for students, and manageable for teachers, as well as to identify a process for their content accommodation and classroom implementation. The tasks below are the outcome of our work toward that goal (Pica, Kang, and Sauro 2006). One follow-up goal is to be able to implement the tasks we have designed on a semester long basis. We are currently at work toward that end (Pica, Sauro, and Lee in preparation).

As was noted above, to provide the long term attention to difficult L2 forms and promote their retention, a task must meet criteria for L2 acquisition as well as classroom authenticity and efficiency. To meet acquisition criteria, it must engage learners in the kinds of interactions that will draw their attention to these forms in a timely manner, i.e. immediately while they are focused on the study of subject content. At the same time, the task must be authentic to classroom participants, both students and teachers, and suited for the content knowledge they need to study and learn. Finally, the task must be uncomplicated and efficient in providing a context for incorporation of content rather than intrusion on it and be able to do so across the span of a curriculum or course. (See Skehan: Chapter 4 of this volume.)

The information-gap task provides a structure that is especially well suited to these criteria for acquisition, authenticity, and efficiency. First, with respect to acquisition, the information-gap task structure has been shown to set up conditions for learners to focus on L2 form. This is because only one outcome or answer is considered possible, appropriate, or correct. Reaching this end point requires a verbal exchange of content information, the use of checks and responses for clarity and comprehensibility (Pica, Kanagy, and Falodun 1993), and the kinds of rephrasing, replacement, and manipulation of phonological and structural features that focus attention on L2 form. (See Pica 1994, for review.)

The three types of information-gap tasks that have been shown to be particularly useful in the content classroom are 'Spot the difference' (for example, Long 1980, 1981; Crookes and Rulon 1988; Pica, Kang, and Sauro 2006), 'Jigsaw' (for example, Doughty and Pica 1986; Pica, Holliday, Lewis, and Morgenthaler 1989; Pica 1991; Pica, Lincoln-Porter, Paninos and Linnell 1996; Swain and Lapkin 2001; Pica, Kang and Sauro 2006), and 'Grammar communication' tasks (for example, Fotos and Ellis 1991; Fotos 1994; Loschky and Bley-Vroman 1993a, Pica, Kang, and Sauro 2006). Versions of these tasks have also appeared in popular student textbooks as well as resource books often used by teachers (for example, Ur 1988). Thus, in addition to providing a good context for FoF in SLA, the tasks are in keeping with criteria for classroom authenticity.

In the tasks that we have designed for our content classroom research and instruction, we use the very texts that students have read and studied for content learning as a basis for form-focus. In each task, learners proceed through five steps.

1 First, they each read the same passage, which is in the form of an excerpt of a content chapter, report, or any other printed material that they have studied for their content learning. The passage should be encoded in L2 forms that are low in salience, difficult to master, and developmentally appropriate.

2 Next, they each read a slightly different version of the passage, without revealing their respective versions to each other. Each of the sentences in the two versions has a phrase in which a form with low salience from the original passage appears identically, in a different order, or with a slightly different encoding.

3 The learners then compare their passages, as they look for the forms, phrases, and sentences that are different. They are asked to choose which ones they think 'sound better' and justify their choices.

4 Next, without looking back at their choices or the passages they have read, they work together to write their choices in a single cloze version of the original passage. Although recalling a phrase with a targeted form is considered a good indicator that the form has been noticed (Robinson 2003), recalling it is not the only goal of this task step. Students' discussions, arguments, and justifications of their form selections are important mechanisms for drawing their attention to form and meaning.

5 Finally, they re-read the original passage, compare it with their cloze version, identify any discrepancies, and pose explanations for them. As with Step 4, it is students' discussion of form that is especially critical to building their awareness of its connection to content.

Figures 11.1 and 11.2 provide a short example of what students would see and do in Steps 1, 2, and 3 of a 'Spot the difference' task. It was developed from a text in the subject content area of applied linguistics (R. Ellis 2003: 160). The passage in Figure 11.1 contains L2 forms that are low in salience, difficult to master, and developmentally appropriate across L2 learning levels. Figure 11.1 displays the original passage. Figure 11.2 displays the passage in versions for articles and determiners. The phrase and form differences are highlighted for purposes of display, only.

(1) Our main concern here is with the structured input stage of a lesson as this involves the use of focused tasks. (2) In R. Ellis (1995: 98–9) I list some general principles for designing this kind of focused task, which I call 'interpretation tasks'. (3) These include the following: An interpretation task consists of a stimulus to which learners must make some kind of response. (4) The stimulus can take the form of spoken or written input. (5) The response can take various forms, for example, indicate true-false, check a box, select the correct picture, draw a diagram, perform an action, but in each case, the response will be completely nonverbal or minimally verbal. (6) The activities in the task can be sequenced to require first attention to meaning, then noticing the form and function of the grammatical structure, and finally error identification. (7) Learners should have the opportunity to make some kind of personal response, i.e. relate the input to their own lives.

FIGURE 11.1 *Passage excerpt from R. Ellis (2003: 160), for Task Step 1*

Version to Student A	Version to Student B
(1) Our main concern here is with the structured input stage of a lesson as this involves the use of focused tasks. (2) In R. Ellis (1995: 98–9) I list *some general principles* for designing this kind of focused task, which I call 'interpretation tasks'. (3) These include the following: An interpretation task consists of a stimulus to which *the learners* must make some kind of response. (4) The stimulus can take *a form* of spoken or written input. (5) The response can take various forms, for example, indicate true-false, check a box, select the correct picture, draw *the diagram*, perform an action, but in each case, the response will be completely nonverbal or minimally verbal. (6) The activities in the task can be sequenced to require first attention to meaning, then noticing the form and function of the grammatical structure, and finally *an error identification*. (7) Learners should have the opportunity to make some kind of personal response, i.e. relate *the input* to their own lives.	(1) Our main concern here is with the structured input stage of a lesson as this involves the use of focused tasks. (2) In R. Ellis (1995: 98–9) I list *the general principles* for designing this kind of focused task, which I call 'interpretation tasks'. (3) These include the following: An interpretation task consists of a stimulus to which *learners* must make some kind of response. (4) The stimulus can take *the form* of spoken or written input. (5) 3. The response can take various forms, for example, indicate true-false, check a box, select the correct picture, draw *a diagram*, perform an action, but in each case, the response will be completely nonverbal or minimally verbal. (6) The activities in the task can be sequenced to require first attention to meaning, then noticing the form and function of the grammatical structure, and finally *error identification*. (7) Learners should have the opportunity to ask some kind of personal response, i.e., relate *input* to their own lives.

FIGURE 11.2   *'Spot the difference' versions for articles and determiners, for Task Steps 2 and 3*

Figure 11.3 displays Step 4, which is the cloze version of the original passage of Figure 11.1. Students must complete the cloze based on what they recall from Steps 1–3.

171

(1) Our main concern here is with the structured input stage of a lesson as this involves the use of focused tasks. (2) In R. Ellis (1995: 98–9) I list _____ for designing this kind of focused task, which I call 'interpretation tasks'. (3) These include the following: An interpretation task consists of a stimulus to which _____ must make some kind of response. (4) The stimulus can take _____ of spoken or written input. (5) The response can take various forms, for example, indicate true-false, check a box, select the correct picture, draw _____, perform an action, but in each case, the response will be completely nonverbal or minimally verbal. (6) The activities in the task can be sequenced to require first attention to meaning, then noticing the form and function of the grammatical structure, and finally _____. (7) Learners should have the opportunity to make some kind of personal response, i.e., relate _____ to their own lives.

FIGURE 11.3 *Cloze version of Figure 11.1 for Task Step 4*

(1) Our main concern here is with the structured input stage of a lesson as this involves the use of focused tasks. (2) In R. Ellis (1995: 98–9) I list *the general principles* for designing this kind of focused task, which I call 'interpretation tasks'. (3) These include the following: An interpretation task consists of a stimulus to which *learners* must make some kind of response. (4) The stimulus can take *the form* of spoken or written input. (5) The response can take various forms, for example, indicate true-false, check a box, select the correct picture, draw *a diagram*, perform an action, but in each case, the response will be completely nonverbal or minimally verbal. (6) The activities in the task can be sequenced to require first attention to meaning, then noticing the form and function of the grammatical structure, and finally *error identification*. (7) Learners should have the opportunity to ask some kind of personal response, i.e., relate *the input* to their own lives.

FIGURE 11.4 *Original passage with article and determiner phrases highlighted, for Task Step 4*

Figures 11.4 and 11.5 display versions for the 'Jigsaw' and 'Grammar communication' tasks.

The directions to the tasks are identical, with a slight variation in Step 3, which is the step in which they make, and justify, their form-focused choices. In the 'Spot the difference' task, students choose between sentences. In the 'Jigsaw' task, students first reorder their sentences to comply with

Version to Student A	Version to Student B
Sentence 1. Our main concern here is with the structured input stage of a lesson as this involves the use of focused tasks.	Sentence 1 Our main concern here is with the structured input stage of a lesson as this involves the use of focused tasks.
Sentence #_____ The stimulus can take a form of spoken or written input.	Sentence #_____ The stimulus can take the form of spoken or written input.
Sentence #_____ These include the following: An interpretation task consists of a stimulus to ask which the learners must make some kind of response.	Sentence #_____ These include the following: An interpretation task consists of a stimulus to which learners must make some kind of response.
Sentence #_____ Learners should have the opportunity to ask some kind of personal response, i.e., relate the input to their own lives.	Sentence #_____ Learners should have the opportunity to ask some kind of personal response, i.e., relate input to their own lives.
Sentence #_____ In R. Ellis (1995: 98–9) I list some general principles for designing this kind of focused task, which I call 'interpretation tasks'.	Sentence #_____ In R. Ellis (1995: 98–9) I list general principles for designing this kind of focused task, which I call 'interpretation tasks'.
Sentence #_____ The response can take various forms, for example, indicate true-false, check a box, select the correct picture, draw a diagram, perform an action, but in each case, the response will be completely nonverbal or minimally verbal.	Sentence #_____ The response can take various forms, for example, indicate true-false, check a box, select the correct picture, draw the diagram, perform an action, but in each case, the response will be completely nonverbal or minimally verbal.

FIGURE 11.5 *Jigsaw task versions for articles and determiners, for Steps 2 and 3*

those in the original passage, and then choose between them, much as they did for 'Spot the difference' task. In the 'Grammar communication' task, students choose among phrases that contain specific forms or features of their sentences.

Our research has shown that all three task types activate processes of interaction and attention that are crucial for learning forms that are difficult

Version to Student A	Version to Student B
(1) Our main concern here is with the structured input stage of a lesson as this involves the use of focused tasks. (2) In R. Ellis (1995: 98–9) I list some general principles for designing this kind of focused task, which I *can call/ could call* 'interpretation tasks'. (3) These include the following: An interpretation task consists of a stimulus to which learners *might make, can make* some kind of response. (4) The stimulus *can take, could take* the form of spoken or written input. (5) The response *should take, takes* various forms, for example, indicate true-false, check a box, select the correct picture, draw a diagram, perform an action, but in each case, the response will be completely nonverbal or minimally verbal. (6) The activities in the task *are sequenced, must be sequenced* to require first attention to meaning, then noticing the form and function of the grammatical structure, and finally error identification (7) Learners *should have, could have* the opportunity to ask some kind of personal response, i.e. relate the input to their own lives.	(1) Our main concern here is with the structured input stage of a lesson as this involves the use of focused tasks. (2) In R. Ellis (1995: 98–9) I list some general principles for designing this kind of focused task, which I *call/ might call* 'interpretation tasks'. (3) These include the following: An interpretation task consists of a stimulus to which learners *could make, might make* some kind of response. (4) The stimulus *should take, takes* the form of spoken or written input. (5) The response *can take, could take* various forms, for example, indicate true-false, check a box, select the correct picture, draw a diagram, perform an action, but in each case, the response will be completely non-verbal or minimally verbal. (6) The activities in the task *can be sequenced, could be sequenced* to require first attention to meaning, then noticing the form and function of the grammatical structure, and finally error identification. (7) Learners *can have, might have* the opportunity to ask some kind of personal response, i.e. relate the input to their own lives.

FIGURE 11.6 *'Grammar communication' task versions for verb forms, for Steps 2 and 3*

to detect in subject content. (See Pica 2005; Pica, Kang, and Sauro 2006.) Interaction processes that relate to targeted forms can occur throughout task implementation. Attention processes can be activated throughout the tasks as well, though noticing has been found to occur more often during Steps 2 and 3, as learners select and justify their phrase choices. Similarly, awareness of form, function, and meaning connections tends to arise as the learners justify their choices in Step 3 and recall them for the cloze of Step 4.

The tasks also provide a context for recasting and other immediate responses of feedback as learners compare their text passages and phrase and sentence selections. Our findings have revealed, for example, that as learners go through Step 3, they often read the erroneous version of a sentence in their passage, and then hear the more appropriate version read to them in response.

To insure that the tasks will be used in the classroom over time, the tasks are designed to be easy to implement and adjust. In a given week, students can read and discuss a chapter from a content volume during their first class meeting. They can then spend the following days completing its companion 'Spot the difference' task for articles and determiners. They might next read and discuss a different chapter and complete its companion 'Jigsaw' task for texts with modals, or for texts with articles and determiners again, or both. Versions of the tasks can be distributed in ways that insure that the students work throughout the week on all categories of form, meaning, and function. The many combinations of forms and passages that are possible provide variety and maintain student interest across the three task types.

Conclusion

This chapter has considered three factors of 'time' and their contributions to FoF instruction, and it has tried to do so in ways that consider the role of teachers in this process. Current and growing demands on teachers to help students learn subject content in an L2 they have yet to master, as well as to implement a FoF approach in so doing, can feel justifiably overwhelming for them to accomplish. Yet it is teachers who are especially crucial to the success of this effort. It is they who can identify optimal times for FoF interventions, select forms that are developmentally timely for students to notice, and extend the time needed for form learning and retention. It is my hope that this chapter can inform FoF practices in the L2 content classroom, and do so with appreciation of teachers who implement them.

12

Using form-focused discovery approaches

BRIAN TOMLINSON

THIS CHAPTER addresses discovery approaches in L2 learning, in particular form-focused discovery activities, as a way of encouraging learners 'to discover language for themselves' (Bolitho and Tomlinson 1980: 1) by searching for patterns and commonalities in instances of the target structures they encounter. Form-focused discovery approaches can be defined as activities that enable learners to discover how a particular language form functions. They are designed so that learners make use of their analysis of linguistic data in the form of examples, sample texts, or concordance lines to develop a language awareness that:

1 Provides a 'growing insight into the way language works to convey meaning' (Hawkins 1984: 4–5).

2 Is 'dynamic and intuitive' and 'gradually develop(s) internally by the learner' (Tomlinson 1994: 123).

3 Develops a 'healthy spirit of enquiry' (Bolitho and Tomlinson 1995: 4).

The main objective of discovery approaches is to promote noticing of how language items are used so that learners become aware of the gaps between their use of target forms and the typical use of highly proficient speakers (see discussions in Swain 1985, 2005; Swain and Lapkin: Chapter 5 of this volume, about 'noticing the gap'), thus achieving learning readiness (Tomlinson 1994: 122–3) to process and acquire the language item.

Other objectives include:

1 Contributing to the development of such cognitive skills as connecting, generalizing, and hypothesizing.

2 Helping learners to become better monitors of their own and other people's output.

3 Helping learners to become independent and autonomous.

4 Helping learners to develop positive attitudes towards the TL.

5 Equipping the learners with the means to gain more from their language exposure outside of the classroom and after their language course.

Theoretical principles underlying discovery approaches

Rod Ellis (2005a) suggests that discovery activities can assist learners to use explicit knowledge to facilitate the acquisition of implicit knowledge but does not offer research findings to prove this conclusively. I recognize that this is an important area for future research, but would argue from experience that developing the type of awareness which results from effective discovery activities can eventually facilitate acquisition. However, participating in discovery activities is an investment in the future and not a short cut to instant acquisition. The word 'awareness', rather than 'knowledge' is used to refer to the internal, dynamic, variable, partial, infinite, intuitions which result from discovery activities.

The following theoretical positions support the view of discovery learning as useful for promoting awareness of specific grammar rules and patterns, enabling FoF to occur within communicative activities, and leading to eventual acquisition.

Experiential learning

It has been suggested that learning can be facilitated if learners first experience a phenomenon before studying it (Kolb 1984). The sequence of apprehension before comprehension promotes the use of the full sensory, motor, affective, and cognitive resources of the brain, and it is suggested that this process can be facilitated through the seven-step form-focused multidimensional version of the discovery approach which is described in the following section.

Deep processing

Deep processing of intake is necessary for effective and durable learning to take place (Craik and Lockhart 1972). Such processing is semantic in that the attention of the learner is primarily on the meaning and significance of the intake and, in particular, on its relevance to the learner. Language drills, controlled practice, and narrowly controlled discovery activities can only achieve shallow processing and can only be an aid to short-term learning. The form-focused multi-dimensional version of the discovery approach can, however, achieve deep processing and can eventually facilitate enduring acquisition.

Self-investment

It has been repeatedly noted that learners will only learn if they need and want to learn and are willing to invest time and energy in the process (Tomlinson 2003b: 19). They need to be motivated both instrumentally and integratively (Dörnyei 2001) and this can be achieved by the discovery approach if it excites the curiosity of the learner in relation to a language feature.

Noticing

Discovery approaches can help learners notice features of their input both in the sense of paying attention to features they might otherwise be unaware of and in the sense of being alerted to 'gaps between their typical interlanguage performance and that of typical proficient users of the language' (Tomlinson 1994: 121). Noticing these gaps helps learners attend to related features of language use in subsequent input and to allocate to them the salience and relevance which can facilitate acquisition (Schmidt and Frota 1986; Schmidt 1992; Tomlinson 1994; Batstone 1996; R. Ellis 2002a, 2005a; Swain 2005; also see Chapter 1).

Psychological readiness

A number of SLA researchers have suggested that language learners best acquire language features when they are mentally ready to do so. (For example, see Dulay, Burt, and Krashen 1982; Piennemann 1985; Piennemann, Johnston, and Brindley 1988.) One way of assisting learners to achieve such readiness is to use discovery approaches. These approaches 'create the curiosity, alertness, and positive valuation which are pre-requisites for the development of communicative competence' (Tomlinson 1994: 121). If learners need and want to learn about a particular language feature, they will make efforts to do so and their discoveries will help them to understand and make use of this feature when they meet it again. This will reinforce and/or modify the generalizations developed in the learner's brain and aid acquisition. This process has been summarized by Tomlinson (in Bolitho *et al.* 2003: 252) as follows:

> The main principle is that most learners learn best whilst affectively engaged, and when they willingly invest energy and attention in the learning process. Another principle is that paying deliberate attention to features of language in use can help learners to notice the

gap between their own performance in the TL, and the performance of proficient users of the language. This noticing can give salience to a feature, so that it becomes more noticeable in future input, and thereby contributes to the learners' psychological readiness to acquire that feature.

However, the above theoretical positions suggest that discovery approaches will only be of value if learners are provided with frequent subsequent encounters with the feature they have made discoveries about, and if these encounters are varied and engaging. Extensive reading, extensive listening, re-reading of texts, and re-cycling of language in textbooks can facilitate this as can the multi-dimensional version of the discovery approach with its emphasis on re-visiting texts and on searching for further samples.

Form-focused discovery activities

A distinction needs to be made between discovery activities using FoFs and those using an FoF (Long 1991). Forms-focused discovery activities typically pre-select a grammatical structure and then create a text or a series of sentences designed to help learners make pre-determined discoveries about the form and/or function of the structure. An example would be an activity designed to focus on the functions of the past perfect tense in which the learners are asked such questions as: 'What is the difference between "The game started when I arrived" and "The game had started when I arrived"?'

In contrast, form-focused discovery activities typically focus on 'linguistic elements as they arise incidentally in lessons whose overriding focus is on meaning or communication' (Long 1991: 45–6). (Also see the discussion in Chapter 1.) The focus might have been predicted by the teacher or textbook writer, it might be chosen during the lesson by the teacher, or it could be selected by the learners after experiencing an engaging text or participating in a challenging task. An example would be:

> Now that you have decided what both the father and the son are trying to achieve in their conversation, go back to the text and locate all the uses of the imperative. For each use decide why the speaker has used it and what the speaker intended to achieve through its use. Then see if you can formulate generalizations about the use of the imperative in this text. For homework, look for examples of the imperative in authentic language use and see if they confirm your generalizations. If they do not confirm them, modify your generalizations so that they do.

When I first started to devise discovery activities I was definitely following a forms focused approach with predetermined discovery points and examples conveniently contrived to lead the learners to a convergent discovery. However, I soon realized the limitations of this approach, both in relation to student motivation and engagement, and to the 'authenticity' and value of the discovery. Now I follow a form-focused approach in which the first objective is to help the learners to achieve deep processing of their representation of a cognitively and affectively engaging text. Having achieved this objective, they are then invited to re-visit the text in order to make discoveries about one or more of its salient features. The following activities are used to support a form-focused discovery approach.

Map-following activities

These direct the learners towards making the discovery which the textbook and/or the teacher want(s) them to make. For example, if learners are given examples of direct speech and are then asked what punctuation mark goes around the actual words spoken, all the learners will arrive at the same conclusion. Many teachers, with some justification, argue that this is a time wasting procedure and suggest that it would be more efficient for the teacher to simply tell the learners such facts rather than require them to discover the rules for themselves.

Aided-discovery activities

Here a text is selected (or written) which provides rich data in relation to a feature which the textbook writer and/or teacher want(s) the learners to investigate. The learners are then invited to analyse the text in order to discover tendencies for themselves. An example of this would be, 'Comment on the writer's choice of direct or indirect speech in this newspaper extract' (Bolitho and Tomlinson 1995: 21). The text contains samples of the feature in use and the learners are aided by these samples to make discoveries for themselves. There are no right answers and all the learners' discoveries are valid providing they can be justified from the evidence in the text.

In my experience, teachers (and learners) prefer these activities as a prelude to subsequent activities because they require deeper investment from the learners and help to develop cognitive skills as well as contribute to language learning. However, many teachers, including myself, are less enthusiastic if the writer or teacher floods the text with many extra examples, writes texts with atypical clusters of the target feature, or uses highlighting to draw attention to the feature. Such attempts to achieve salience often result in unnatural exemplifications of language in use and a distortion of the reading or listening process.

Open-ended discovery activities

In open-ended activities the learners experience a text and then re-visit it to investigate a feature they noticed during their first encounter with the text. This could mean, for example, that the same story was read by all the learners in a class after which some learners tried to make discoveries about reported speech, some about the present perfect, some about modal verbs, and others about relative clauses. This approach has the advantage that the learners focus on what is salient for them and then subsequently share their discoveries. However, some teachers may be reluctant to use this approach as they lose control of what the learners are doing, they cannot prepare the lesson in advance and they might not be able to answer learners' questions.

Form-focused multi-dimensional activities

My own preference is for a form-focused multidimensional approach that allows learners to notice different aspects of the TL as they perform a series of related activities drawing on their creativity and communicative skills. This type of approach incorporates the following steps:

1 The learners begin with a *readiness activity* which activates their minds in relation to the content of the text they will experience. For example, they visualize an interesting old woman they know before reading a poem narrated by an old woman.

2 Then they are given an *initial response activity* which helps them to experience the text rather than to study it. For example, they are told to change the picture in their minds to that of the woman in the poem as they listen to the poem being read aloud in the voice of an old woman.

3 They perform an *intake response activity* which helps them to develop and articulate their mental representation of the text. For example, they discuss their answers to the question, 'Do you like the old lady?' or they decide which of three photos portrays the lady who wrote the poem.

4 They do a *development activity* in which they re-visit the text before making use of it as the basis of a creative writing activity. For example, they re-read the poem before writing a letter as the old lady to her son in Australia.

5 They do an *input response activity* in which they re-visit the text in order to investigate one of its salient features. For example, they decide in

groups why the old lady wrote the poem almost entirely in the simple present tense and then they make generalizations about the function(s) of the tense. This links the target form with its communicative function.

6 They do a *research activity* in which they look for other samples of the feature they investigated in Step 5 above. For example, they look for samples of the present simple tense in use in newspapers, novels, textbooks, etc., and then use these samples to confirm or modify their generalizations. This activity exposes the learners to other meaningful usages of the target form.

7 They do a *revision activity* in which they use discoveries from Steps 5 and 6 to improve their texts in Step 4 (as well as other texts they have previously written).

Such a form-focused multidimensional approach can take considerable time but is rich in learning opportunities and offers something to learners with different learning style preferences and different interests. It makes use of sensory imagery, the inner voice, affective associations, connections with previous experience, and cognitive strategies which are typically used in L1 multi-dimensional processing but which are less frequently used in FoFs FL processing rendered uni-dimensional by a narrow concern on linguistic decoding and encoding. (For more descriptions and examples of this approach, see Tomlinson 1994, 2003a. For information about multi-dimensional processing, see Kaufman 1996; Masuhara 1998, 2003, 2005; Berman 1999; Tomlinson 2000a, 2000b, 2001, 2003a.)

Personal experience using form-focused discovery approaches

The following section presents my language teaching experience using form-focused discovery approaches. I first used these approaches in 1969 while working with Rod Ellis at what was then Mankoya Secondary School in Western Province, Zambia. I encouraged students to answer practice reformulation questions and then to increase their awareness by using the correct answers to make discoveries regarding grammar regularities. For example, if a question involved changing active voice sentences to the passive voice, students would use the correct answers to work out how the passive was formed and when and why it should be used instead of the active voice. The approach was very much forms focused (R. Ellis 2005a; Long 1991) in that the target discovery points were pre-determined grammatical items and context free.

R. Ellis and I published a series of course books called *English Through Situations* (Ellis and Tomlinson 1973) in which grammar and vocabulary were taught through providing generalizations, examples, and practice. We requested students to perform such activities as 'answer these questions and you will see how we use the simple present tense' (Book 1: 16). In our book *Teaching Secondary English* (Ellis and Tomlinson 1980), we did not refer explicitly to discovery approaches but did include in some chapters discovery activities for the teachers reading/using the book. I also included activities in which students compared their answers with model answers to make discoveries for themselves in a book written for Longman on *O-level Summary and Composition* (Tomlinson 1981). These early attempts at using discovery approaches were based on the belief that thinking about how a language worked facilitated its acquisition. However, no explicit theories were articulated and there were no theories or research in the literature to support these activities.

It was when working with Rod Bolitho at Bell College, Saffron Walden and on RSA Dip TEFL teacher courses in Cambridge that I began to develop theories about the value to learners of discovering things about the language for themselves. Bolitho and I developed a series of activities to help teachers and advanced learners to become more positive and curious about the TL and to make discoveries about problematical aspects of language use. We trialled these activities and then published them as *Discover English: A Language Awareness Workbook* (Bolitho and Tomlinson 1980, 1995, 2005). This book was innovative in that it was neither prescriptive nor descriptive but aimed to help teachers and advanced learners to explore the English language through guided analysis of examples of English in use and through comparing their answers to open ended questions with the possible answers suggested in the commentary.

This approach has stimulated my development of activities for use in teacher training courses and workshops around the world for the last 20 years. These activities are aimed at encouraging learners to develop excitement and positive curiosity about English and to make original and valid discoveries about language use from their experience and analysis of authentic texts. As we have seen, my version of the discovery approach is based on theories of experiential learning, noticing, and psychological readiness. Descriptions, justifications, and demonstrations of the discovery approach can be found in Bolitho *et al.* (2003) and Tomlinson (1994, 2003a). A description of a similar but slightly different language awareness approach can be found in Wright and Bolitho (1993) and Bolitho (2003).

I have always enjoyed using this approach and have made many discoveries myself during lessons or demonstrations, for example, that the main use of modals in English is manipulation, that the main difference between 'some' and 'any' and between 'a' and 'the' is the difference between unmarked and marked forms, that one of the uses of 'in case of' is to protect the owners of factories from prosecution and that the imperative is more frequently used to seek help than it is to give commands.

In the PKG Programme, a training program for 50,000 teachers in Indonesia, I introduced an approach that became known as EGRA (experience, generalization, reinforcement, application) (Tomlinson 1990). One teacher requested her 12-year-old students to act out a birthday party story, then to identify the words in the script that indicated how something was done (for example, 'slowly', 'loudly') and then to distinguish between two different types of such words. Suddenly a boy jumped up to celebrate a Eureka moment and to articulate his discovery that it was necessary to add '-ly' to a word to say how something was done, but there were some words like 'often' which were different types of 'how' words. This learner's enthusiastic discovery about regular and irregular adverbs showed the initially sceptical but very creative teacher that it is possible to use discovery approaches profitably with children if the teacher does not emphasize metalanguage, but provides the students with a meaningful experience of a text and excites their curiosity (Bolitho *et al.* 2003). When using such approaches with young adults at a university in Japan, it was clear that at lower linguistic levels more discoveries are made and articulated if the learners are allowed to use their L1 to discuss features of the TL.

Teacher attitudes towards form-focused discovery approaches

Throughout my 30 years of using and advocating discovery approaches, I have observed that teachers in many different countries have reacted in very similar ways. In the main they have been persuaded of the potential value of such approaches but some have either not used them or limited their use because they have not realized that:

1 *Discovery approaches can be used with any age of learners.*

The popular feeling seems to be that children and young teenagers do not have the cognitive maturity to make discoveries for themselves. This is counter to what is known about the pattern-detecting capacity of the brain. If the teacher does not insist on the use of metalanguage and if the discovery activity is set up as a problem solving or exploration challenge, children can discover (but not always articulate) language patterns and norms.

2 *Discovery approaches can be used with any level of learners.*

Many teachers make the false equation between linguistic level and intellectual level. Even complete beginners can make discoveries if they are not asked to discuss and articulate them in the TL. For example, I have succeeded many times in helping beginning learners of Japanese as a FL discover norms of Japanese word order, number, and morphology. The discoveries were made after experiencing Japanese in use and then thinking about and discussing perceivable patterns in English.

3 *Discovery approaches lead to eventual, rather than immediate, acquisition.*

Discovery approaches are an investment in the future and can lead to eventual acquisition. No approach leads to instant acquisition, although some drill-based approaches can give the illusion of doing so. (See Chapter 1.)

4 *Discovery approaches are intended to disturb learners by revealing to them that they do not really know what they think they know.*

Creating a slight disturbance is one of the means by which discovery approaches challenge rule-based knowledge and replace it with norm-based awareness. (See Swain and Lapkin: Chapter 5 in this volume.) This could, for example, involve presenting learners with language samples in which 'some' and 'any' do not follow the prescriptive rules often presented in course books and then helping the learners to realize that, although the language samples do not conform to absolute rules, they are used in normative ways. For example, as one group discovered, 'some' is usually an unmarked form whereas 'any' tends to mark attitudes and expectations. The important point for the teacher to bear in mind is that learners should not be left disturbed at the end of such a lesson, but should begin to see the convergent realities which can replace the false certainties they relied on previously.

5 *Discovery approaches take up time in an efficient and effective way.*

Discovery approaches do take up time and this has been the main complaint over the years. My response has always been that, in a discovery activity, the learners learn much more than just information about a language feature. They develop cognitive skills, positive attitudes, and learner autonomy, and are helped to eventually acquire not only the target feature but other syntactic, lexical, and pragmatic features which they notice in the text(s). Discovery approaches, because of their comparative richness and depth, are actually more economical and efficient than presentation or practice activities.

6 *Discovery approaches are most useful for those learners with studious learning style preferences but can be made valuable for experiential learners too.*

The favouring of studious learners is a serious limitation of those discovery approaches which directly require learners to perform a detailed analysis of language samples. However it is not true of the form-focused multi-dimensional approach described above, which starts by providing the learners with a potentially engaging experience of language in use before inviting them to revisit the text to make discoveries for themselves. Such activities can appeal to experiential learners as well as to studious learners, and in particular to those many learners who enjoy both holistic and affective engagement as well as discrete cognitive analysis.

Questionnaire responses

At present there is very little research on teachers' attitudes towards form-focused discovery approaches, although Mohamad (2001, 2004) has examined student attitudes towards consciousness-raising tasks, and is currently researching teacher attitudes to consciousness-raising activities. In an attempt to gain some information about teacher attitudes to form-focused discovery approaches, I sent out a questionnaire by email to various teachers and teacher trainers around the world, who then sent them on to teachers, and I received 38 responses from teachers in the following countries: UK (9), New Zealand (7), Turkey (5), China (2), Ethiopia (2), Ireland (2), Japan (2), Singapore (2), Bangladesh (1), Germany (1), Hong Kong (1), Libya (1), Portugal (1), Russia (1), Thailand (1).

Thirty-two of the respondents said they used form-focused discovery approaches. Six said they did not. Although the limited responses constitute a very small sample of teachers' attitudes towards form-focused discovery approaches and might or might not be typical, their responses are interesting to consider.

One open-ended question asked 'Why do you make use of discovery approaches?' The responses are presented in Figure 12.1 below.

A majority of the teachers in the sample gave reasons related to the development of cognitive skills and to the cognitive processing of information. Memory seemed to be one of the main concerns, as well as the affective realm of learning (mainly in relation to the stimulating of interest and motivation). As language teachers, the development of *language awareness* was also given as a reason by many of them.

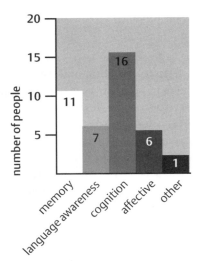

FIGURE 12.1 *Reasons for using discovery approaches*

Here are some of the teachers' comments regarding their use of discovery approaches:

1 I think the things that children discover themselves are much more memorable. Even if they don't discover anything, they are then much more open to hearing an explanation than they would have been before trying.

2 My impression is that students tend to remember 'rules' more effectively if they work them out for themselves from well-supported material (you get out what you put in).

3 By discussing what they are discovering, learners develop other skills at the same time for example, negotiating, explaining, reformulating, etc.

4 It facilitates a more learner-centred classroom which is more productive in terms of learner output.

5 It limits the problems inherent in teacher explanation, i.e. the potential for misunderstanding, monotony, lack of learner involvement, etc.

6 If the context is rich enough, there is potential for more 'accidental' learning (what we teach is not what they learn).

7 It makes the students active learners since they remember better what they learn when they discover the rules/topic themselves. Students also have to make use of their past knowledge of the language to understand a new grammatical point. Such an approach develops the students' critical thinking.

8 Discovery learning requires the students to work together in groups. That way, they come to know each other better and see the benefit of studying together.

9 An important part of language learning is the ability to become a 'language detective'. We all have this skill, but to be an efficient language learner we need to practise and develop it. Hopefully, students will do this on their own later outside the classroom.

A second open-ended item asked about the benefits of discovery approaches for form-focused teaching. The responses are summarized in Figure 12.2.

Both the affective and the cognitive contributions to learning were considered to be very important. The contribution to memory also seemed to be important, but the development of language awareness was only considered to be a significant benefit by 10 per cent of the respondents. Below are comments regarding the benefits of form-focused discovery approaches mentioned by the teachers.

1 It is economical in terms of time for the students. Form is given in context.

2 When students are faced with the challenge of discovering the rule for themselves, they are more active and thus take more responsibility for their own learning. When they are more active, they learn more effectively.

3 Students can be more involved in their learning process and teachers can monitor more effectively.

4 Students are stimulated to think about language.

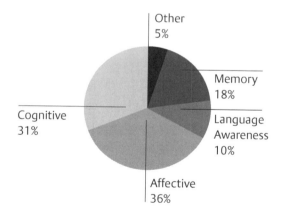

FIGURE 12.2 *Benefits of discovery approaches in form-focused teaching*

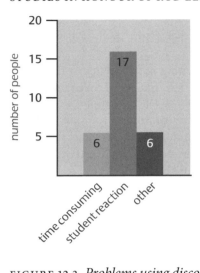

FIGURE 12.3 *Problems using discovery approaches*

The next section presents problems and solutions identified by the participants in their responses to open ended questions.

As indicated in Figure 12.3, the majority of the teachers in the sample mentioned negative student reactions as the main problem when using discovery approaches in the classroom.

Solutions to the problems pointed out by the teachers mainly involved training students to use and appreciate discovery approaches and the use of different classroom techniques to introduce the methodology in the classroom. See Figure 12.4

Here is a brief selection of some of the specific problems and solutions mentioned by the participants. Because of space limitations, it is not possible to present all participants' comments or all problems and solutions.

Participant 1

Problems	Solutions
Learners don't always see the point and are impatient. They want to be told the form.	Persevere with the approach, but sometimes throw in some more deductive teaching.

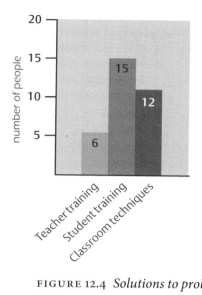

FIGURE 12.4 *Solutions to problems using discovery approaches*

Participant 2

Problems	Solutions
Learner resistance to/unfamiliarity with the discovery approach.	Gradual introduction. With higher levels and older groups, making sure there is a strong element of intellectual engagement in the activities to give them 'credibility'.
The demands of the syllabus mean that only a limited time is available to perform the form-focused discovery activities.	Organizing activities so that a substantial part of the work is undertaken by learners outside the classroom.

Participant 3

Problems	Solutions
When trying to do a jigsaw task as part of the discovery method, the students focused more on the task and not enough on the form.	Using simpler texts and tasks when focusing on grammar or lexical objectives.

Sometimes students prefer to be told what the objective is and don't want to figure out rules for form, meaning, and use.	Using a variety of different techniques seems to work best. Explaining how our memories work—we remember more and make stronger connections when we have to figure out the rules for ourselves.

Thus, the participants seem to think that the problems of negative student reactions can be prevented/overcome by explaining the approach and by varying the nature of the activities.

Conclusion

In conclusion, my recommendations to teachers would be:

- Use form-focused multi-dimensional discovery approaches as a way of helping learners to increase their language awareness.
- Introduce discovery approaches from the very beginning of a course so that they are accepted as the norm rather than treated as a disturbing surprise.
- Explain to learners why they are performing discovery activities and what the potential benefits are.
- Give learners the opportunity to reflect on and to report their experience of participating in discovery activities.
- Make sure that discovery lessons include experiential as well as analytical phases.
- Make sure that the learners use their discoveries to revise work they have previously produced and to inform work that they subsequently produce.
- At the beginning of a course provide the learners with loose-leaf files on which they write their name as the author of a book on the language. Then request them to insert all their discovery examples and notes in their files. Check the files occasionally, not for marking, but to suggest further sources of data to help them to revise, modify, and develop their generalizations. At the end of the course, the learners take away a grammar of the language written by themselves. This can work wonders for self-esteem and confidence.

13
Learning or measuring? Exploring teacher decision-making in planning for classroom-based language assessment

PAULINE REA-DICKINS

DECISION-MAKING in language testing and assessment has been investigated from a number of different perspectives. Typically, this has focused on test or examination development and administration (for example, Bachman and Palmer 1996; Milanovic, Saville, and Shuhong 1998), teacher assessment processes (for example, Rea-Dickins and Gardner 2000), or on the development of pedagogically appropriate assessment procedures (for example, O'Malley and Valdez Pierce 1996; TESOL Standards 1997). In this chapter, I explore the types of decisions that teachers make when *planning* for classroom-based language assessment, with specific reference to the assessment of learners with English as an Additional Language (EAL), aged 6 and 7, within mainstream classes in the English school system. In so doing it problematizes the role of the teacher on the one hand, as assessor of curriculum attainment and, on the other, as facilitator of language development, thus positioning the teacher 'at the interface' between language assessment and second language acquisition (SLA). The data are derived from semi-structured teacher interviews over one school year and are analysed using winMax (Kukartz 1998). The research, of which this study forms a part, adopted a broad sociocultural approach that recognized the need to understand language assessment practices within the social and cultural context in which they take place.

Learning through EAL in English schools

The language needs of children working in mainstream schooling and using EAL[1] cannot be ignored. It is estimated that in English schools, around 10 per cent of children are learning through an additional (second or even a third) language (Department for Education and Skills 2003: 29). The learning needs of these children are distinctive from L1 English monolingual speakers in several respects. An obvious significant difference is that these school learners are learning specialist subject knowledge through a language that is not their L1 and, at the same time, they are acquiring and developing their English language proficiency. They may have distinct needs for a number of other diverse reasons, too. For example, they may enter (in this case) English schools at a non-standard age and have varied previous experiences of schooling and in other languages (for example, Breen *et al.* 1997; National Association for Language Development in the Curriculum (NALDIC) 1999). Their home and community contexts may have different cultural expectations of schooling and the pupils' support structures at home and in the community may vary. As R. Ellis has observed: 'the E2L [EAL] learner is faced with a struggle to reconcile the culture and language of the school with the culture and language of the home' (R. Ellis 1985: 21). As bilinguals or multilinguals, learners with EAL also have particular linguistic characteristics. For example, the development of L1 impacts on their progress in L2 (see, Collier 1987, 1992, 1995; NALDIC 1999); it is also maintained that learners with EAL may have above average meta-linguistic skills (Gravelle 2000).

Further, in addition to the above diversity, research points to several ways in which assessment for EAL is distinctive from assessment for English L1 learners and how the English National Curriculum assessment is inappropriate for learners with EAL. A few examples illustrate this. Firstly, EAL learners' performance may be more contingent on context than monolingual children so that to increase the validity of assessment the linguistic performance of learners with EAL needs to be assessed using different tasks and task types *and* across the different school subject areas. This point has been made by Gravelle (1996), as well as much earlier by R. Ellis (1985: 10, based on McEwan *et al.* 1975) who criticized the National Foundation for Educational Research (NFER) tests on account of their exclusive focus on grammatical knowledge across the four skills, emphasizing that they:

> do not assess to what extent the pupils will be able to *use* this knowledge in the kinds of communicative tasks required by the school curriculum and public examinations.

Secondly, EAL learners may perform better in oral subject content but may not demonstrate this achievement in their written performance, as reflected through the English National Curriculum Levels, i.e. the assessment framework (Department for Education and Skills 2003). In this respect, Cline and Shamsi (2000: 4) have this to say: 'It is important to look for multiple sources of evidence wherever possible and sample children's performance and behaviours in different roles and different situations'. As a third issue, the English National Curriculum Levels do not show *progression* in EAL—the target levels are common for all school learners (for example, Leung 1996); neither do they (at the time of writing) take sufficient account of language performance across the curriculum.

When it comes to the policy context in England, the position of central government in relation to the assessment of EAL is firm. Firstly, all school-aged children are to be judged by the National Curriculum assessment levels, with minimal special arrangements for EAL learners operationalized in the form of two pre-Level 1 'Steps' to the National Curriculum Levels (Qualifications and Curriculum Authority 2000). Secondly, in recognition of the need for learners with EAL to continue to develop their L2 language proficiency in order not to hold back their cognitive development, policy requires all teachers to be responsible for both subject knowledge learning and the development of English language acquisition, thus presenting dual challenges for teachers of mainstream classes: the need to raise achievement in all subjects and to support learners with EAL 'in becoming competent English language users as quickly and effectively as possible' (School Curriculum and Assessment Authority (SCAA) 1996: 2). In addition, teachers should be clear about the purpose of the assessment, distinguishing summative, formative, and diagnostic aims (Department for Education and Skills 2003: 1), together with the expectation that 'all EAL pupils receive regular and appropriate feedback on their use of English including sensitive, positive correction' with 'demonstration of alternative ways of expressing meanings in English ... ' (ibid.: 14).

From the foregoing, there are potentially significant numbers of school learners in a vulnerable position if their specific social, academic, and linguistic needs are not being taken into account and addressed. It is argued here that assessment is an important tool in supporting the educational and, in particular the linguistic development of learners with EAL. Firstly, appropriate assessment opportunities may provide teachers with diagnostic data as the basis for their instructional planning. Secondly, appropriate teacher assessment strategies have the potential to provide learners with formative language development opportunities on tasks and activities that have cross-curricula relevance. (See, for example, McKay, Hudson, and Sapuppo 1994; McKay 2000; TESOL 2001.) As seen from the policy context above, these should be goals for *all* teachers—an observation made by R. Ellis two decades ago in the conclusion to his chapter on policy and provision for EAL (R. Ellis 1985: 22):

LIVERPOOL JOHN MOORES UNIVERSITY
LEARNING SERVICES

> Ideally the ability to teach ESL must become the repertoire of teaching
> skills that any teacher working in the multilingual classroom must
> possess. ... If ESL teaching is to be seen as something more than a pal-
> liative, it must be integrated within mainstream curricular activity.

This chapter engages with some of the issues and implied challenges highlighted above for effective teaching and learning within the context of
learners with EAL. It does this through the lens of teacher decision-making
in relation to their assessment planning processes for learners using EAL.
Specifically, an analysis of teacher self-reports of their planning intentions
and decisions for classroom assessment allows us to highlight a number of
issues about classroom assessment and to identify (1) their assessment
purposes, (2) the criteria they use in appraising learner performance, (3)
the content orientation of teachers' assessment activities and whether, and
if so how, they integrate both the linguistic and content demands, as well as
to gain insights into (4) their selection of assessment tasks. More generally, it
also allows an exploration of teacher understandings of how they perceive
and plan for *language assessment* in mainstream content classrooms. In so
doing it brings us, centrally, to the interface between formative language
assessment, i.e. assessment that may be formative for the learners in terms of
their language development, and instructed SLA (for example, R. Ellis 1990,
2003).

The study

The data presented here derive from research studies in inner city primary
(elementary) schools, in one education service in England.[2] (See also Rea-
Dickins 2001, 2006.) These schools all had a high density of minority ethnic
children using EAL in the mainstream. This chapter focuses on the nature of
the decisions taken by the teachers in relation to their assessment of these
minority ethnic children so as to be able to address the following research
question:

> How do teachers decide on the design and the focus of their assess-
> ment activities to support their learners with EAL who are as yet
> unable to access the National Curriculum?

With this aim in view, each teacher through a pre-observation interview had
been asked to identify in advance any activity that they planned to use as an
assessment activity, i.e. an activity through which they specifically set out to
obtain information about any aspect of a learner's language ability. This
activity was then audio and video recorded. The teachers were also inter-

viewed after the implementation of the assessment, using loosely structured interview questions. The data were managed and analysed using WinMAX (Kuckartz 1998). To develop the categories underpinning the different facets of the teachers' decisions about their classroom-based assessment, the individual teachers' self-reports (i.e. their interviews) were analysed, and specific strategies identified and coded.

The findings

In the analysis that follows, extracts from teacher interviews—both pre- and post-activity—are presented. All were qualified primary teachers with extensive experience of working with learners with EAL, some of whom had specific responsibilities for 'language support'.[3] They were working at Key Stage 1 in the English National Curriculum, with children aged between 6 and 7 years old.

Overview

During the initial 'readings' of the interviews and the early coding of the data, four central stages in the assessment process—delineated by time— were represented by the teachers when talking about their assessments (see Rea-Dickins 2001), as shown in Table 13.1.

The relationships between these stages are explained as follows. Firstly, planning is an essential stage for all the teachers and is multifaceted. (See Table 13.2 and analysis below.) This was distinguished from the implementation phase during which teachers guide their learners through an activity that is assessed either as part of routine instruction (i.e. assessment activity embedded within the flow of teaching and learning) or as a stand-alone activity (for example, a story re-tell, an explanation of how an electric circuit works, or a written task). The third stage that emerged from the teachers' discourse related to decision-making at the 'local level' as when teachers

---

Stage 1 Planning for assessment

Stage 2 Implementation of the assessment activities

Stage 3 Monitoring the learners and the assessment data

Stage 4 Formal recording of the assessment 'results' and their dissemination

---

TABLE 13.1 *Stages in teachers' decision-making for classroom assessment*

within a specific year group used the information from an assessment for the specific purpose of formulating learning targets for a class, as well as for individual learners; such data would be used routinely during teachers' weekly planning meetings. The fourth stage was defined as qualitatively different in that learner assessment data were used for more formal reporting purposes, for example for school, local authority, or national records.

These broad categories were then used to organize other emergent aspects that characterized a teacher's decision-making about assessment: a more detailed analysis and coding of the data was undertaken in relation to the strategies reported by the teachers for each of these main stages. Table 13.2 below presents the range of decisions related to *planning for* classroom language assessment. Within this main category, teachers explained in their interviews, for example, how they identified their reasons for assessing the children on a given occasion, what they believed to be the most appropriate assessment activity, and why they selected a specific content focus for a given assessment.

The strategies associated with teacher decision-making during the planning for assessment stage are set out below.

1 Identifying assessment purpose	e.g. referenced to a review of curriculum (content knowledge) goals, or language targets thus achievement focused cf. monitoring individual learner progress
2 Selecting assessment focus	i.e. what precisely is to be assessed
3 Selecting assessment activity	i.e. how learners are to be assessed
4 Checking the activity is appropriate for the children	e.g. is there adequate contextual embedding? Are the learners linguistically 'ready'?
5 Preparing the children for the assessment	e.g. through a review of specific lexis
6 Selecting the level of formality for the implementation of the assessment activity	e.g. whether the performance will be unaided or scaffolded
7 Deciding how the learner performance is to be 'recorded'	e.g. in the form of a set of language samples, ticks on a grid, as a set of sentences, or list
8 Identifying the assessment criteria	e.g. related to elements of grammar,

	functional language use such as the ability to express 'cause and effect' relations, or to write a description of a process
9 Agreeing who implements the assessment	i.e. in contexts where there are two teachers (mainstream subject and language support), one will take the lead in any given assessment activity
10 Deciding how the assessment information is to be used	e.g. to provide formative support for student learning, to inform an individual teacher, or to be added to a learner's record?
11 Deciding on the nature of the feedback	e.g. immediate (verbal) feedback through teacher–learner interaction, a smiley face, a written comment
12 Acting on modifications to the assessment activity	i.e. deciding how to improve on a classroom assessment activity that had been used previously
13 Deciding when to implement the assessment activity	e.g. as part of routine instruction, at the end of a unit of work, during small group work
14 Agreeing on who makes the final assessment decisions	i.e. this is relevant in cases where there is more than one teacher in a class for example, class and language support teacher?

TABLE 13.2 *Teacher planning strategies for classroom language assessment*

From the above, we can see that in planning to assess their learners with EAL, teachers take a wide range of decisions. Some of these are predictable, such as deciding when to assess and which criteria to use to evaluate learner performance and, indeed, would apply equally to all assessment contexts. Given, however, the specific and diverse needs of children with EAL highlighted earlier, and the implications of these for classroom language assessment practices, this chapter probes further the kinds of factors teachers take into account when making their assessment decisions.

Some data

The extracts I have selected are typical of those that appear in the full data set. These appear next, followed by my commentary on each. The meanings and interpretations that I attribute to these are based on my previously mentioned knowledge of the assessment contexts of the teachers gained though an ongoing dialogue with a group of teachers over an extensive period of time working in schools. The first set of comments is grouped around the teachers' expressed purposes for assessment, see decision 1 in Table 13.2.

1 Deciding on assessment purpose

a X [teacher names a learner] I think he'll move back down again and I just need the evidence to prove my instincts (G/1/LST/57–8).[4]

b ... I've got to do an assessment, it's the end of the autumn term, have I got samples of language across these areas (M/1/LST/211–12).

c It's the end of a half term and with some of the ongoing procedures it's quite useful to keep regularly assessing because otherwise it can get lost and you don't know at what stage the children achieved a certain level (G/1/LST/5–8).

d ... the writing I keep ... I think X (class teacher names LST] showed you the samples which they do weekly without any help (E/1D/CT/223–5).

In (a) above the teacher is referring to a learner who had been previously placed in a higher set but whom she now feels would have his needs better addressed in a lower ability set. Her purpose for assessing this child is to confirm this view. As such she will be assessing his attainment level—a summative purpose—but at the same time she is using her assessment diagnostically, for purposes of better student placement that also links with decision 10 in Table 13.2. She is, thus, proposing to use assessment data for both summative and formative purposes.

From the teachers' reference to time (decision 13 in Table 13.2) in both (b) and (c): 'the end of the autumn term' and the 'end of a unit', we may infer the teachers' priority to establish the attainment levels of their learners at the end of a teaching unit (decision 1). In (b) we may also note as significant the mention of 'language samples' and 'across these areas'. Firstly, the language samples frequently mentioned by the teachers refer to the notes they record about their learners' classroom performances (see Gardner and Rea-Dickins 2002) and this reflects a decision both about how learners are to be assessed (decision 3) and how the learners' performances will be captured (decision 7). These are written down as, for example, verbatim classroom talk or as an observation about a learner or learners as they use language in the classroom. (See Rea-Dickins and Gardner 2000.) A class and a language support teacher explain:

> I will jot down a few notes and modify something I was going to do if I've overestimated, or if it's obvious that more children understood than I expected.
> (F/1/CT/149–51)

> And there'll always be somebody doing [language] samples. And in the oracy groups that we do, we jot down while we're actually doing that. And I have my notebook with me all the time so I do it all the time.
> (F/1/LST/211–14)

These samples of learners' actual classroom performance may then be used for a variety of purposes that include an assessment of whether individual children have reached the set attainment targets. This use is explicitly stated by the language support teacher in (c) above, reflecting the concern with gaining an accurate record of a child's level of attainment. In practice, this frequently means checking off curriculum related (i.e. content) targets against subject knowledge criteria (decision 8), as part of the ongoing monitoring of curriculum learning. Secondly, the use in (b) of 'across these areas' refers to the need to gather learner performance data across curriculum subjects: in other words to obtain authentic language samples from diverse curriculum contexts.

A different point is revealed in (d) when the teacher refers to children's writing samples that have been produced unaided. What can be inferred from this is a concern about whether the children can independently access the national curriculum, i.e. to participate in the same way as their monolingual peers. As such it relates to the decision taken not to provide learners with scaffolded support on this assessment occasion, as captured by decision 6 in Table 13.2.

2 Deciding on the assessment activity

This next set of teachers' comments has to do with planning for the 'how' of assessment, i.e. decision 4 in Table 13.2, in relation to deciding on an appropriate assessment activity.

e We take the learning objectives and the learning outcomes and then we express those in, you know, in terms of the kinds of activities we'll do (E/1D/CT/70–2).

f I had four set questions to ask each group and they sort of rotated around the class and it was: 'Why is a jar made out of glass?' 'Why are toys made out of plastic?' 'Why is a radiator made out of metal?' So I asked the same question to each child (E/1C/LST/148–52).

Comment (e) provides further evidence of the way in which mainstream class teachers have a keen eye on subject learning with reference to the learning objectives and outcomes articulated in the English National Curriculum Levels (for example, Department for Education and Skills 2003). But this criterion-referenced approach to the development of assessment activities is not exclusive to the decisions of mainstream teachers, and is also widely evidenced in language support teachers' comments, as exemplified in (f) and the reference to the mainstream curriculum content of 'materials' in science, thus linking to decision 8. This last comment (f) also reveals other constructs at play. The notion of standardization of the assessment 'procedure' itself can be detected, linked to issues of reliability and with providing equal performance opportunities for each child. There is, thus, a strong linking between decisions about the procedure itself (decision 3) and those connected with whether the child's performance will be facilitated in some way by the teacher and/or other learners (decision 6). In subsequent discussions with this teacher, she confirmed that her aim in providing the same stimulus was to enable her to assess each child individually in terms not only of their individual linguistic performances and their ability to express their understandings of 'materials' within a science curriculum context but also the way in which they were 'accessing the curriculum', as compared with their monolingual peers. Thus, whilst concerned with gauging 'levels' of learner performance from a summative perspective decision, there lies an implicit use of the assessment data to inform her planning in respect of further formatively oriented support for individual learners (decision 10). Again, this provides an instance of the same assessment data being used for both formative and summative purposes.

Extracts (g) to (i) below, further illustrate the teachers' concerns to integrate language and content and to gather learner performance data across the curriculum through activities that have both curriculum authenticity and instructional relevance.

g I've learnt quite a lot from X [mainstream CT] because she does set up some really good language activities around say a topic. Like for example with the plants and the leaves and the roots ... and all those sorts of things where you can be really sort of focused (E/1C/LST/305–8).

h There are some assessments that are built into the curriculum (E/1C/LST/139).

i Well on the QCA scheme of work that I was using you know basically that was the final activity. So that was I suppose the main prompt really (E/3A/LST/105–7).

From these last two observations, we also learn that teachers use ready-made instructional activities from available curriculum texts (decisions 2 and 3).

The 'language' dimension in the above comments is implied, in the sense that teachers have planned to assess the extent to which within the context of subject learning their learners are able to engage effectively and/ or independently and to demonstrate attainment of content targets. The next comments provide instances of teachers talking more specifically about 'language'.

3 Focus on language

Extracts (j) and (k) provide a class teacher's perspective on the assessment of EAL learner performance, through the lens of learner attainment referenced to generic subject objectives.

j The biggest input for me with the language samples is actually the curriculum input ... X [LST] uses it more for language structures but I actually use it more for what they are saying about what they have learnt. So whether they are demonstrating understanding of a point or whether they are demonstrating they haven't understood a point (F/1/CT/4–7).

k Their structures ... cause and effect ... 'if this then that' because that shows the applications and that's what gets a Level 3 ... so I really broke it down ... level 1, level 2, level 3 in the science descriptors and the linguistic level it almost means the same thing cos without those struc-tures they couldn't get a level 3 (E/1/D/CT/28–31).

Thus, in terms of the planning stages presented earlier, the language sam-ples (decision 7, Table 13.2) derived from jointly constructed activities (decision 14) will be assessed by the class teacher through benchmarking learner attainment against the National Curriculum science descriptors (decision 8). This teacher mentions specific facets of classroom language use: linguistic structures and an ability to express the academic language function of 'cause and effect'. In this latter case, this could also relate to the ability to engage with the appropriate register, as in expressing 'cause and effect' in the formulation of hypotheses in science. She also draws attention to a 'glass ceiling effect', recognizing that a hesitant grasp in areas such as these will inhibit a learner's ability to be rated at the higher levels for curriculum attainment, her primary concern.

By way of contrast, the teacher with responsibility for language sup-port identifies in (l) and (m) below particular linguistic elements that she intends to focus on (or has already done so), reflecting decision 2, Table 13.2. Her comments on accuracy are also interesting.

1 Now each half term, I'm having a main priority, a main focus. This half term it was adjectives and noun-verb agreement because I thought the two would go together in describing objects, singulars and plurals and apart from running around … getting all these [objects] when it's a new topic like Growth, it'll be seed trays and compost and pots and watering cans, and we gear the lesson to the required elements in science in the National Curriculum (M/1C/LST/9–15).

m I was doing a lesson on fiction and non-fiction, and linking that in with a topic, we're going to do some noun-verb agreement and past tense, and really get the accuracy … getting a full correct sentence … I tend to use the correct grammatical form … (M/1C/LST/28–32).

As in previous extracts, we observe a strong teacher perspective on 'language through the lens of curriculum content'. But, additionally, there is explicit, rather than implied, mention of linguistic targets linked to academic functional objectives of 'description'. In relation to accuracy, she talks about how she tries to elicit full and accurate sentences from her learners—a fairly common practice in the classes observed—and makes explicit reference to her scaffolding/feedback strategy and her use of corrective feedback 'I tend to use the correct grammatical form'—again a common practice to provide learners with EAL with the correct model. What is interesting for me in this comment is that she makes this feedback strategy (decision 11) explicit, a facet that has a low profile in the data set. In other words, the interactional dimension of classroom formative assessment, that includes specific teachers' feedback strategies, does not emerge in the data overall as a central factor—in that it is made explicit—in a teacher's assessment planning. On the other hand, a focus on rating student performance levels does. In this sense, we can infer that the teachers' positioning of their roles in classroom assessment associate more with that of 'rater' rather than of 'facilitator' of language development.

Discussion

In this section, I focus on points that arise from the distinctiveness of the EAL teaching and learning context and the ways in which teachers problematize their planning decisions for classroom-based assessment. These relate to the validity of teacher assessment practices as well as to the specific assessment roles with which teachers are expected to be fully conversant (Leung and Rea-Dickins 2007).

The first part of this chapter has summarized key issues, some of them raised over two decades ago (for example, R. Ellis 1985), underpinning the quality and equitable educational provision for EAL learners with diverse and distinctive needs in mainstream curriculum contexts. Whilst not always framed as imperatives for assessment each, I would argue, carries implications for the effective implementation of valid assessment opportunities for learners with EAL. Examples of these include:

1 assessment that moves beyond a narrow linguistic focus for EAL assessment—what R. Ellis has called 'system-referenced' testing (for example, R. Ellis 2003: Chapter 9)—to the use of context-embedded tasks through which to assess language performance—operationalizing 'performance-referenced' assessment (ibid.);

2 differentiation in terms of assessment task types, characterized (but not shown in this chapter) by several of the features in R. Ellis' framework for describing tasks (for example, R. Ellis 2003: 21);

3 comprehensive sampling of learners' language performance across subject learning contexts implying, in turn, different modes of performance (for example, speaking and writing);

4 multiple sources of evidence on learners' classroom performances;

5 a closer integration of language and content;

6 the assessment of attainment in subject learning;

7 the assessment of learners' language achievement; and

8 classroom support that nurtures language development.

In my view, in the context of this study, there is evidence of greater *a priori* validity of teacher assessment activities in terms of instructional and curriculum relevance, with the former referring to the appropriacy of the activity within the interaction of teaching and learning processes and the latter with validity in terms of curricula content. In turn, this has brought about the language sampling of a wide range of children's performance right across the curriculum (for example, Rea-Dickins and Gardner 2000).

On validity, Weir (2005: 18) states: 'We can never escape from the need to define what is being measured, just as we are obliged to investigate how adequate a test is in operation'. Mapping this perspective on to the teachers' comments above, it seems to me, that they (1) exemplify understandings of the 'what' and 'how' of assessing learners with EAL in relation to the achievement of curricular targets within their specific instructional contexts, (2) provide evidence of awareness of the language demands implicit within such targets and (3) demonstrate that teachers want to know which levels are within the grasp of their learners in terms of subject curriculum attainment targets and whether or not a child can demonstrate the accomplishment of a specific curriculum learning objective, or achieve a specific level. What I am far less clear about, however, is the *strength* of the validity evidence for the kind of routine classroom assessment, i.e. formative assessment (for example, Rea-Dickins 2001), that supports *progression* in EAL. In other words, what evidence is there that the learners' English language proficiency is being developed through appropriate teacher feedback strategies and interactional opportunities both of which are at the very core of effective language assessment that is formative in terms of its impact on the learners themselves? (See Scott 2003.) Do all teachers with EAL learners in their classes assist the language development of these children systematically and effectively? And, if so, how?

My positioning on formative language assessment and the opportunities that this may afford learners in strengthening their language abilities connects directly to SLA research. In this respect, the research of Rod Ellis on FFI (for example, R. Ellis 1988, 1999b, 2001a, 2002a, 2003; see also Ellis, Basturkmen, and Loewen 2001a; Loewen 2004), as well as his notion of the 'acquisition-rich classroom' (for example, R. Ellis 1999b), have significant contributions to make. However, this view of formative language assessment, or so it appears to me, runs somewhat counter to current government policy in England that has adopted a universalist approach to the educational provision for learners with EAL from both an assessment and a language development perspective. In other contexts, frameworks exist that explicitly support the assessment of the specific needs of learners with EAL. They do this through detailed guidance for teachers in the form of, for example, observation frameworks, a range of structured activities, and explanations of SLA processes (for example, TESOL 2001; McKay, Hudson, and Sapuppo 1994; see also Scott and Erduran 2004). In England, however, the formal assessment of learners with EAL is approached in the same way as it is for English L1 children, with the exception of two specifically prepared 'pre-level step descriptors' (Qualifications and Curriculum Authority 2000). Further, all children share almost identical experiential processes of learning in the mainstream, thus portraying the development of English as a mother tongue as the underlying model for both learners with EAL and monolingual English children.

All this reflects, perhaps, the view that the ability to comprehend subject knowledge texts and to use language appropriately in subject classes, for example, to handle the registers of science or mathematics and engage in scientific argumentation (see Erduran, Simon, and Osborne 2004) is part of scientific knowledge. But, research has shown that language competence may be a barrier for some additional language learners in their school learning. Hargreaves (1997: 410–11), for example, found that learners with EAL are unable to perform fully their academic competence if their English is limited and goes on to suggest that the process of mathematical achievement may be accelerated by increased attention to language at an early age. Further it has always been maintained and evidenced (for example, Cummins 1992, 2000; Collier 1987, 1992, 1995) that it takes an extensive period of time for learners with EAL to become fully competent in English —a point, rather ironically, that is also recognized in government documentation (for example, Office for Standards in Education (OfSTED) 2001).

It should therefore be of some concern that very little knowledge about SLA is either explicitly articulated or referred to in the teacher interviews in this research (but see Rea-Dickins 2002, 2006; Scott 2003; Gardner 2004). However, as Brindley has maintained, it would be wrong to view teachers as ignorant of appropriate assessment practices. Indeed he points out how:

> they assess constantly through such means as observation, recycling of work, diagnostic testing, learner self-assessment, various forms of corrective feedback and *ad hoc* tests. With experience, many teachers will become skilled judges and observers capable of evaluating the quality of language performances and making fine-grained diagnoses of learners' difficulties.
> (Brindley 2001: 127)

The implication, he suggests, is for appropriate professional development opportunities for teachers. However, in England—the context of this study—it is only very recently that any formal training or accreditation for teachers working with EAL have begun to emerge.

Conclusion

This chapter has explored the nature of teacher decision making in relation to planning for the class-based assessment of learners with EAL. Methodologically, whilst it would have been possible to present a frequency count for each of the listed categories, there has been no attempt to do this, as the opportunities for teachers to talk about their assessment were not strictly comparable. In any case, my purpose has been to elaborate what precisely teachers make decisions about and thus to develop the 'broadest' picture possible of the decision-making points.

With reference to the analysis itself, it should be borne in mind that whilst these planning sub-categories are listed as discrete elements (see Table 13.2), they do not operate in practice as fixed and separate entities. Rather, they should be viewed as interdependent facets of planning strategies with which teachers engage in developing appropriate classroom-based assessments. Thus, a decision taken about 'when' to use a specific activity will be linked to assessment purpose and may also involve identifying what specific information a teacher needs about a particular learner or group of learners, a decision about 'content' that is relevant to the phase of instruction, a decision about the design of the activity itself and how it will be implemented. Such connections provide evidence for the *a priori* validity of teacher assessments.

Whilst this chapter has focused on teacher decision-making for assessment, it is clear that this does not occur in a vacuum and a number of researchers (for example, Scott 2005; Yin 2005; Rea-Dickins 2006; Leung and Rea-Dickins 2007) have all identified some of the external influences on teachers' classroom assessment practices that are important to our overall understanding of teacher assessment. Yin, for example, has posited an 'assessment cognition network' (2005: 144). In his research with teachers in an English for Academic Purposes context, he found that: 'when teachers assessed students in the classroom, a wide array of mental processes, resources, and considerations were involved' (ibid.: 144). He also observes 'how classroom assessment is situated at the intersection of so many demands and considerations, and how personal experiences and (always limited) knowledge shape teachers' judgments of students' (ibid.: 160). Leung and Rea-Dickins (forthcoming) have analysed English government policy for the assessment of learners with EAL and have demonstrated, in particular, the tensions and contradictions that prevail in a context in which issues of 'target setting' are a prominent part of the educational discourse. Further, the interview data in this chapter has provided a means through which we can begin to learn more about teachers' cognitions about assessment and whether and how teachers' language assessment practices are influenced by and informed by current thinking beyond the conventional assessment boundaries and the extent to which these include understandings of SLA processes and how learners can engage in language rich interactional opportunities in mainstream classroom discourse. Findings such as these are all highly relevant to our overall understanding of teacher assessment as socially situated practice.

Returning to the title of this chapter, there is plenty of evidence that a considerable amount of benchmarking of EAL learner performance is taking place with reference to national curriculum level descriptors, i.e. the measuring and rating of learner attainment. This, in large part, is attributable to the fact that the teachers participating in this research work within a policy context that has adopted a universalist approach to assessment through National Curriculum English levels. At the same time, however, there is an urgent need to augment our knowledge of SLA processes of younger learners developing their English language proficiency in mainstream classrooms. Much SLA research has involved the older language learner in EFL classrooms but young children using EAL in primary classrooms may have very different processing capacities when it comes to comprehension (for example, VanPatten 1990) and the use of, say, corrective feedback. There might be an attention deficit aggravated by a teacher's focus on the subject area: they are focusing on concept development and problem-solving in, say, science, rather than language *per se*. Further research has the potential to inform theoretically on both additional language development in mainstream classroom interaction and the appropriateness of the universalist approach discussed here.

In this chapter, I have attempted to demonstrate a case for much stronger connections between formative language assessment and SLA research. In the primary curriculum context, in particular, this is a critical educational stage for the development and enhancement of the linguistic skills embedded within effective school literacies. It thus becomes crucially important to know how well the linguistic skills of learners with EAL are actually developed alongside the acquisition of school subject knowledge (i.e. in subject meaning-focused lessons), as such language development is a core element in the demonstration of this knowledge through National Curriculum assessments. The challenge, then, is to develop teachers' understandings of SLA processes and how learners can acquire language through rich interactional formative assessment opportunities in mainstream classroom discourse (for example, what features of a teacher's FoF influence learner uptake?). At the same time, they need to develop their classroom pedagogy so that language learning does take place alongside subject learning in mainstream classrooms (for example, to what extent do teachers provide corrective feedback directed at linguistic form and subject content in mainstream lessons? Are some teacher corrective strategies more likely to be successful than others?). The research by Rod Ellis and colleagues has made and will continue to make a significant contribution towards this goal.

Notes

1 The term English as an Additional Language (EAL) has replaced ESL in the context of mainstream education in the UK, although the latter is still used in Australia and North America.

2 The data presented here are from research studies carried out between 1998 and 2002 and funded by (1) Minority Group Support Services, Coventry Education Service and (2) the ESRC (Economic and Social Research Council), ESRC Major Research Grant R000238196.

3 These schools were part of a larger education service initiative to support learners with EAL in the early years of school. This project enabled language support teachers and bilingual education assistants to work collaboratively with mainstream teachers.

4 The first letter refers to school (for example, E), followed by the interview number (for example, 1D), then by whether the teacher is a mainstream teacher (CT) or a language support teacher (LST); the final numbers are those that appear on the individual interview transcript.

14

Learning through the looking glass: teacher response to form-focused feedback on writing

TRICIA HEDGE

OVER THE LAST 25 years we have gained increasing insight into the strategies used by successful writers, particularly for revising and improving their work. In response to these insights, teachers have explored strategies for supporting learners in developing an understanding of their own writing processes. This chapter will focus on one such strategy—teacher-taped commentary on learner writing—and will analyse how this enables writers to receive feedback focused on both the substance and form of their writing, the latter constituting form-focused instruction (FFI). When the writers in question are teachers or teacher trainees, their responses to taped commentary can be explored to raise issues they will need to address with their own learners.

Action research for teacher development

In an early article, R. Ellis (1986: 92) asks the question

> Do trainers, in fact, really influence what teachers do in the classroom by making them think about the principles and practice of teaching in training sessions remote from the classroom? It is all too easy to assume that a better-informed teacher will become a better teacher.

His question reflected the growing concern of that period about teacher education and how it can encourage teachers to reflect on the principles underlying their professional practice and to make these available for modification.

As R. Ellis points out, it is difficult to do this in contexts where teachers have left their workplaces to study on long courses, often geographically remote from their own classrooms. One possible solution is to provide such teachers with opportunities to learn 'through the looking glass', by inviting them to engage as learners in pieces of action research undertaken by their tutors. This allows the processes of action research both to provide opportunities for reflection and to provide teachers with some of the skills they might require if they later decide to investigate their own classrooms. As one teacher in this study expressed it: 'Thank you for inviting me to take part in this experiment. It has given me some confidence to try something similar with my own students'.

The exploratory study discussed in this chapter demonstrates a well-established cycle: (1) reflection on some problematic area of teaching and learning, (2) planning a change in teaching strategy which might be more effective, (3) action in trying out this possible solution, and (4) observation and analysis of the outcomes as a prompt to further reflection and action (Kemmis and McTaggert 1988). This cycle exemplifies the type of investigation through which teachers can create and internalize their own approach to language teaching (Kagan 1992). This particular study, which I undertook as both teacher and teacher educator, has also provided data to feed into sessions with teachers, encouraging them to reflect on their own roles in responding to their learners' writing.

Feedback on writing as FFI

It is suggested that presenting writers with audio-taped feedback on their writing constitutes a type of explicit reactive FFI (R. Ellis 2001a, 2002a, 2003; also see Chapter 1). The concept of FFI has been suggested by R. Ellis (2001a: 1–2) to include 'any planned or incidental instructional activity that is intended to induce learners to pay attention to linguistic form'. As the name suggests, reactive FFI is initiated in response to perceived learner need, and explicit FFI constitutes direct indication of problematic forms and organization. Thus, one of the aims of this investigation is to explore writer responses to FFI delivered through taped commentary, one type of intervention in the process of writing.

Our approach to feedback is embedded in understanding of revision as demonstrated by good writers and this understanding has been steadily increasing over the last 30 years. (See reviews in Ferris 2001; Ferris and Hedgcock 2005.) Well-known early studies by Perl (1979), Sommers (1980), Faigley and Witte (1981), and Zamel (1983) offered similar findings on revision. Good writers engaged in a recursive and generative process, re-reading their work in meaningful chunks such as paragraphs, and evaluating it for possible improvement. They tended to evaluate throughout the whole process, often making substantial changes, and the amount of revision was often related to the amount of planning, the purpose of the writing, the level of formality required, and the genre.

Current procedures for feedback on writing aim to encourage learners to take responsibility for their own improvement with support from the teacher or from peers, often both, in a multi-draft process. Through their response to explicit feedback on their errors and their subsequent self correction, it has been found that learners are able to attend to problematic areas in their writing, thus increasing the likelihood that they will acquire a deeper understanding of them and, in the case of the second language (L2) learner, eventually acquire them (R. Ellis 2002a). As Swain (2000, 2005) has observed, when L2 writers receive corrective feedback on written output, they are able to notice the gap between what they wish to say and what they are able to say. The noticing process is suggested to promote development of new linguistic knowledge and consolidate prior knowledge (Schmidt 2001). (Also see the discussion of noticing in Chapter 1.)

Teacher-taped commentary as a feedback strategy

Teacher-taped commentary appears to have been less researched than other methods of feedback such as peer conferencing or reformulation, yet several writers have commented on its values (McAlpine 1989; Patrie 1989; Cohen and Cavalcanti 1990; Hyland 1990; Boswood and Dwyer 1995; Jongekrijg and Russell 1999). Its potential can perhaps be seen in this extract of taped commentary and the response of the writer, Concepta. It is taken from the author's early experiments with this method.

> TUTOR I've just read the introductory paragraph and that I think is fine, because you've taken the title and reformulated it in your own words, which immediately demonstrates that you understand what the title wants you to do. I also like the quotation from H which gets the point across particularly effectively. As I look at the third paragraph, what strikes me here is that you've launched into a very interesting discussion on the bilingual individual, but you haven't actually sign-posted your reader by saying, you know, first I'm going to define what we mean by bilingualism and discuss the factors that we need to consider when we look at it. In other words, you're not actually providing a link back to the title or to your introduction. You need to give your reader a sense of direction as to where the essay is actually going.

> CONCEPTA'S RESPONSE As you went through my paper, it gave me lots of things to think about. On re-reading the assignment I realize

now the blatant lack of linking sentences and a definite need for an introduction to the paper that provides the reader with an outline (...) My paper reminded me in some ways of someone just learning how to use a standard transmission and popping the clutch from paragraph to paragraph.

I found this method of critiquing extremely convenient. I've been able to listen to the tape a couple of times. I would now be self-critical about the style of comment and this will be taken up later, but what seems to be evident here is what Patrie (1989: 88) has called the naturalness of taped commentary: 'You will naturally respond to the writing as a whole piece of discourse and your responses will also become a dialogue between you and the writer'.

The study

Participants

The participants in this study were 16 teachers taking a module in Language Teaching for a Master's degree in a UK university. It was a mixed nationality group, with a combination of British, Canadian, Chinese, Greek, Japanese, Korean, Malaysian, Portuguese, and Taiwanese teachers. Their English language proficiency levels ranged between 6 IELTS and native speaker competence. Module assessment required the teachers to produce an essay of 3000 words selected from a range of titles in the field of applied linguistics and English language teaching, for example:

> A process approach to writing has been described as one in which
> the focus is as much on the writer as the piece of writing. Discuss the
> implications of this dual focus for L2 writing pedagogy in relation
> to a group of learners you know.

Workloads during the day would have made it difficult to hold individual writing conferences. Taped commentary seemed to have potential as a form of feedback which could be done during the tutor's quieter periods. Its use was underpinned by a belief that assignment writing is a major means of teacher development. These teachers were highly motivated towards professional development and were engaged in the process of questioning the relevance of their educational goals and practices.

Goals

Given my dual role as writing tutor and as teacher educator, the exploration had several goals. The first was a course goal: to foster the development of the learners' writing skills through instruction focused on both content and form, calling their attention to problematic structures, syntax, organizational challenges, and other aspects of academic writing, thus assisting their future acquisition of improved content and form (Schmidt 2001). The second was to explore the ways in which teachers perceived the advantages and disadvantages of using taped commentary during the drafting process. The third was to reflect on these perceptions and to consider what modifications might be desirable to improve effectiveness of the method. The fourth aim was to experiment with ways of using the data for teacher development.

Procedure

The procedure for this investigation was to record commentaries on the writing of the teachers. The procedure followed the steps described in Hedge (2005: 134). Each essay was marked with numbers in the margin of the essay drafts at points where the tutor wished to comment orally. The taped commentary referred to the numbers and both the essay draft and the taped commentary were returned to the teachers. They were advised that the numbers indicated points at which the tutor stopped reading in order to record requests for clarification, or to express confusion, or to advise on linguistic problems, etc. Recorded comments were made on content, organization, coherence and more specific problems with form, for example, grammatical errors, faulty sentence structure, inappropriate vocabulary. These linguistic inaccuracies were also marked on the essay draft. However, the commentary began with advice to leave consideration of these until later and to wait for any summary comments on language at the end of the commentary.

Examples of comments are as follows:

You start your final paragraph with 'In sum' but, in fact, you don't really go on to give a summary of the whole essay. You focus on what you think is the most important issue for teachers. So perhaps you could write something like 'The main or central issue arising from this discussion'. If you look at the concluding paragraphs of articles in some ELT journals you will find other useful phrases, depending on exactly what the function is of the paragraph.

I've read several times now 'lots of' or 'a lot of' or 'a big number of' in your essay. In formal writing it's better to use 'a substantial amount of' or 'a substantial number of'. There are some dictionaries, like the Oxford Compact dictionary, that give advice on formality.

This paragraph is all one long sentence. Could you divide it into three shorter ones? It would help your reader.

In addition, teachers were given a feedback sheet containing a written summary from the tutor and an invitation to respond to the taped commentary, either on the tape or on the feedback sheet. They were also asked for their opinions about the advantages and disadvantages of this feedback method over the traditional method of receiving written comments from the tutor.

Results

Feedback sheet responses

Responses written by the learners on the feedback sheets varied between 47 words divided into bullet points and 500 words of continuous prose. They listed between two and fourteen points in relation to advantages and disadvantages of taped commentary, many expressing similar perceptions. The

Teacher-taped commentary	No. of times mentioned
Advantages	
1 *The writing*	
1.1 Detail	15
1.2 Meaningful interaction between reader and writer	12
1.3 Progressive negotiation with the text	9
1.4 Ideas generation from critique	11
1.5 Ease of understanding	7
1.6 Combined comment on content and form	5
2 *The writer*	
2.1 Sense of value as an individual	10
2.2 Motivation/excitement	5
2.3 Seriousness of teacher endeavour	8
Disadvantages	
3.1 Time-consuming for teacher	5
3.2 Problems with technology	3
3.3 Difficulty in listening	3
3.4 Cost	2

N = 16

TABLE 14.1 *Advantages and disadvantages of taped commentary*

responses were first comprehensively listed, thereby providing one type of data for later use with the teachers. As shown in Table 14.1, they were then categorized into 'Advantages', producing six subcategories under 'The writing' and three under 'The writer', and into 'Disadvantages', producing four subcategories. Indications were given of the number of similar comments made and sample responses presented. This provided a second type of data for discussion with the teachers.

Discussion

In the section 'The writing' the first subcategory involved learner noticing and continued awareness of the tutor's remarks about writing form and detail, a particular aim of FFI. This was expressed in various ways.

> More thorough and informative feedback about what I've written. The many questions you asked helped me to think about details.

> I felt that I received comments on every little bit of my essay.

> The main advantage is that the spoken protocol provides much more detailed feedback (hundreds of words of comment as opposed to a summative response which provides a general review only).

Almost all teachers remarked on the amount of comment, but it is also significant that they used the words 'detail' and 'thorough'. It would be possible in speech, which is less dense lexically and allows digression more easily than writing, to take longer to say what could be said in a succinct written comment. Certainly it is possible to make much lengthier comment on tape. For example, a quick comparison between verbal comments on grade B papers in this investigation and written comments on similar work in the previous year shows an approximate difference between 250–400 words (written) and 900–1600 words (spoken). However, teacher-taped feedback was perceived by the learners as more 'informative', such awareness being one of the goals of reactive FFI (R. Ellis 2001a).

The second subcategory relates to interaction between reader and writer, as expressed in the following responses:

> It was like talking to a person, like a tutorial session, but with the advantage of being able to re-listen and review the essay again.

> It is immediate compared with written comments. I felt involved.

If we add the third category in Table 14.1 to this perception of 'immediacy', the major value of taped commentary becomes clear: it allows progressive negotiation with the text in the reader/writer interaction. One teacher expressed this very clearly:

This kind of feedback helps the student to see how his/her tutor is progressively reacting to the work. It really helps to follow a tutor's train of thought. It allows the student to see what each section of the work means to the reader in terms of the whole project.

The commentaries as FFI

A significant point of this procedure is that the reader is usually not able to ask for clarification while reading and must therefore negotiate or interpret a text by moving recursively through it to make sense of its meaning. If the writer becomes aware of this struggle through the evidence of the commentary, it provides support for improvements in the clarity of the text, thus stimulating the noticing process described above. Verbal FFI is particularly useful in providing evidence of weaknesses in overall organization and local coherence, because the tutor can express confusion, or report having to make a leap in logic because part of the argument is missing. However, the nature of the comment deserves careful consideration.

In the example of tutor/teacher interaction given earlier in this paper, Concepta is remarkably responsive to what many might describe as an over-directive style on the part of the tutor. She is informed as to what she failed to do and told what she needs to do instead, thus developing her awareness of areas that require remediation, a goal of reactive FFI. However, the directness of the feedback should be softened. Ideally, the role of the tutor would be more collaborative than evaluative and allow for shared responsibility with the ultimate goal of transferring control to the writer for successful improvement of the essay. In this way the procedure has potential for implementing Applebee's 'instructional scaffolding' (1986: 110) which highlights the development of a learner's self regulation.

Asking questions to promote noticing and FFI

It may be effective to indicate confusion or non-comprehension and to ask questions in order to elicit improvement. The work of Graves (1983) with much younger learners provides useful pointers for question types that would allow writers to exert authority over their writing and make their own decisions about revision. To borrow some question types from his framework, opening questions might take such forms as: What would you say is the main aim of this section? Do you think you have clarified this aim? Can your reader find it stated somewhere? Or do you think it's implicit in what you've written? Subsequent questions might be: How does this section develop the ideas in the last one? What kind of link have you provided between sections? Focused questions could highlight a variety of problems: Can you think of an example from your own experience to illustrate this point? Or: I was confused by this connective. Are you now turning to a contrasting point? What other connectives could you use?

There is always a danger that the tutor's attempt to create dialogic interaction can easily lapse into monologic mediation (Lantolf 2000b, Chapter 3 of this volume) and the ultimate risk is that writers might perceive the tutor as appropriating their texts. A similar study with another group of teachers elicited the response:

> I wanted to enter into the spirit of things and respond to the comments you were making but had to wait until the end. Hearing the comments vocalized made me want to interrupt you out loud and it was a bit annoying that the tape just rolled on.

Writing teachers need to be wary of taking over a student's writing to such an extent that the student's effort to develop writing ability is subverted. Any feeling that a text is being appropriated by the tutor can lead to breakdown of rapport. To guard against this, it is possible to ask writers to annotate their drafts requesting feedback on particular points of uncertainty.

A further subcategory relates to ideas generated by the critique. This writer had developed an effective procedure for listening to the taped comments:

> As I listened to your comments and questions, *I re-read that part of the material and thought about it.* I also made notes from the commentary. This process got me thinking how to develop my ideas.

This response acknowledges the process of becoming aware of the gap between what the writer wants to express and what she has been able to express. Here, learning through FFI has been mediated through collaborative dialogue.

Others commented on how the commentary had helped them to appreciate the requirements of the UK academic tradition which were different from their own. For example:

> When you said: Do you think you could make a list of your own here, and incorporate the others? I was surprised. I haven't thought of doing it. Is this the criticality criteria?

Her reference is to faculty criteria for assessment of work, which she was clearly using to review her writing, and she had not appreciated some points under the general criterion 'degree of criticality'.

Content of the taped commentaries: substance versus form

On analysing the data, it was possible to reflect on the amount of time devoted to substance and form. A good deal of comment was devoted to issues of substance as the study took place early in the academic year. A key point, in fact, was to encourage a critical perspective, not just to 'collect heads' from authoritative sources, but to create a personal framework incorporating those of others, or to compare ideas from different writers rather than listing them, or to trace historical development of an idea with comment. Another was to encourage a teacher to develop points further into supporting points and thus develop a fuller argument. Yet another was to encourage the reformulation of ideas in authoritative sources rather than to use quotation and to continue by giving a personal example of the point being made. All of these strategies were intended to move the writer from 'knowledge-telling' to 'knowledge transformation' (Scardamalia and Bereiter 1987) and it had proved much easier to do this quickly and to provide the writer with points for reflection in a non-threatening way through taped commentary. In comparison, oral comment in the face-to-face tutorial situation can be intimidating, particularly when students are listening to a foreign language and when their work is problematic.

Comments in subcategory 1.5 related to the difficulty sometimes experienced in making sense of terse written comments, as in 'It was easier to follow than some written comments I've had which can be too condensed to understand' and 'I feel that written comments could almost be more meaningful to the tutor than the student as they are stripped of context'.

The final subcategory consisted of comments on the combination of feedback encouraging micro-text-based changes and macro-text-based changes (Faigley and Witte 1981). The former refers to reworking of sentences and paragraphs and the latter to changes in the overall organization of the text. Some teachers commented on the technique of marking problems with micro features on the writing and then summarizing some major problematic areas on the cassette, for example:

> Different tutors have different ways of marking error. In this method tutor can mark mistakes, but also give some summary of my main weaknesses, for example, using article and connectives, and how I can find help. It would take a lot of time to write all this down.

Thus, the provision of explicit, reactive FFI on academic writing drafts through taped commentary appears to have enabled the participants to notice problematic areas of their writing and increased their awareness of what needed to be amended.

Learner reactions to the taped commentaries

A different type of response is categorized in the section entitled 'The writer'. Affect is in the foreground here, as demonstrated in these comments:

> I found this procedure very exciting, personalized, and helpful.
>
> It's motivating. I was keen to hear your comments.
>
> I thought that it gave a personal approach as I could hear your voice.
>
> It felt like personal attention. I enjoyed it.

Comments on the personal touch, on valuing, on attention, on motivation and excitement, all point to the building of rapport, for which taped commentary seems to have valuable potential. As teachers themselves, some were also clearly reflecting on their future roles and felt that using taped commentary would benefit their relationship with learners, by demonstrating the seriousness of teacher endeavour: 'In this method it is clear to students that the teacher has considered them carefully and is prepared to try out something new that will help them'.

Comments on disadvantages were fewer in number, though the novelty of this first experience of taped commentary might have generated a positive response. Some teachers were reflecting on how they might use the technique in their own professional contexts. Cost, time, and problems with technology all deserve careful thought before embarking on the use of taped commentary. Subcategory 3.3. 'Experiencing problems in listening', is a universally relevant point:

> Occasionally there were words I couldn't understand and it's hard to work out the spelling to check them in a dictionary.
>
> You spoke fast at times and I couldn't hear all words.

Such difficulties would increase with students of lower language ability and this points to a potential constraint of taped commentary and the need to address it with appropriate strategies.

These reflections are, of course, personal, and partly based on knowledge of the students, their abilities, attitudes, and personalities. But that is in keeping with the aims of action research, to uncover what is happening in one's own classroom and to reflect on it. However, the data is useful for wider purposes than personal reflection.

Using the data for teacher development

Different forms of the data can be used to support several aims for teacher development.

1 To reflect on their possible roles in feedback and to review one alternative for responding to learners' writing.

2 To understand that each learner will perceive, experience, and gain from any procedure according to their differing prior experience and expectations.

3 To see the value of engaging in enquiry into their own professional practice and to understand some of the issues in doing it.

4 To appreciate that such enquiry can enable them to make more rationally based decisions about the design of teaching procedures in their own context.

Categorizing activity

It was reported above that the tutor compiled the teacher responses to feedback in two formats. The first format, the unsorted list of responses, can enrich a session on action research, in which the aim would be to build both competence and confidence in gathering and analysing data from learners. Teachers can be asked to attempt a categorization of the responses. Analysis of the feedback forms had yielded some 95 propositions in total, a manageable number for students working in small groups. The first step would be a general review within the class to suggest major categories within the responses. A technique such as key word analysis could be suggested and demonstrated. Small groups could then further categorize the data. When some categories have been determined, these can be allocated to subgroups. The advantage of this method is the inevitability of different interpretations among groups and subgroups, the way in which it demonstrates the problems of finding patterns in the data without misrepresentation, and the need to refine categories.

Pedagogy development activity

The second format, the categorized data, with sample responses attached, can also be used to raise awareness of issues in feedback. Teachers can reflect on the responses from writers and formulate principles for giving explicit FFI through feedback on writing. These could be created independently by more experienced teachers or, with those of less experience, some prompts could be given to start discussion and reflection on the task. For example,

The writer
- to motivate through praise and encouragement
- to focus on strengths as well as weaknesses in order to build confidence
- to move learners towards independence

The context
- to give feedback appropriate to the age and level of learners
- to take account of the learners' educational experiences and expectations of methodology
- to be in tune with IT potential/constraints

The writing
- to be appropriately detailed and informative
- to encourage effective interaction with the text
- to promote noticing and continued awareness of what constitutes good quality writing through reactive FFI

TABLE 14.2 *Goals for a principled approach to FFI through feedback on writing*

Dörnyei (2001) gives some useful starting points in his guidelines on motivating through feedback such as using praise, encouraging the development of develop self-confidence, and providing specific focus that will enable students to work on those areas that need improvement.

Table 14.2 shows the kind of framework of principles that could be employed in a fuller or more reduced form.

Conclusion

This chapter has set out to demonstrate how teachers can become researchers into their own professional practice and the classroom experiences of their learners in order to extend their personal understanding of the functioning and effects of a particular classroom procedure—in this case, providing explicit reactive FFI on learner writing through taped feedback. It has also set out to demonstrate the value of engaging teachers as participants in action research, as motivation and support for teachers' future attempts to explore their own classrooms and in this way to add to the available repertoire of reflective practice activities. The investigation was based on the belief that we need to assert our experience and expertise as teachers and as teacher educators to find ways of enabling our learners to speak, and then to listen to their voices. In this way both parties can learn from the experience and develop improved confidence and morale.

15

Explicit language knowledge and focus on form: options and obstacles for TESOL teacher trainees[1]

CATHERINE ELDER, ROSEMARY ERLAM, and JENEFER PHILP

RESEARCH ON form-focused instruction (FFI) suggests a role for grammar instruction within a communicative approach (R. Ellis 1994b, 1995, 1997a, 1998; Long 1996, 2000; Spada 1997; Doughty and Williams 1998a; Long and Robinson 1998; Norris and Ortega 2000; Nassaji and Fotos 2004). This recommendation derives from three sources: long-term outcomes of meaning-focused instruction and non-instructed (naturalistic) language learning, theoretical work on processes of language acquisition, and evidence from experimental and classroom-based research on focus on form (FoF), as set out in Chapter 1.

Much research in second language (L2) classrooms has reported on the relative frequency and effectiveness of reactive, incidental feedback, particularly recasts, provided to learners in response to non-target like utterances across both second and foreign language (FL) contexts. (For review, see Nicholas, Lightbown, and Spada 2001; Long 2006b.) As noted in Chapter 1, while some researchers note the benefits of such feedback for acquisition (for example, Doughty 2001), others (Lyster 1998b, 2004) maintain that more explicit, less ambiguous corrective feedback is preferable in certain classroom contexts where learners may not perceive implicit feedback as corrective.

Implicit feedback may however be the preferred option for many teachers both in terms of classroom management and continuity of interaction (Doughty 1994; Ellis, Basturkmen, and Loewen 2001a; Loewen and Philp 2006; Long 2006b), but also because it allows teachers to fall back on their implicit knowledge of the L2. Errors corrected through explicit feedback, on the other hand, require metalinguistic knowledge and, in some instances, a command of metalanguage (the technical or semi-technical words for grammatical categories and functions), which teachers may not possess.

While metalinguistic knowledge is clearly not the same as language proficiency, and a number of studies have shown only moderate positive correlations between the two (Alderson, Clapham, and Steel 1997; Elder, Warren *et al.* 1999; Renou 2000), both are regarded as critical for effective language teaching. Andrews (2003), citing Wright and Bolitho's (1997) model of classroom language content and use, emphasizes the interconnection between proficiency and language awareness and argues that a teacher's language awareness (TLA) incorporates both knowledge *about* the language and knowledge *of* the language. Particular to TLA is a metacognitive aspect, drawing from both types of knowledge, which enables the teacher to plan learning activities, modify and mediate input from other sources, and respond to learner production and questions in the context of such activities. As Wright (2002: 115) notes, 'a linguistically aware teacher not only understands how language works, but understands the student's struggle with language and is sensitive to errors and other interlanguage features'.

Similarly, Elder (1994, 2001), exploring the construct of teacher language proficiency for testing purposes, proposes that language teachers need to (a) be proficient enough in the target language (TL) to provide rich and well formed models for their learners, (b) tailor their input to make it comprehensible to learners, and, most importantly for the current study, (c) have sufficient metalinguistic knowledge both to explain grammatical rules and to respond to learner error (using whatever strategies are appropriate to the particular learning context).

Work on TLA, however, suggests that not all teachers are well equipped to offer such explanations or to exploit the potential of different options within FFI (Bolitho 1988; Wright 1991; Wright and Bolitho 1997; Andrews 1999, 2003; Mitchell 2000). Bolitho (1988) and Andrews (1994, 2003) report a perceived inadequate grammatical knowledge or awareness among teacher trainees in the English speaking West, but Andrews (2003), citing Wright (1991), suggests this is less true of 'non-native' L2 teacher trainees from 'periphery' contexts (Canagarajah 1993) because of the inclusion of explicit grammar pedagogy in their prior education, and as part of teacher training programmes.

This latter claim has not been tested, however, and is based on the assumption that learning the explicit rules of TL grammar will result in the ability to produce acceptable TL explanations for L2 learners. Such an assumption would seem highly questionable given that grammar instruction in FL teaching contexts (even those espousing the communicative approach) is typically delivered to L2 learners in their mother tongue rather than through the medium of the TL (Mitchell 1988; Duff and Polio 1990; Polio and Duff 1994; Kim and Elder 2005). Also worth noting are the results

226

of previous research assessing learners' levels of metalinguistic knowledge (Green and Hecht 1992; Alderson, Clapham, and Steel 1997; Elder *et al.* 1999; Renou 2000; Elder and Manwaring 2004). These show that the ability to verbalize grammatical rules in the TL is often quite limited, even amongst advanced undergraduate learners of the FL with many years of prior formal instruction. Whether this is due to conceptual confusion about the workings of the language, limited language proficiency, a lack of appropriate metalanguage, or a combination of these is not entirely clear, but it is a matter for concern given that university language departments are usually the recruiting ground for language teachers.

The present study

In the present study, both a Metalinguistic Knowledge test (MKT) and a Grammaticality Judgement test (GJT) were used to test the explicit language knowledge of a group of advanced English language learners from Malaysia who were trainee English language teachers. The research questions which the study addressed are as follows:

1 What level of metalinguistic knowledge do advanced English learners from Malaysia have?
2 What kinds of rules/metalinguistic terms present particular difficulties for advanced learners?
3 Is metalinguistic knowledge associated with the ability to recognize error?
4 What are the implications of these findings for the teaching of focus on form (FoF) in L2 classrooms?

Methodology

Participants

The participants were 61 students enrolled in a one-and-a-half year foundation programme at an international languages teacher training institute in Malaysia.

At the time of the study, the students were nearing completion of their foundation programme and preparing to embark on a four-year BEd degree, the middle two years of which were to be completed at universities in either New Zealand, Australia, or the United Kingdom. On completion of this 'sandwich' degree, students would be expected to take up positions as English language teachers in primary or secondary schools in Malaysia.

All students had studied English as a second language (ESL) from the age of seven, at primary and secondary schools in Malaysia. They had been selected for admission to the institute on the basis of their high school grades, in particular their English language marks. Their results on the diagnostic English language needs assessment (DELNA), a test used to identify their language support needs in reading, listening, and writing, confirmed that the vast majority of them performed above the threshold deemed to be necessary to cope with the academic language demands of an English-medium university. All students were between 19 and 21 years of age. During the one-and-a-half years of foundation studies, students attended a variety of English classes, namely English studies (literature), language description (grammar), and language development (proficiency). A social studies class was also conducted in English. The language description classes were of approximately three hours duration per week and were taught over a period of 18 months (120 contact hours in total). The content of the course dealt with such areas as word classes, phrases and clauses, sentences patterns, sentence types, cohesive devices, words and meanings, and lexical relationships.

Test

Two tests of explicit knowledge were used in the present study, a MKT and an unspeeded GJT. The MKT was an adaptation of an earlier test of metalanguage devised by Alderson, Clapham, and Steel (1997). The first part of the test (Part 1), which is the focus of the current study,[2] presented students with 15 ungrammatical sentences, each of which contained a typical learner error in relation to a specific language structure.[3] The part of the sentence containing the error was, in each case, underlined. Participants were asked to write an explanatory rule for the identified error. (A sample item is provided in Appendix A.)

The GJT consisted of 68 sentences, evenly divided between grammatical and ungrammatical. There were four sentences to be judged for each of 17 grammatical structures, the 15 that were targeted in the MKT, plus two more (3rd person 's', dative alternation).[4]

Test administration

Participants completed the two tests during a period in which one of the researchers was visiting Malaysia along with another colleague to administer DELNA to these and other students from the institute. The present test was administered as a pen and paper test with no time limit. It was completed along with and subsequent to a Grammaticality Judgment test (see below).

Scoring

Responses to Part 1 of the MKT were scored according to two criteria. The first was the formulation of a rule to account for the underlined error (rule score). For each item, criteria were established that would determine whether a given explanation was an *adequate* formulation of the appropriate rule or not. It is important to note here that the criteria for adequate formulation of a rule did not require the use of metalinguistic terminology, but simply the ability to articulate the concept/s deemed to be central in each case. We were, in other words, attempting to avoid, in so far as possible, any confusion between what was being assessed (knowledge of language) and the means used to express this knowledge (metalanguage) (Berry 2005). The judgements of two expert applied linguists were used as a basis for deciding the criteria for each item, with reference to relevant pedagogic or descriptive grammar texts as required. Participants scored one mark for an adequately formulated rule and a maximum of 15 for this part of the test.

For each item, participants were also given a score for their use of metalinguistic terminology (metalang. score). While, as already noted, the test rubric did not *require* them to use metalanguage, the two examples provided before starting the test (see Appendix A) did demonstrate the use of metalinguistic terminology (which is extremely hard to avoid in some cases). For each item, a list of acceptable metalinguistic terms was generated. Participants had only to use one of the specified terms to score one mark for each item in this category. The maximum score possible in this section was 15.

For each item, the scoring criteria (see Appendix B for examples) were first 'trialled' with a selection of 'sample' answers taken from participants' scripts. The marking key was then reworked (where necessary) by the researchers and an additional rater was 'trained' with respect to the criteria and given the sample items to rate independently. Any differences were discussed and in the few cases where discussion did not resolve differences, the ratings of the researcher were taken as the final scores.

The GJT items were objectively scored as either correct (1 point) or incorrect (0 points). The maximum score for this test was 68.

Test reliability

The internal consistency of Part 1 of the MKT was calculated using Cronbach's alpha, yielding $\alpha = .81$. Inter-rater reliability was also established for the Rule item. The correlation between *initial* scores (i.e. before joint discussion of differences in ratings) given by the two raters for participants' attempts at rule formulation was: $r = .96$. For the GJT for each item, participants were required to indicate whether the sentence was (a) grammatical or (b) ungrammatical. Internal consistency of the judgement accuracy scores was calculated using Cronbach's alpha, yielding $\alpha = .66$.

Results

Descriptive statistics for participants' performance on Part 1 of the MKT are presented in Table 15.1. Results show that participants scored a mean of 7.41 (out of a maximum total score of 15) for their ability to formulate an acceptable rule in relation to the 15 targeted grammatical structures. They scored a mean of 5.07 (out of a maximum total score of 15) for their ability to use appropriate metalinguistic terminology in their rule explanations. Performance ranged widely on both these components as evidenced by the relatively large standard deviations, however no candidate achieved a perfect score.

A correlation was carried out between the two sets of scores on Part 1 of the test to see to what extent participants' ability to formulate a rule was related to their ability to use metalinguistic terms. There was a significant correlation, $r = .66, p = .01$.

Table 15.2 presents the percentage correct of rule formulation scores for each of the 15 items of Part 1 of the MKT, in order of increasing difficulty. It also presents information for each item that shows the percentage of responses that were marked incorrect because of poor rule formation and the percentage of non suppliance of response. The structures for which the participants performed best in terms of formulating an adequate rule were (in order of increasing difficulty) regular past tense, plural 's', possessive 's', and comparatives. The structures that were most difficult for students (from most to least difficult) were ergatives, verb complements, and unreal conditional.

Descriptive statistics for participants' performance on the GJT are presented in Table 15.3. Participants scored highly on this test, $M = 60.21$ out of a possible maximum score of 68, showing that they were able to perform to a high level when required to judge the grammatical accept-

	M	SD	N	Max score	Range	Percentage mean
Part 1: rule	7.41	2.91	61	15	1–14	49.40
Part 1: metalang.	5.07	2.93	61	15	0–14	33.80
Part 1: total	12.48	5.33	61	30	3–28	41.60

TABLE 15.1 *Descriptive statistics for Part 1 of the MKT*

ability of sentences containing the targeted structures. In fact there was a ceiling effect on this test, with a number of participants obtaining perfect or near perfect scores.[5] It is interesting to note that they performed at a similar level when judging both the grammatical ($M = 29.66$) and ungrammatical sentences ($M = 30.56$), given that results from a larger study in which the same test was used have suggested that the two types of item are tapping different types of knowledge—implicit knowledge in the case of the grammatical items and explicit knowledge in the case of the ungrammatical. (For further discussion of the implicit/explicit knowledge distinction in relation to these different kinds of items see R. Ellis 2005b.)

Item no.	Grammatical structure	Percentage correct	Percentage incorrect	Percentage missing answers
8	Regular past tense	78.69	18.03	3.28
5	Plural 's'	73.77	16.39	9.84
7	Possessive 's'	73.77	18.03	8.20
4	Comparatives	70.49	21.31	8.20
9	Indefinite article	63.93	24.59	11.48
13	Question tags	63.93	24.59	11.48
12	Adverb placement	60.66	27.87	11.48
15	Relative clauses	45.90	31.15	22.95
11	Yes/no questions	42.62	24.59	32.79
14	*Since* and *for*	42.62	29.51	27.87
1	Modal verbs	37.70	50.82	11.48
10	Embedded questions	29.51	50.82	19.67
3	Unreal conditional	21.31	37.70	40.98
2	Verb complements	19.67	63.93	16.39
6	Ergatives	16.39	52.46	31.15

TABLE 15.2 *Percentage correct, percentage incorrect and percentage missing answers for rule formulation scores, Part 1 MKT*

GJT	M	SD	N	Max score	Range	Percentage mean
Ungrammatical sentences	30.56	2.89	61	34	22–34	89.88
Grammatical sentences	29.66	2.72	61	34	23–34	87.24
Total	60.21	4.24	61	68	51–68	88.54

TABLE 15.3 *Descriptive statistics for GJT*

Grammatical structure	Percentage correct
Modal verbs	95.49
Indefinite article	95.08
Adverb placement	95.08
Indefinite article	95.08
Possessive 's'	93.85
Verb complements	93.44
Question tags	93.44
Regular past tense	89.34
Since and *for*	88.52
Dative alternation	88.52
Yes/no questions	86.48
Ergatives	84.84
Relative clauses	83.61
Embedded questions	82.38
Plural 's'	81.97
Unreal conditional	80.74
Comparatives	77.46

TABLE 15.4 *Percentage correct for items in GJT*

Table 15.4 presents the percentage correct for items in the GJT according to each grammatical structure tested (there were four items testing for participants' ability to judge the grammaticality of sentences in relation to each target structure). It is interesting to note that the three structures for which participants scored highly when required to formulate a rule, that is, regular past tense, plural 's', and possessive 's', were not among the three structures that they found easiest in terms of making a grammaticality judgement. Accuracy rates were nevertheless high on these items (89, 82 and 94 per cent respectively), far higher than for the corresponding items on the rule explanation section of the MKT.

Table 15.5 presents correlations between performances on all parts of the MKT and performances on the GJT (grammatical items, ungrammatical items, total score). Results show that there were significant correlations between scores on the rule and metalanguage components of the MKT and both total scores and scores for ungrammatical items on the GJT. Interestingly, the correlation between metalanguage scores (based on use of relevant terminology) and the ungrammatical items on the GJT was consistently higher than that for Part 1 rule scores (indicating the appropriateness of the explanations provided).

Test	GJT total	GJT–gram.	GJT–ungram.
Part 1 rule score	.30*	.11	.34**
Part 1 metalang. Score	.35**	.07	.45**
Part 1 total	.36**	.10	.43**

*$p<.05$ **$p<.01$

TABLE 15.5 *Correlational matrix for performance on Part 1 of MKT and performance on GJT*

Discussion

The discussion will be organized around the research questions set out above.

1 What level of metalinguistic knowledge do English teacher trainees from Malaysia have?

Results of the MKT show that, in spite of their extensive English training which includes an explicit focus on the formal features of English, these trainee teachers vary widely in their level of metalinguistic knowledge and as a group perform rather poorly on this test. Even with a scoring system which accepts approximate explanations of errors, the participants achieve less than 50 per cent of acceptable responses on the rule explanation task. Their command of metalinguistic terminology (which correlates moderately with the ability to verbalize rules) is even weaker, although we must concede that participants may have deliberately chosen *not* to use technical language in this section of the test.

The poor results on the rule formulation task correspond to the findings of previous research (Sorace 1985; Green and Hecht 1992), which indicate that learners, even those with considerable experience of traditional instruction with an FoF orientation, do not necessarily learn the rules about language that they have been taught. However, as Bialystok (1979), Green and Hecht (1992), and Renou (2000) also found, the participants in the current study appear to have understood some grammatical rules better than others. We will speculate further about the reasons for this below.

2 What kinds of rules/metalinguistic terms present particular difficulties for advanced learners?

It is interesting to see that the rule explanations which these advanced Malaysian learners of English found easiest to formulate (plural 's', possessive 's', and comparative) all appear frequently in elementary English text books, whereas the more difficult ones—ergatives, verb complement, and unreal conditional—are not generally introduced until later in the pedagogical sequence. There may therefore be some relationship between pedagogical exposure (to English grammar) and item difficulty. Structures which are taught early are likely to be recycled and consolidated at later stages of learning with the result that learners achieve a stronger grasp of them. But there are also likely to be other factors involved in determining difficulty, for example processing constraints (Pienemann 1998) and the transparency of form-meaning links (DeKeyser 2005b). In the case of plural and possessive 's', the link between the morphemes and their respective pluralizing and ownership functions seems reasonably transparent and the relevant rule may for this reason be more readily verbalizable (N. Ellis 1996, 1999). Other forms are less frequent in the input and do not regularly appear as a focus of instruction, such as the need to use the active verb form with ergative verbs like 'improve'. Rules for such forms are also more complex and hence less amenable to explanation. To explain why 'His grades *were improved* last year' is an erroneous sentence; candidates would require knowledge of the class of ergative verbs and its specific exemplars, as well as an understanding of the distinction between the active and passive mode, including the concept of (hidden) agency. N. Ellis (1999) argues that such structures are more likely to be learnt implicitly on an item-by-item basis, initially as formulaic utterances. It is therefore feasible that the participants in this study may never have encountered or needed to articulate the relevant rule and this may explain why over 30 per cent of them failed even to attempt an explanation for this item. The rule for the formulation of the unreal conditional is similarly complex, involving an understanding of complex verb forms and some notion of syntactic interdependency between clauses. Perhaps for this reason there was a 41 per cent non-suppliance rate on this item and only 21 per cent of correct responses.

As for metalinguistic terms, it is clear from some of the garbled explanations supplied by the participants that many are confused about both their meaning and application. Take the following example produced as an explanation of the wrong verb form in the question:

Does Liao *has* a Chinese wife?

In this context, 'has' should be written in past 'had'. It is universally acknowledged that 'had' refers to possessive nouns, and referring to the sentence, which means Liao had a Chinese wife.

In the following example, the testee has confused metalinguistic terms in explaining the overuse of modals:

I *must have* to wash my hands.

You do not have to put 'must' there because you cannot put a noun before a noun.

These examples, and there are many others besides, suggest that many of the participants, for a range of reasons, have poor understanding of both the explicit rules of English and the terms in which such rules are traditionally couched. Although space precludes an extensive discussion of the nature of learner misunderstandings, it is clear from the language of the examples presented above that they are in many cases attempting to mimic the discourse of pedagogical grammars making reference to notions of generality (for example, 'it is universally acknowledged') and constraint (for example, 'you cannot put') or obligation (for example, 'should be written') which are characteristic of pedagogical rules, without having a clear conceptual understanding. Some participants, perhaps more aware of their limited understanding, confined themselves to correcting the targeted error with no attempt at generalization beyond the particular instance, for example:

The cake *that you baked it* tastes very nice.

You should omit 'it'.

Such a response, while it was not deemed acceptable on our test, is arguably more useful as feedback for a learner than the confused explanations exemplified above.

3 Is metalinguistic knowledge associated with the ability to recognize error?

Results reported in Table 15.5 above show a moderate (and statistically significant) correlation ($r = .43$) between scores on the MTK and those derived from the ungrammatical GJT sentences which measure different exemplars of the same set of structures. Both the rule and metalinguistic terminology sections contribute significantly to this relationship suggesting that detection and explanation go hand in hand at least to some extent, probably because explicit knowledge contributes to the resolution of both types of item (N. Ellis 2005). However, given the substantial difference in the difficulty of the two tests, as indicated by the difference in means (42 per cent on MTK and 89 per cent on the GJT), we cannot take for granted that if a L2 learner can recognize an error in a sentence s/he will be able to explain why the item is wrong or invoke the relevant TL rule. (See also Brumfit, Mitchell, and Hooper 1996; Alderson, Clapham, and Steel 1997; Elder *et al.* 1999 for a similar conclusion.)

At the item level there were also some notable differences in difficulty across the tests (and see Clapham 2001 and Hu 2002 who report a similar variation in performance on particular items according to task demands). Whereas errors in the use of a modal verb, adverb placement, and an indefinite article were the easiest to recognize, these were not, as we have seen above, the easiest items to explain. Conversely, there are some items, such as the comparative, which were harder on the GJT than the MKT. It seems then that an incorrect answer on an error detection item does not always imply absence of metalinguistic knowledge.

4 What are the implications of these findings for the teaching of FoF in L2 classrooms?

Findings of the study suggest that this particular group of teacher trainees, in spite of being handpicked to participate in the off-shore Bachelor of Education course on the basis of a strong prior academic record and a high level of English proficiency, have a disturbing lack of knowledge about the rules of English grammar as well as, in many cases, a limited command of the technical terms required to explain these rules to L2 learners, if or when the need arises. This conforms with the findings of other investigations of metalinguistic knowledge involving advanced FL learners (Alderson, Clapham, and Steel 1997; Elder *et al.* 1999; Renou 2000; Elder and Manwaring 2004). Although Wright (1991: 69), in relation to non-native teacher trainees from Malaysia, describes them as 'metalinguistically well equipped at the outset—i.e. they knew basic grammatical terminology', he notes that they nevertheless had difficulty in applying that metalanguage and lacked confidence. If non-native teacher trainees have such gaps in their knowledge, it is likely to be all the more the case for native speakers who have often not had any formal experience of language study in their class-rooms (Bolitho 1988; Andrews 1994, 2003). A poor command of metalin-guistic knowledge is likely to impact negatively on the quality of FFI, both in traditional grammar-based classrooms and in other meaning-focused teaching where FoF instruction is incidental rather than systematic. Although reactive FoF feedback which is accompanied by some kind of metalinguistic explanation has been found to account for a proportion of teacher feedback moves (Lyster and Ranta 1997; Havranek 2002; Loewen and Philp 2006), little attention has been paid in FoF studies to the quality of this feedback or, more precisely, to the accuracy and intelligibility of the metalinguistic information imparted to learners and its possible effect on learner uptake. This is clearly an area where further research is needed.

In the meantime it seems reasonable to propose that where there are gaps in teachers' metalinguistic knowledge, it may be better to adopt alternatives to FoF teaching strategies which draw less heavily on command of technical terminology and the ability to verbalize grammatical rules. As far as pre-emptive FoF is concerned, the generally poor explanations offered for certain structures (such as ergatives) by this group of participants suggest that such structures may be better avoided altogether as the target for explicit instruction and left for learners to acquire implicitly via positive evidence alone (N. Ellis 1999). As for reactive strategies, since the participants in this study appear to have had little difficulty with detecting grammatical errors (as indicated by their high level of performance on the GJT and their tendency to correct errors rather than explain the relevant rules), they might be advised to resort where possible to prompts and recasts, rather than metalinguistic explanations, as an alternative means of drawing learners' attention to errors in their production.

Ideally, however, a teacher should have the necessary knowledge and skill to draw on the full range of FoF options, including the provision of explicit grammatical information when learners signal the need for it. As N. Ellis (1999: 30) maintains, 'Learning the patterns, regularities or underlying concepts in a complex domain with advance organizers and instruction is always better than learning without cues' and explicit language knowledge has a clear role to play in planning and implementing FFI, whether of the FoF or FoFs variety.

Conclusion

This chapter has argued the case for FFI in L2 classrooms, drawing on evidence from a range of different sources, and has considered the kinds of knowledge and skill which teachers need to deliver such instruction effectively. We have argued that language teachers need not only high levels of language proficiency to be able to provide rich and well-formed input for learners but also sufficient explicit knowledge about language to be able to plan FFI and respond appropriately to learner needs through judicious use of a range of FoF options. Responding to claims that many language teachers are ill-equipped for this task, we have explored the levels of explicit language knowledge and language proficiency among a group of Malaysian TESOL teacher trainees especially selected to participate in an off-shore teacher education course.

To do so we have drawn on a range of custom-built instruments which allow us to explore performance across different task types, including grammaticality judgement and rule explanation tasks targeting parallel sets of structures. While the English language proficiency of these teacher trainees was found to be quite high, our investigation revealed significant lacunae in their knowledge about language and a highly uneven performance across the different task types. We believe that these lacunae need to be addressed in teacher education programmes to ensure that any FoF activity in which such teachers engage will be conducive to L2 learning.

The findings of this study signal the need for diagnostic testing of trainee teachers' metalinguistic knowledge (not just their ability to use the TL, which, as noted above, may be an unreliable predictor of such knowledge), using an instrument similar to the MKT described in this paper. The advantage of both the MKT and the GJT is their systematic sampling of a range of grammatical structures (although others could certainly be added) and, in the case of the MKT, the careful attention paid to establishing criteria which (a) identify critical 'bottom line' indicators of grammatical understanding rather than insisting on perfect rule formulations, and (b) attempt to assess grammatical understanding independently of the use of metalinguistic terminology. Separating the two is clearly important given the debates about the utility (or otherwise) of such terminology for teaching purposes (Berry 2005).

Diagnostic testing could provide a basis for individualized strategic advice about alternatives to explicit FoF instruction in the communicative classroom and about the range of options available when teachers wish to draw their learners' attention to an error in learner production which they feel ill-equipped to explain. Such testing could also identify priorities for formal teaching intervention or for self-instruction in relation to particular TL structures in order to strengthen L2 teachers' explicit knowledge base. Future research will, however, need to monitor the effectiveness of such intervention, given the apparent failure of formal instruction to produce high levels of understanding about the workings of English and other target languages. There are also dangers in an undue focus on the testing and development of metalinguistic knowledge independently of pedagogical skill. The cognitive sophistication involved in the former may sometimes be in conflict with the simplification skills required for the latter, as Elder (2001) and others have pointed out. Teacher trainees need to be mindful of the distinction between displaying what they know for testing purposes and using what they know to plan and deliver FoF instruction in ways that will be sensitive to learner needs. Teacher education programmes have an important role here as discussed in the other papers in this volume.

Notes

1 The research involving the development and trialling of the test described in this paper was funded by a Marsden Fund grant awarded by the Royal Society of Arts of New Zealand to Rod Ellis and Cathie Elder. Other researchers who contributed to the research are, along with Rosemary Erlam and Jenefer Philp, Shawn Loewen, Satomi Mizutani and Shuhei Hidaka. The authors wish to thank Susan McKenna for her hard work and consistent help with the analysis of data for this paper.

2 The second part of the test tested the ability to match grammatical features to their linguistic realizations in written texts. We have excluded any discussion of this section due to space constraints.

3 See R. Ellis (2005b) for a rationale for selection of the 15 structures and a detailed analysis of the tests as measures of explicit knowledge.

4 The structure 3rd person 's' was unintentionally omitted from the MKT and the item testing for dative alternation had to be eliminated from the data set because there were difficulties in deciding on appropriate criteria for scoring it.

5 This may explain the relatively low reliability index of this test for the population in question.

Appendix A

Instructions and sample items from the MKT (Part 1)

In this part, there are 15 sentences. They are all ungrammatical. The part of the sentence containing the error is underlined. For each sentence, if you know a rule which explains why the sentence is ungrammatical, write it in English in the space provided. If you do not know a rule, leave it blank and go on to the next sentence.

Here is an example.

Example 1

I have lost <u>mine</u> ring.
Before a noun, you have to use the possessive adjective, not the pronoun.

Appendix B

Sample scoring criteria for individual test items

Question 1

I *must have to* wash my hands.

Rule: (1 mark) 'must' and 'have to' both express same meaning/
obligation—you don't need both

OR 'must' and 'have to' are both modal verbs/or a semi
modal and a modal—you don't need both

Metalanguage: modal/semi modal/auxiliary
(1 mark)

Question 3

If Jane had asked me, I *would give* her money.

Rule: (1 mark) answer must contain some reference to the relationship
(syntactic interdependency) between the two parts of the
sentence

Metalanguage: past perfect/conditional/present perfect
(1 mark)

Glossary of acronyms

CALL	Computer assisted language learning	MKT	Metalinguistic Knowledge Test
CT	Class teacher	NALDIC	National Association for Language Development in the Curriculum
DELNA	Diagnostic English language needs assessment		
DfES	Department of Education and Skills	NCC	Neural correlates of consciousness
EAL	English as an additional language	NFER	National Foundation for Educational Research
EEG	Electro-encephalographic	NfM	Negotiation for meaning
EFL	English as a foreign language	NoF	Negotiation of form
ESL	English as a second language	OfSTED	Office for Standards in Education
ESRC	Economic and Social Research Council	QCA	Qualifications and Curriculum Authority
FFEs	Focus on form episodes	RFFE	Reactive focus on form episodes
FFI	Form-focused instruction		
FL	Foreign language	SCAA	School Curriculum and Assessment Authority
fMRI	Functional Magnetic Resonance Imaging		
FoF	Focus on form	SCOBA	Schema for the Orienting Basis of Action
FoFs	Focus on forms	SCT	Sociocultural theory
GJT	Grammaticality Judgement Test	SLA	Second language acquisition
IELTS	International English Language Testing System	SPSS	Statistical Package for the Social Sciences
IRF	Initiation—response—feedback	TL	Target language
		TLA	Teacher language awareness
L1	First language	TESOL	Teachers of English to Speakers of Other Languages
L2	Second language		
LST	Language support teacher		

Notes on the contributors

Rob Batstone is a Senior Lecturer in the Department of Applied Language Studies and Linguistics at the University of Auckland. His chief research interest is in developing socio-cognitive accounts of second language acquisition.

Catherine Elder is an Associate Professor of Applied Linguistics and Director of the Language Testing Research Centre at the University of Melbourne. Her research spans the areas of second/foreign language teaching, testing, and program evaluation.

Nick Ellis is a Research Scientist at the English Language Institute and Professor of Psychology at the University of Michigan. His research interests include cognitive, psycholinguistic, and emergentist aspects of SLA.

Rosemary Erlam is a Lecturer in the Department of Applied Language Studies and Linguistics at the University of Auckland. Her research interests include instructed second language learning, language testing, and form-focused instruction.

Sandra Fotos is a Professor of English in the School of Economics at Senshu University, Tokyo. Her research interests include form-focused grammar teaching and learning, CALL, and bilingualism.

Tricia Hedge has held appointments in Uppsala, Thames Valley, Temple, Warwick, and Nottingham universities and is currently a Visiting Guest Lecturer in the School of Education at King's College, University of London. Her research interests are in reading and writing pedagogy and teacher education. Her major publications are *Teaching and Learning in the Language Classroom* (Oxford University Press 2000) and *Writing* (2nd edition, Oxford University Press 2005).

Eli Hinkel teaches applied linguistics and ESL at Seattle University. She has published numerous books and articles on learning L2 culture, grammar, writing, and pragmatics.

James P. Lantolf is Greer Professor in Language Acquisition and Applied Linguistics at Penn State University and is Director of the Center for Language Acquisition and Co-director of the Center for Advanced Language Proficiency, Education, and Research. His most recent book, co-authored with Steve Thorne, is *Sociocultural Theory and the Genesis of Second Language Development* (Oxford University Press 2006).

Sharon Lapkin is a Professor in the Modern Language Centre and Second Language Education Program at the Ontario Institute for Studies in Education, University of Toronto. She is Co-President of the Canadian Association of Applied Linguistics. Her research interests centre on French L2 education in the Canadian context.

Shawn Loewen is an Assistant Professor in the Second Language Studies Program at Michigan State University. Previously he was at the University of Auckland. His research interests include SLA and L2 classroom interaction.

Hossein Nassaji is an Associate Professor of Applied Linguistics in the Department of Linguistics at the University of Victoria, Victoria, Canada. His research interests include form-focused instruction, interactional feedback, and classroom discourse.

Jenefer Philp is a Lecturer in the Department of Applied Language Studies and Linguistics at the University of Auckland. Her experimental and classroom-based research centres on the role of interaction in second language development by adults and children.

Teresa Pica is a Professor in the Graduate School of Education at the University of Pennsylvania. Her research addresses questions on classroom practice in light of second language acquisition theory and research.

Pauline Rea-Dickins is a Professor of Applied Linguistics in Education at the University of Bristol. Her research interests include language program evaluation, language testing, and assessment with specific reference to additional/second language learning contexts.

Jack Richards has published extensively in the fields of language teaching and applied linguistics. He is also the author of many widely used classroom texts. He has taught at universities in the USA, Hong Kong, and New Zealand, and is currently an Adjunct Professor at Macquarie University, Sydney, and at the Regional Language Centre, Singapore.

Peter Skehan teaches in the English Department at the Chinese University of Hong Kong. He researches psycholinguistic factors in second language performance, focusing on task-based instruction and language aptitude.

Merrill Swain is a Professor in the Second Language Education Program in the Ontario Institute for Studies in Education, University of Toronto. Her interests include sociocultural theory and second language learning and teaching. She is Past President of the American Association of Applied Linguistics, and is currently a Vice-President of the International Association of Applied Linguistics.

Brian Tomlinson is the Head of the Post-Graduate, Research, and Consultancy Team in the School of Languages at Leeds Metropolitan University, and is the founder and President of the Materials Development Association (MATSDA). His main research interests in language learning are materials development, inner speech and visualization, awareness approaches, and language through literature.

Bibliography

Alderson, J., C. Clapham, and **D. Steel.** 1997. 'Metalinguistic knowledge, language aptitude, and language proficiency'. *Language Teaching Research* 1/2: 93–121.

Aljaafreh, A. and **J. Lantolf.** 1994. 'Negative feedback as regulation and second language learning in the zone of proximal development'. *The Modern Language Journal* 78/4: 465–83.

Allen, P., M. Swain, B. Harley, and **J. Cummins.** 1990. 'Aspects of classroom treatment: toward a more comprehensive view of second language education' in B. Harley, P. Allen, J. Cummins, and M. Swain (eds.). *The Development of Second Language Proficiency.* Cambridge: Cambridge University Press.

Allwright, R. 1981. 'What do we want teaching materials for?' *ELT Journal* 36/1: 5–19.

Anderson, J. 1983. *The Architecture of Cognition.* Cambridge, Mass.: Harvard University Press.

Anderson, J. 1992. 'Automaticity and the ACT-super(*) theory'. *American Journal of Psychology* 105/2: 165–80.

Anderson, J. 1996. 'ACT: a simple theory of complex cognition'. *American Psychologist* 51/4: 355–65.

Andrews, S. 1994. 'The grammatical knowledge/awareness of native-speaker EFL teachers' in M. Bygate, A. Tonkyn, and E. Williams. *Grammar and the Language Teacher.* Hemel Hempstead: Prentice Hall.

Andrews, S. 1999. 'Why do L2 teachers need to "know about language"?: teacher metalinguistic awareness and input for learning'. *Language and Education* 13/3: 161–77.

Andrews, S. 2003. 'Teacher language awareness and the professional knowledge base of the L2 teacher'. *Language Awareness* 12/2: 81–95.

Applebee, A. 1986. 'Problems in process approaches: towards a reconceptualisation of process instruction' in A. Petrosky and D. Bartholomae (eds.). *The Teaching of Writing.* Chicago: Chicago University Press.

Baars, B. 1988. *A Cognitive Theory of Consciousness.* Cambridge: Cambridge University Press.

Baars, B. 1997. 'In the theatre of consciousness: global workspace theory, a rigorous scientific theory of consciousness'. *Journal of Consciousness Studies* 4/4: 292–309.

Baars, B., W. Banks, and **J. Newman** (eds.). 2003. *Essential Sources in the Scientific Study of Consciousness.* Cambridge, Mass.: MIT Press/Bradford Books.

Baars, B. and **S. Franklin.** 2003. 'How conscious experience and working memory interact'. *Trends in Cognitive Science* 7/4: 166–72.

Bachman, L. and **L. Palmer.** 1996. *Language Testing in Practice.* Oxford: Oxford University Press.

Barsalou, L. 1999. 'Perceptual symbol systems'. *Behavioral and Brain Sciences* 22/4: 577–609.

Bartlett, F. 1932. *Remembering: A Study in Experimental and Social Psychology.* Cambridge: Cambridge University Press.

Batstone, R. 1996. 'Noticing Key Concepts in ELT'. *ELT Journal* 50/3: 273.

Batstone, R. 2002. 'Making sense of new language: a discourse perspective'. *Language Awareness* 11/1: 14–29.

Batstone, R. 2005. 'Planning as discourse activity: a sociocognitive view' in R. Ellis (ed.). *Planning and Task Performance in a Second Language.* Amsterdam: John Benjamins.

Beauvois, M. 1998a. 'E-talk: computer-assisted classroom discussion—attitudes and motivation' in J. Swaffar, S. Romano, P. Markley, and K. Arens (eds.). *Language Learning Online: Theory and Practice in the ESL and L2 Computer Classroom.* Austin, Tex.: Labyrinth.

Beauvois, M. 1998b. 'Write to speak: the effects of electronic communication on the oral achievement of fourth semester French students' in J. Muyskens (ed.). *New Ways of Learning and Teaching: Focus on Technology and Foreign Language Education.* Boston: Heinle and Heinle.

Beglar, D. and **A. Hunt.** 2002. 'Implementing task-based language teaching' in J. Richards and W. A. Renandya (eds.). *Methodology in Language Teaching.* Cambridge: Cambridge University Press.

Berman, M. 1999. 'The teacher and the wounded healer'. *IATEFL Issues* 152: 2–5.

Berry, R. 2005. 'Making the most of metalanguage'. *Language Awareness* 14/1: 3–20.

Bialystok, E. 1979. 'Explicit and implicit judgments of L2 grammaticality'. *Language Learning* 29/1: 81–103.

Bialystok, E. 1982. 'On the relationship between knowing and using linguistic forms'. *Applied Linguistics* 3/3: 181–206.

Bialystok, E. 1990. 'The competence of processing: classifying theories of second language acquisition'. *TESOL Quarterly* 24/4: 635–48.

Bialystok, E. 1994. 'Representation and ways of knowing: three issues in second language acquisition' in N. Ellis (ed.). *Explicit and Implicit Learning of Languages.* London: Academic Press.

Birch, B. 2005. *Learning and Teaching English Grammar, K-12.* White Plains, NY: Prentice Hall.

Blake, W. 1790. 'The marriage of heaven and hell'. Retrieved 20 June 2005 from http://www.blakearchive.org:80/cgi-bin/nph-dweb/blake/Illuminated-Book/MHH/mhh.c/@Generic__BookTextView/4351;cv = java#X.

Blake, R. and **E. Zyzik.** 2003. 'Who's helping whom? Learner/heritage-speakers' networked discussions in Spanish'. *Applied Linguistics* 24/4: 519–44.

Block, D. 2003. *The Social Turn in Second Language Acquisition.* Edinburgh: Edinburgh University Press.

Bod, R., J. Hay, and **S. Jannedy** (eds.). 2003. *Probabilistic Linguistics.* Cambridge, Mass.: MIT Press.

Bolinger, D. 1991. *Essays on Spanish: Words and Grammar.* Newark, Del.: Juan de la Cuesta.

Bolitho, R. 1988. 'Language awareness on teacher training courses' in T. Duff (ed.). *Explorations in Teacher Training: Problems and Issues.* Harlow: Longman.

Bolitho, R. 2003. 'Materials for language awareness' in B. Tomlinson (ed.). *Developing Materials for Language Teaching.* London: Continuum.

Bolitho, R., R. Carter, R. Hughes, R. Ivanič, H. Masuhara, and **B. Tomlinson.** 2003. 'Ten questions about language awareness'. *ELT Journal* 57/3: 251–59.

Bolitho, R. and **B. Tomlinson.** 1980, 1995, 2005. *Discover English.* Oxford: Macmillan.

Boswood, T. and **R. Dwyer.** 1995. 'From marking to feedback: audiotaped responses to student writing'. *TESOL Journal* 95/96: 20–3.

Braidi, S. 2002. 'Reexamining the role of recasts in native-speaker/nonnative-speaker interactions'. *Language Learning* 52/1: 1–42.

Breen, M., C. Barratt-Pugh, B. Derewianka, H. House, C. Hudson, T. Lumley, and **M. Rohl.** 1997. *How Teachers Interpret and Use National and State Assessment Frameworks.* Volumes 1–3. Canberra: Department of Employment, Education, Training and Youth Affairs.

Brindley, G. 2001. 'Language assessment and professional development' in C. Elder, A. Brown, E. Grove, K. Hill, N. Iwashita, T. Lumley, T. McNamara, and K. O'Loughlin (eds.). *Experimenting with Uncertainty, Essays in Honour of Alan Davies.* Studies in Language Testing 11. Cambridge: Cambridge University Press.

Brinton, D., M. Snow, and **M. Wesche.** 1989. *Content-based Second Language Instruction.* New York: Newbury House.

Brock, M. and **M. Pennington.** 1999. 'A comparative study of text analysis and peer tutoring as input to writing on computers in an ESL context' in M. Pennington (ed.) *Writing in an Electronic Medium: Research with Language Learners.* Houston, Tex.: Athelstan.

Brown, G. and **G. Yule.** 1983. *Teaching the Spoken Language.* Cambridge: Cambridge University Press.

Brumfit, C., R. Mitchell, and **J. Hooper.** 1996. ' "Grammar", "language" and classroom practice' in M. Hughes: *Teaching and Learning in Changing Times.* Oxford: Blackwell Publishers.

Bruner, J. 1966. 'Some elements of discovery' in L. Shulman and E. Keislar (eds.). *Learning by Discovery: A Critical Appraisal.* Chicago: Rand McNally.

Bull, W. 1965. *Spanish for Teachers*. Malabar, Fla.: Robert E. Krieger Publishing Company.

Bull, W. 1971. *Time, Tense, and the Verb. A Study in Theoretical and Applied Linguistics with Particular Attention to Spanish*. Berkeley, Calif.: University of California Press.

Bybee, J. and **P. Hopper** (eds.). 2001. *Frequency and the Emergence of Linguistic Structure*. Amsterdam: Benjamins.

Bygate, M. 2001. 'Effects of task repetition on the structure and control of oral language' in M. Bygate, P. Skehan, and M. Swain (eds.). *Researching Pedagogic Tasks: Second Language Learning, Teaching and Testing*. New York: Longman.

Byrd, P. 2005. 'Instructed grammar' in E. Hinkel (ed.). *Handbook of Research in Second Language Teaching and Learning*. Mahwah, N.J.: Lawrence Erlbaum Associates.

Canagarajah, A. 1993. 'Critical ethnography of a Sri Lankan classroom: ambiguities in student opposition to reproduction through ESOL'. *TESOL Quarterly* 27/4: 600–26.

Cantoni-Harvey, G. 1987. *Content-Area Language Instruction: Approaches and Strategies*. Reading, Mass.: Addison-Wesley.

Carpay, J. 1974. 'Foreign language teaching and meaningful learning. A Soviet Russian point of view'. *I.T.L. Review of Applied Linguistics* 25–26: 161–87.

Carpay, J. and **B. Van Oers.** 1999. 'Didactic models and the problem of intertextuality and polyphony' in Y. Engeström, R. Miettinen, and R. Punamaki (eds.). *Perspectives on Activity Theory*. Cambridge: Cambridge University Press.

Cazden, C. 2001. *Classroom Discourse: The Language of Teaching and Learning*. Portsmouth, N.H.: Heinemann.

Celce-Murcia, M. 1991. 'Grammar pedagogy in second and foreign language teaching'. *TESOL Quarterly* 25/3: 459–80.

Celce-Murcia, M. (ed.). 2001. *Teaching English as a Second or Foreign Language*. Third edition. Boston: Heinle and Heinle.

Celce-Murcia, M. and **S. Hilles.** 1988. *Techniques and Resources in Teaching Grammar*. New York: Oxford University Press.

Chamot, A. and **J. O'Malley.** 1994. *The CALLA Handbook: Implementing the Cognitive Academic Language Learning Approach*. Reading, Mass.: Addison-Wesley.

Chandler, J. 2003. 'The efficacy of various kinds of error feedback for improvement in the accuracy and fluency of L2 student writing'. *Journal of Second Language Writing* 12/3: 267–96.

Chandler, J. 2004. 'A response to Truscott'. *Journal of Second Language Writing* 13/4: 345–48.

Chapelle, C. 2001. *Computer Application in Second Language Acquisition*. Cambridge: Cambridge University Press.

Chaudron, C. 1977. 'A descriptive model of discourse in the corrective treatment of learners' errors'. *Language Learning* 27/1: 29–46.

Chen, H. 1996. 'A study of the effect of corrective feedback on foreign language learning: American students learning Chinese classifiers'. PhD dissertation. University of Pennsylvania, Philadelphia.

Christiansen, M. and **N. Chater** (eds.). 2001. *Connectionist Psycholinguistics.* Westport, Colo.: Ablex.

Christie, F. 1998. 'Learning the literacies of primary and secondary schooling' in F. Christie and R. Misson (eds.). *Literacy and Schooling: New Directions.* London: Routledge.

Clapham, C. 2001. 'The assessment of metalinguistic knowledge' in C. Elder, A. Brown, E. Grove, *et al.* (eds.). *Experimenting with Uncertainty: Essays in Honour of Alan Davies.* Studies in Language Testing 11. Cambridge: Cambridge University Press.

Cline, T. and **T. Shamsi.** 2000. *Language Needs or Special Needs? The Assessment of Learning Difficulties in Literacy Among Children Learning English as an Additional Language: A Literature Review.* DFEE Research Report No. 184. Nottingham: Department for Education and Employment Publications.

Cohen, A. and **M. Cavalcanti.** 1990. 'Feedback on compositions: teacher and student verbal reports' in B. Kroll (ed.). *Second Language Writing: Research Insights for the Classroom.* Cambridge: Cambridge University Press.

Cole, M. 1991. 'On socially shared cognitions' in L. B. Resnick, J. M. Levine, and S. D. Teasley (eds.). *Perspectives on Socially Shared Cognitions.* Hillsdale, N.J.: Lawrence Erlbaum Associates.

Collier, V. 1987. 'Age and rate of acquisition of second language for academic purposes'. *TESOL Quarterly* 21/4: 617–41.

Collier, V. 1992. 'A synthesis of studies examining Collier: long-term language minority student data on academic achievement'. *Bilingual Research Journal* 16/1–2: 187–212.

Collier, V. 1995. *Promoting Academic Success for ESL Students.* Elizabeth, N.J.: New Jersey Teachers of English to Speakers of Other Languages—Bilingual Educators.

Collins. 1990. *COBUILD English Grammar.* London: Collins ELT.

Connors, K. and **B. Ouellette.** 1996. 'Describing the meanings of French pronominal-verbal constructions for students of French-English translation'. *Language Sciences* 18/1–2: 213–26.

Coxhead, A. 2000. 'A new academic word list'. *TESOL Quarterly* 34/2: 213–38.

Craik, F. and **R. Lockhart.** 1972. 'Levels of processing: a framework for memory research'. *Journal of Verbal Learning and Verbal Behaviour* 11: 671–84.

Crandall, J. 2000. 'Language teacher education'. *Annual Review of Applied Linguistics* 20: 34–55.

Crookes, G. 1989. 'Planning and interlanguage variation'. *Studies in Second Language Acquisition* 11/4: 367–83.

Crookes, G. 1997a. 'SLA and language pedagogy: a socio-educational perspective'. *Studies in Second Language Acquisition* 19/1: 93–116.

Crookes, G. 1997b. 'What influences what and how second and foreign language teachers teach?' *The Modern Language Journal* 81/1: 67–79.

Crookes, G. 1998. 'On the relationship between second and foreign language teachers and research'. *TESOL Journal* 7/3: 6–11.

Crookes, G. and **K. Rulon.** 1988. 'Topic and feedback in native speaker/non-native speaker conversation'. *TESOL Quarterly* 22/4: 675–81.

Cummins, J. 1992. 'Language proficiency, bilingualism and academic achievement' in P. Richard-Amato and M. Snow (eds.). *The Multicultural Classroom.* New York: Longman.

Cummins, J. 2000. *Language, Power and Pedagogy.* Clevedon: Multilingual Matters.

Day, E. and **S. Shapson.** 1991. 'Integrating formal and functional approaches in language teaching in French immersion: an experimental study'. *Language Learning* 41/1: 21–58.

de Graaff, R. 1997. *Differential Effects of Explicit Instruction on Second Language Acquisition.* The Hague: Holland Institute of Generative Linguistics.

Dehaene, S. and **J.-P. Changeux.** 2004. 'Neural mechanisms for access to consciousness' in M. Gazzaniga (ed.). *The Cognitive Neurosciences.* Third edition. Cambridge, Mass.: MIT Press.

Dehaene, S., A. Jobert, L. Naccache, P. Ciuciu, J.-B. Poline, D. Le Bihan, *et al.* 2004. 'Letter binding and invariant recognition of masked words'. *Psychological Science* 15: 307–13.

Dehaene, S., C. Sergent, and **J.-P. Changeaux.** 2003. 'A neuronal network model linking subjective reports and objective physiological data during conscious perception'. *Proceedings of the National Academy of Science USA* 100: 8520–5.

DeKeyser, R. 1995. 'Learning second language grammar rules: an experiment with a miniature linguistic system'. *Studies in Second Language Acquisition* 17/3: 379–410.

DeKeyser, R. 1997. 'Beyond explicit rule learning: automatizing second language morphosyntax'. *Studies in Second Language Acquisition* 19/2: 195–221.

DeKeyer, R. 1998. 'Beyond focus on form: cognitive perspectives on learning and practicing second language grammar' in C. Doughty and J. Williams (eds.). *Focus on Form in Second Language Acquisition.* Cambridge: Cambridge University Press.

DeKeyser, R. 2001. 'Automaticity and automatization' in P. Robinson (ed.). *Cognition and Second Language Acquisition.* Cambridge: Cambridge University Press.

DeKeyser, R. 2005a. 'Implicit and explicit learning' in E. Hinkel (ed.). *Handbook of Research in Second Language Teaching and Learning.* Mahwah, N.J.: Lawrence Erlbaum Associates.

DeKeyser, R. 2005b. 'What makes learning second language grammar difficult? A review of issues'. *Language Learning* 55/1: 1–25.

DeKeyser, R. and **A. Juffs.** 2005. 'Cognitive considerations in L2 learning' in E. Hinkel (ed.). *Handbook of Research in Second Language Teaching and Learning.* Mahwah, N.J.: Lawrence Erlbaum Associates.

DeKeyser, R., R. Salaberry, P. Robinson, and **M. Harrington.** 2002. 'What gets processed in processing instruction? A commentary on Bill VanPatten's "Processing instruction: an update" '. *Language Learning* 52/4: 805–24.

DeKeyser, R. and **K. Sokalski.** 1996. 'The differential role of comprehension and production practice'. *Language Learning* 46/4: 613–42.

DeKeyser, R. and **K. Sokalski.** 2001. 'The differential role of comprehension and production practice'. *Language Learning* 51/Supplement: 81–2.

Dennett, D. 2001. 'Are we explaining consciousness yet?' *Cognition* 79/1–2: 222–37.

Department for Education and Skills (DfES). 2003. *The Assessment of Pupils Learning English as an Additional Language.* London: DfES.

Di Pietro, R. 1987. *Strategic Interaction.* Cambridge: Cambridge University Press.

Donato, R. 1994. 'Collective scaffolding in second language learning' in J. Lantolf and G. Appel (eds.). *Vygotskian Approaches to Second Language Research.* Norwood, N.J.: Ablex.

Dörnyei, Z. 2001. *Motivational Strategies in the Language Classroom.* Cambridge: Cambridge University Press.

Doughty, C. 1994. 'Fine-tuning of feedback by competent speakers to language learners' in J. Alatis (ed.). *Georgetown University Round Table on Languages and Linguistics.* Washington, D.C.: Georgetown University Press.

Doughty, C. 2001. 'Cognitive underpinnings of focus on form' in P. Robinson (ed.). *Cognition and Second Language Instruction.* Cambridge: Cambridge University Press.

Doughty, C. 2004. 'Effects of instruction on learning a second language: a critique of instructed SLA research' in B. VanPatten, J. Williams, S. Rott, and M. Overstreet (eds.). *Form-meaning Connections in Second Language Acquisition.* Mahwah, N. J.: Lawrence Erlbaum Associates.

Doughty, C. and **T. Pica.** 1986. '"Information gap tasks": an aid to second language acquisition?' *TESOL Quarterly* 20/3: 305–25.

Doughty, C. and **E. Varela.** 1998. 'Communicative focus on form' in C. Doughty and J. Williams (eds.). *Focus on Form in Classroom Second Language Acquisition.* Cambridge: Cambridge University Press.

Doughty, C. and **J. Williams** (eds.). 1998a. *Focus on Form in Classroom Second Language Acquisition.* Cambridge: Cambridge University Press.

Doughty, C. and **J. Williams.** 1998b. 'Issues and terminology' in C. Doughty and J. Williams (eds.). *Focus on Form in Classroom Second Language Acquisition.* Cambridge: Cambridge University Press.

Doughty, C. and **J. Williams.** 1998c. 'Pedagogical choices in focus on form' in C. Doughty and J. Williams (eds.). *Focus on Form in Classroom Second Language Acquisition.* Cambridge: Cambridge University Press.

Douglas, D. 2001. 'Performance consistency in second language acquisition and language testing research: a conceptual gap'. *Second Language Research* 17/4: 442–56.

Duff, P. and **C. Polio.** 1990. 'How much foreign language is there in the foreign language classroom?' *The Modern Language Journal* 74/2: 154–66.

Dulay, H., M. Burt, and **S. Krashen.** 1982. *Language Two.* New York: Oxford University Press.

Egbert, J. 2005. *CALL Essentials: Principles and Practice in CALL Classrooms.* Waldorf, Md.: TESOL.

Egbert, J. and **E. Hanson-Smith.** 1999. *CALL Environments: Research, Practice and Critical Issues.* Alexandria, Va.: TESOL.

Eichenbaum, H. 2002. *The Cognitive Neuroscience of Memory.* New York: Oxford University Press.

Elder, C. 1994. 'Proficiency testing as benchmark for language teacher education'. *Babel* 29/2: 8–19.

Elder, C. 2001. 'Assessing the language proficiency of teachers: are there any border controls?' *Language Testing* 18/1: 149–70.

Elder, C. and **D. Manwaring.** 2004. 'The relationship between metalinguistic knowledge and learning outcomes among undergraduate students of Chinese'. *Language Awareness* 13/3: 145–62.

Elder, C., J. Warren, J. Hajek, D. Manwaring, and **A. Davies.** 1999. 'Metalinguistic knowledge: how important is it in studying a language at university?' *Australian Review of Applied Linguistics* 22/1: 81–95.

Ellis, A. and **A. Young.** 1988. *Human Cognitive Neuropsychology.* Hove, Sussex: Erlbaum Associates.

Ellis, N. 1993. 'Rules and instances in foreign language learning: interactions of explicit and implicit knowledge'. *The European Journal of Cognitive Psychology* 5/3: 289–318.

Ellis, N. (ed.). 1994. *Implicit and Explicit Learning of Languages.* San Diego: Academic Press.

Ellis, N. 1995. 'Consciousness in second language acquisition: A review of field studies and laboratory experiments'. *Language Awareness* 4/2: 123–46.

Ellis, N. 1996. 'Sequencing in SLA: phonological memory, chunking and points of order'. *Studies in Second Language Acquisition* 18/1: 91–126.

Ellis, N. 1999. 'Cognitive approaches to SLA'. *Annual Review of Applied Linguistics* 19: 22–42.

Ellis, N. 2002a. 'Frequency effects in language processing: a review with implications for theories of implicit and explicit language acquisition'. *Studies in Second Language Acquisition* 24/2: 143–88.

Ellis, N. 2002b. 'Reflections on frequency effects in language processing'. *Studies in Second Language Acquisition* 24/2: 297–339.

Ellis, N. 2005. 'At the interface: dynamic interactions and explicit and implicit language knowledge'. *Studies in Second Language Acquisition* 27/1: 305–52.

Ellis, N. 2006a. 'Language acquisition as rational contingency learning'. *Applied Linguistics* 27/1: 1–24.

Ellis, N. 2006b. 'Selective attention and transfer phenomena in SLA: salience, contingency, interference, overshadowing, blocking, and perceptual learning'. *Applied Linguistics* 27/2: 164–194.

Ellis, N. and **N. Laporte.** 1997. 'Contexts of acquisition: effects of formal instruction and naturalistic exposure on second language acquisition' in A. M. DeGroot and J. F. Kroll (eds.). *Tutorials in Bilingualism: Psycholinguistic Perspectives.* Mahwah, N.J.: Lawrence Erlbaum Associates.

Ellis, N. and **D. Larsen-Freeman** (eds.). (In press, December 2006.) 'Language Emergence: Implications for Applied Linguistics'. Special issue. *Applied Linguistics* 27(4).

Ellis, R. 1982. 'Informal and formal approaches to communicative language teaching'. *ELT Journal* 36/2: 73–81.

Ellis, R. 1984. 'Can syntax be taught? A study of the effects of formal instruction on the acquisition of wh questions by children'. *Applied Linguistics* 5/1: 138–55.

Ellis, R. 1985. 'Policy and provision for ESL in schools' in C. Brumfit, R. Ellis, and J. Levine (eds.). *English as a Second Language in the United Kingdom: Linguistic and Educational Contexts.* ELT Documents 121. Oxford: Pergamon Press for The British Council.

Ellis, R. 1986. 'Activities and procedures for teacher training'. *ELT Journal* 40/2: 91–9.

Ellis, R. 1987. 'Interlanguage variability in narrative discourse: style shifting in the use of the past tense'. *Studies in Second Language Acquisition* 9/1: 1–20.

Ellis, R. 1988. *Classroom Second Language Development.* London: Prentice Hall.

Ellis, R. 1989 'Are classroom and naturalistic second language acquisition the same? A study of the classroom acquisition of German word order rules'. *Studies in Second Language Acquisition* 11/3: 305–28.

Ellis, R. 1990. *Instructed Second Language Acquisition: Learning in the Classroom.* Oxford: Blackwell Publishing.

Ellis, R. 1994a. *The Study of Second Language Acquisition.* Oxford: Oxford University Press.

Ellis, R. 1994b. 'A theory of instructed second language acquisition' in N. Ellis (ed.). *Implicit and Explicit Learning of Languages.* San Diego, Calif.: Academic.

Ellis, R. 1995. 'Interpretation tasks for grammar teaching'. *TESOL Quarterly* 29/1: 87–105.

Ellis, R. 1997a. *SLA Research and Language Teaching*. Oxford: Oxford University Press.

Ellis, R. 1997b. 'SLA and language pedagogy: an educational perspective'. *Studies in Second Language Acquisition* 19/1: 69–92.

Ellis, R. 1998. 'Discourse control and the acquisition-rich classroom' in W. Reynandya and G. Jacobs. *Learners and Language Learning*. Singapore: SEAMEO RELC.

Ellis, R. 1999a. 'Input-based approaches to the teaching of grammar'. *Annual Review of Applied Linguistics* 19: 64–80.

Ellis, R. 1999b. *Learning a Second Language Through Interaction*. Studies in Bilingualism 17. Amsterdam: John Benjamins.

Ellis, R. 2000. *Learning a Second Language through Interaction*. Amsterdam: John Benjamins.

Ellis, R. 2001a. 'Introduction: investigating form-focused instruction'. *Language Learning* 51. Supplement 1: 1–46.

Ellis, R. (ed.). 2001b. *Form-focused Instruction and Second Language Learning. Best of Language Learning* 4. Oxford: Blackwell Publishing.

Ellis, R. 2001c. 'Non-reciprocal tasks, comprehension and second language acquisition' in M. Bygate, P. Skehan, and M. Swain (eds.). *Researching Pedagogical Tasks*. New York: Longman.

Ellis, R. 2002a. 'Does form-focused instruction affect the acquisition of implicit knowledge?' *Studies in Second Language Acquisition* 24/2: 223–6.

Ellis, R. 2002b. 'The place of grammar instruction in the second/foreign language curriculum' in E. Hinkel and S. Fotos (eds.). *New Perspectives on Grammar Teaching in Second Language Classrooms*. Mahwah, N.J.: Lawrence Erlbaum Associates.

Ellis, R. 2002c. 'Grammar teaching—practice or consciousness raising' in J. Richards and W. A. Renandya (eds.). *Methodology in Language Teaching*. Cambridge: Cambridge University Press.

Ellis, R. 2003. *Task-based Language Learning and Teaching*. Oxford: Oxford University Press.

Ellis, R. 2004a. 'The definition and measurement of L2 explicit knowledge'. *Language Learning* 54/2: 227–75.

Ellis, R. 2004b. 'Principles of instructed second language learning'. *System* 33/2: 209–24.

Ellis, R. 2005a. 'Instructed language learning and task-based teaching' in E. Hinkel (ed.). *Handbook of Research in Second Language Teaching and Learning*. Mahwah, N.J.: Lawrence Erlbaum Associates.

Ellis, R. 2005b. 'Measuring implicit and explicit knowledge of a second language'. *Studies in Second Language Acquisition* 27/1: 141–72.

Ellis, R. (ed.). 2005c. *Planning and Task Performance in a Second Language.* Amsterdam: John Benjamins.

Ellis, R. 2005d. 'Planning and task-based performance: theory and research' in R. Ellis (ed.). *Planning and Task Performance in a Second Language.* Amsterdam: John Benjamins.

Ellis, R. 2006. 'Current issues in the teaching of grammar: an SLA Perspective'. *TESOL Quarterly* 40/1: 83–107.

Ellis, R. and **G. Barkhuizen.** 2005. *Analysing Learner Language.* Oxford: Oxford University Press.

Ellis, R., H. Basturkmen, and **S. Loewen.** 2001a. 'Learner uptake in communicative ESL lessons'. *Language Learning* 51/2: 281–318.

Ellis, R., H. Basturkmen, and **S. Loewen.** 2001b. 'Preemptive focus on form in the ESL classroom'. *TESOL Quarterly* 35/3: 407–31.

Ellis, R., S. Loewen, and **R. Erlam.** 2006. 'Implicit and explicit corrective feedback and the acquisition of L2 grammar'. *Studies in Second Language Acquisition* 28/2: 339–68.

Ellis, R. and **B. Tomlinson.** 1973. *English Through Situations.* Lusaka: Longman Zambia.

Ellis, R. and **F. Yuan.** 2004. 'The effects of planning on fluency, complexity, and accuracy in second language narrative writing'. *Studies in Second Language Acquisition* 26/1: 59–84.

Ellis, R. and **F. Yuan.** 2005. 'The effects of careful within-task planning or oral and written task performance' in R. Ellis (ed.). *Planning and Task Performance in a Second Language.* Amsterdam: John Benjamins.

Elman, J., E. Bates, M. Johnson, A. Karmiloff-Smith, D. Parisi, and **K. Plunkett.** 1996. *Rethinking Innateness: a Connectionist Perspective on Development.* Cambridge, Mass.: MIT Press.

Erduran, S., S. Simon, and **J. Osborne.** 2004. 'Tapping into argumentation: developments in the use of Toulmin's argument pattern in studying science discourse'. *Science Education* 88/6: 915–33.

Faigley, L. and **S. Witte.** 1981. 'Analysing revision'. *College Composition and Communication* 32/4: 400–14.

Ferris, D. 1999. 'The case for grammar correction in L2 writing classes: a response to Truscott (1996)'. *Journal of Second Language Writing* 8/1: 1–11.

Ferris, D. 2001. 'Teaching writing for academic purposes' in J. Flowerdew and M. Peacock (eds.). *Research Perspectives in English for Academic Purposes.* Cambridge: Cambridge University Press.

Ferris, D. 2002. *Treatment of Error in Second Language Student Writing.* Ann Arbor, Mich.: University of Michigan Press.

Ferris, D. 2004. 'The "grammar correction" debate in L2 writing: where are we, and where do we go from here? (and what do we do in the meantime ... ?)'. *Journal of Second Language Writing* 13/1: 49–62.

Ferris, D. and **J. Hedgcock.** 2005. *Teaching ESL Composition: Purpose, Process and Practice.* Second edition. Mahwah, N.J.: Lawrence Erlbaum Associates.

Ferris, D. and **B. Roberts.** 2001. 'Error feedback in L2 writing classes. How explicit does it need to be?' *Journal of Second Language Writing* 10/3: 161–84.

Firth, A. and **J. Wagner.** 1997. 'On discourse, communication, and (some) fundamental concepts in SLA research'. *The Modern Language Journal* 81/3: 286–300.

Foster, P. and **P. Skehan.** 1996. 'The influence of planning on performance in task-based learning'. *Studies in Second Language Acquisition* 18/3: 299–324.

Fotos, S. 1993. 'Consciousness raising and noticing through focus on form: grammar task performance versus formal instruction'. *Applied Linguistics* 14/4: 126–41.

Fotos, S. 1994. 'Integrating grammar instruction and communicative language use through grammar consciousness raising tasks'. *TESOL Quarterly* 28/3: 323–51.

Fotos, S. 1998. 'Shifting the focus from forms to form in the EFL classroom'. *ELT Journal* 52/4: 301–7.

Fotos, S. 2002. 'Structure-based interactive tasks for the EFL grammar learner' in E. Hinkel and S. Fotos (eds.). *New Perspectives on Grammar Teaching in Second Language Classrooms.* Mahwah, N.J.: Lawrence Erlbaum Associates.

Fotos, S. 2004. 'Writing as talking: e-mail exchange for promoting proficiency and motivation in the foreign language classroom' in S. Fotos and C. Browne (eds.). *New Perspectives on CALL for Second Language Classrooms.* Mahwah, N.J.: Lawrence Erlbaum Associates.

Fotos, S. 2005. 'Traditional and grammar translation methods for second language teaching' in E. Hinkel (ed.). *Handbook of Research in Second Language Teaching and Learning.* Mahwah, N.J.: Lawrence Erlbaum Associates.

Fotos, S. and **R. Ellis.** 1991. 'Communicating about grammar—a task-based approach'. *TESOL Quarterly* 25/4: 605–28.

Fotos, S. and **C. Browne** (eds.). 2004. *New Perspectives on CALL for Second Language Classrooms.* Mahwah, N.J.: Lawrence Erlbaum Associates.

Frackowiak, R., K. Friston, C. Frith, R. Dolan, C. Price, S. Zeki *et al.* (eds.). 2004. *Human Brain Function.* Second edition. London: Academic Press.

Freud, S. 1966. *The Standard Edition of the Complete Psychological Works of Sigmund Freud, Volume 1: 1886–1899.* Edited by J. Strachey. London: The Hogarth Press.

Frodesen, J. 2001. 'Grammar in writing' in M. Celce-Murcia (ed.). *Teaching English as a Second or Foreign Language.* Third edition. Boston: Heinle and Heinle.

Gaer, S. 1999. 'Classroom practice: an introduction to e-mail and World Wide Web projects' in J. Egbert and E. Hanson-Smith (eds.). *CALL Environments: Research, Practice and Critical Issues.* Alexandria, Va.: TESOL.

Gal'perin, P. 1967. 'On the notion of internalization'. *Soviet Psychology* 5/3: 28–33.

Gardner, S. 2004. 'Four critical features of teacher-guided reporting in infant science and literacy contexts'. *Language and Education* 18/3: 361–78.

Gardner, S. and **P. Rea-Dickins.** 2002. *Focus on Language Sampling: A Key Issue in EAL Assessment.* England: NALDIC (National Association for Language Development in the Curriculum) Publications Group.

Gass, S. 2003. 'Input and interaction' in C. Doughty and M. Long (eds.). *Handbook of Second Language Acquisition.* Oxford: Blackwell Publishing.

Gould, S. 1982. *The Panda's Thumb: More Reflections on Natural History.* New York: W. W. Norton.

Gravelle, M. 1996. *Supporting Bilingual Learners in Schools.* Stoke-on-Trent: Trentham Books.

Gravelle, M. 2000. *Planning for Bilingual Learners: An Inclusive Curriculum.* Stoke-on-Trent: Trentham Books.

Graves, D. 1983. *Writing: Teachers and Children at Work.* London: Heinemann Educational Books.

Green, P. and **K. Hecht.** 1992. 'Implicit and explicit grammar: an empirical study'. *Applied Linguistics* 13/2: 168–84.

Greenfield, R. 2003. 'Collaborative e-mail exchange for teaching secondary ESL: a case study in Hong Kong'. *Language Learning and Technology* 7/1: 46–70. http://llt.msu.edu/vol7/num1/greenfield.

Gumperz, J. (ed.). 1982. *Language and Social Identity.* Cambridge: Cambridge University Press.

Gumperz, J. 1992. 'Contextualization and understanding' in A. Duranti and C. Goodwin (eds.). *Rethinking Context: Language as an Interactive Phenomenon.* Cambridge: Cambridge University Press.

Hammerly, H. 1991. *Fluency and Accuracy.* Clevedon, UK: Multilingual Matters.

Han, Z. 2002. 'Rethinking the role of corrective feedback in communicative language teaching'. *RELC Journal* 33/1: 1–34.

Haneda, M. 2004. 'The joint construction of meaning in writing conferences'. *Applied Linguistics* 25/2: 178–219.

Hargreaves, E. 1997. 'Mathematics assessment for children with English as an Additional Language'. *Assessment in Education* 4/3: 401–11.

Harley, B. 1989. 'Functional grammar in French immersion: a classroom experiment'. *Applied Linguistics* 10/4: 331–59.

Harley, B. 1993. 'Instructional strategies and SLA in early French immersion'. *Studies in Second Language in Acquisition* 15/2: 245–60.

Harley, B. and **M. Swain.** 1984. 'The interlanguage of immersion students and its implications for second language teaching' in A. Davies, C. Criper, and A. P. R. Howatt (eds.). *Interlanguage.* Edinburgh: Edinburgh University Press.

Havranek, G. 2002. 'When is corrective feedback most likely to succeed?' *International Journal of Educational Research* 37/3: 255–70.

Hawkins, E. 1984. *Awareness of Language: An Introduction.* Cambridge: Cambridge University Press.

Hebb, D. 1949. *The Organization of Behaviour.* New York: John Wiley and Sons.

Hedge, T. 2005. *Writing.* Oxford: Oxford University Press.

Hendrickson, J. 1978. 'Error correction in foreign language teaching: recent theory, research, and practice'. *The Modern Language Journal* 62: 387–98.

Herron, C. 1991. 'The garden path correction strategy in the second language classroom'. *The French Review* 64/6: 708–18.

Hinkel, E. 2002. *Second Language Writer's Text: Linguistic and Rhetorical Features.* Mahwah, N.J.: Lawrence Erlbaum Associates.

Hinkel, E. 2003. 'Simplicity without elegance; features of sentences in L1 and L2 academic texts'. *TESOL Quarterly* 37/2: 275–302.

Hinkel, E. 2004. *Teaching Academic ESL Writing: Practical Techniques in Vocabulary and Grammar.* Mahwah, N.J.: Lawrence Erlbaum Associates.

Hinkel, E. 2005a. 'Functions of personal examples and narratives in L1 and L2 academic prose' in D. Atkinson, W. Grabe, V. Ramanathan, and W. Eggington (eds.). *Studies in Applied Linguistics: English for Academic Purposes, Discourse Analysis, and Language Policy and Planning. Essays in Honor of Robert B. Kaplan on the Occasion of His 75th Birthday.* Clevedon, UK. Multilingual Matters.

Hinkel, E. 2005b. *Handbook of Research in Second Language Teaching and Learning.* Mahwah, N.J.: Lawrence Erlbaum Associates.

Holliday, L. 1999. 'Theory and research: input, interaction and CALL' in J. Egbert and E. Hanson-Smith (eds.). *CALL Environments: Research, Practice and Critical Issues.* Alexandria, Va.: TESOL.

Hu, G. 2002. 'Psychological constraints on the utility of metalinguistic knowledge in second language production'. *Studies in Second Language Acquisition* 24/3: 347–86.

Hulstijn, J. 1995. 'Not all grammar rules are equal: giving grammar instruction its proper place in foreign language teaching' in R. Schmidt (ed.). *Attention and Awareness in Foreign Language Learning.* Hawaii: University of Hawaii Press.

Hulstijn, J. 2005. 'Theoretical and empirical issues in the study of implicit and explicit second-language learning'. *Studies in Second Language Acquisition* 27/2: 129–40.

Hulstijn, J. and **R. DeKeyser** (eds.). 1997. 'Testing SLA theory in the research laboratory'. *Studies in Second Language Acquisition* 19/2. Special issue.

Hunt, K. 1970. 'Syntactic maturing in school children and adults' in *Monographs of the Society for Research in Child Development* 53. Chicago: University of Chicago Press.

Hyland, K. 1990. 'Providing productive feedback'. *ELT Journal* 44/4: 279–85.

Iwashita, N. 2001. 'The effect of learner proficiency on interactional moves and modified output in nonnative–nonnative interaction in Japanese as a foreign language'. *System* 29/2: 267–87.

Iwashita, N. 2003. 'Negative feedback and positive evidence in task-based interaction'. *Studies in Second Language Acquisition* 25/1: 1–36.

Izumi, S. 2002. 'Output, input enhancement, and the noticing hypothesis'. *Studies in Second Language Acquisition* 24/4: 541–77.

Jackendoff, R. 1987. *Consciousness and the Computational Mind.* Cambridge, Mass.: MIT Press.

Jacoby, S. and **E. Ochs.** 1995. 'Co-construction: an introduction'. *Research on Language and Social Interaction* 28/3: 171–83.

James, C. 1980. *Contrastive Analysis.* London: Longman.

James, C. 1998. *Errors in Language Learning and Use.* London: Longman.

James, W. 1890. *The Principles of Psychology.* Volume 1. New York: Holt.

Jenkins, J. 2001. *The Phonology of English as an International Language.* Oxford: Oxford University Press.

Jerison, H. 1976. 'Paleoneurology and the evolution of mind'. *Scientific American* 234: 90–101.

Jongekrijg, R. and **J. Russell.** 1999. 'Alternative techniques for providing feedback to students and trainees: a literature review with guidelines'. *Educational Technology* November/December: 54–8.

Kabanova, O. 1985. 'The teaching of foreign languages'. *Instructional Science* 14/1: 1–47.

Kagan, D. M. 1992. 'Implications of research on teacher belief'. *Educational Psychologist* 27/1: 65–90.

Kanda, M. and **D. Beglar.** 2004. 'Applying pedagogical principles to grammar instruction'. *RELC Journal* 35/1: 105–19.

Kandel, E., J. Schwartz, and **T. Jessell.** 2000. *Principles of Neural Science.* Fourth edition. New York: McGraw-Hill.

Karpov, Y. V. 2003. 'Vygotsky's doctrine of scientific concepts. Its role in contemporary education' in A. Kozulin, B. Gindis, V. S. Ageyev, and S. M. Miller (eds.). *Vygotsky's Educational Theory in Cultural Context.* Cambridge: Cambridge University Press.

Karpov, Y. V. and **H. Haywood.** 1998. 'Two ways to elaborate Vygotsky's concept of mediation: implications for instruction'. *American Psychologist* 53/1: 27–36.

Karpova, S. N. 1977. '*The Realization of Language in Children*'. Paris: Monton.

Kaufman, G. 1996. 'The many faces of mental imagery' in C. Cornoldi *et al.* (eds.). *Stretching the Imagination: Representation and Transformation in Mental Imagery.* Oxford: Oxford University Press.

Keck, C. M., G. Iberri-Shea, N. Tracy, and **S. Wa-Mbaleka.** 2006. 'Investigating the empirical link between interaction and acquisition: a quantitative meta-analysis' in L. Ortega and J. Norris (eds.). *Synthesizing Research on Language Learning and Teaching.* Amsterdam: John Benjamins.

Kelly, L. 1969. *Twenty-five Centuries of Language Teaching.* Rowley, Mass.: Newbury House.

Kemmis, S. and **R. McTaggert** (eds.). 1988. *The Action Research Planner*. Third edition. Geelong: Deakin University Press.

Kern, R. 1995. 'Restructuring classroom interaction with networked computers: effects on quantity and characteristics of language production'. *Modern Language Journal* 79/4: 457–76.

Kim, S. and **C. Elder.** 2005. 'Language choices and pedagogic functions in the foreign-language classroom: a cross-linguistic function analysis of teacher-talk'. *Language Teaching Research* 9/4: 1–26.

Koch, C. 2004. *The Quest for Consciousness: a Neurobiological Approach.* Englewood, Colo.: Roberts and Company.

Kolb, D. 1984. *Experiential Learning: Experience as the Source of Learning and Development*. Englewood Cliffs, N.J.: Prentice Hall.

Kowal, M. and **M. Swain.** 1994. 'Using collaborative language production tasks to promote students' language awareness'. *Language Awareness* 3/2: 73–93.

Kozulin, A. 1995. 'The learning process. Vygotsky's theory in the mirror of its interpretations'. *School Psychology International* 16/2: 117–29.

Kramsch, C. 1986. 'From language proficiency to interactional competence'. *The Modern Language Journal* 70/4: 367–72.

Krashen, S. 1981. *Second Language Acquisition and Second Language Learning.* Oxford: Pergamon Press.

Krashen, S. 1982. *Principles and Practice in Second Language Acquisition.* Oxford: Pergamon Press.

Krashen, S. 1985. *The Input Hypothesis: Issues and Implications.* Oxford: Pergamon Press.

Krashen, S. 1993. 'The effect of formal grammar teaching: still peripheral'. *TESOL Quarterly* 27/4: 722–25.

Kuckartz, U. 1998. *WinMAX Scientific Text Analysis for the Social Sciences: User's Guide.* London: Scolari Sage Publications (http://www.scolari.co.uk).

Lado, R. 1957. *Linguistics Across Cultures: Applied Linguistics for Language Teachers.* Ann Arbor, Mich.: University of Michigan Press.

Lalande, J. 1982. 'Reducing composition errors: an experiment'. *The Modern Language Journal* 66/spring: 140–9.

Lantolf, J. (ed.). 2000a. *Sociocultural Theory and Second Language Learning.* Oxford: Oxford University Press.

Lantolf, J. 2000b. 'Second language learning as a mediated process'. *Language Learning* 50/1: 79–96.

Lantolf, J. and **M. Poehner.** 2004. 'Dynamic assessment of L2 development: bringing the past into the future'. *Journal of Applied Linguistics* 1/1: 49–74.

Lantolf, J. and **S. Thorne.** 2006. *Sociocultural Theory and the Genesis of Second Language Development.* Oxford: Oxford University Press.

La Pierre, D. 1994. 'Language output in a cooperative learning setting: determining its effects on second language learning'. PhD Thesis. Toronto: University of Toronto (OISE).

Lapkin, S. 2003. 'Untangling second language writers' and teachers' knots with reformulation' in S. Peterson (ed.). *Untangling Some Knots in K-8 Writing Instruction*. Newark, Del.: International Reading Association.

Larsen-Freeman, D. and **N. Ellis** (eds.). 2006. 'Language emergence: implications for applied linguistics'. *Applied Linguistics* 27/4. Special issue.

Larsen-Freeman, D. and **M. Long.** 1991. *An Introduction to Second Language Acquisition Research*. London: New York: Longman.

Leeman, J. 2003. 'Recasts and second language development'. *Studies in Second Language Acquisition* 25/1: 37–63.

Leontiev, A. 1981. *Problems of the Development of the Mind*. Moscow: Progress.

Leow, R. 1997. 'Attention, awareness, and foreign language behavior'. *Language Learning* 47/3: 467–505.

Leow, R. 1998. 'Towards operationalizing the process of attention in SLA: evidence for Tomlin and Villa's (1994) fine-grained analysis of attention'. *Applied Psycholinguistics* 19/1: 133–59.

Leow, R. 2001a. 'Attention, awareness and foreign language behavior'. *Language Learning* 51/Supplement 1: 113–55.

Leow, R. 2001b. 'Do learners notice enhanced forms while interacting with the L2? An online and offline study of the role of written input enhancement in L2 reading'. *Hispania* 84/1: 496–509.

Leow, R. 2002. 'Models, attention, and awareness in SLA: A response to Simard and Wong's "Alertness, orientation, and detection: the conceptualization of attention functions in SLA" '. *Studies in Second Language Acquisition* 24/1: 113–19.

Leung, C. 1996. 'English as an additional language within the national curriculum: a study of assessment practices'. *Prospect* 7/3: 58–68.

Leung, C. and **P. Rea-Dickins.** 2007. 'Teacher assessment as policy instrument— contradictions and capacities'. *Language Assessment Quarterly*.

Levelt, W. 1989. *Speaking: from Intention to Articulation*. Cambridge, Mass.: MIT Press.

Levenston, E. 1978. 'Error analysis of free comparison: the theory and the practice'. *Indian Journal of Applied Linguistics* 4/1: 467–505.

Levy, M. 1997. *Computer-Assisted Language Learning: Content and Conceptualization*. Oxford: Clarendon Press.

Lightbown, P. 1998. 'The importance of timing on focus on form' in C. Doughty and J. Williams (eds.). *Focus on Form in Classroom Second Language Acquisition*. Cambridge: Cambridge University Press.

Lightbown, P. 2000. 'Classroom SLA research and second language teaching'. Anniversary article. *Applied Linguistics* 21/4: 431–62.

Lightbown, P. and **N. Spada.** 1990. 'Focus on form and corrective feedback in communicative language teaching'. *Studies in Second Language Acquisition* 12/4: 429–48.

Lightbown, P. and **N. Spada.** 1999. *How Languages are Learned.* Second edition. Oxford: Oxford University Press.

Lightbown, P. and **N. Spada.** 2006. *How Languages are Learned.* Third edition. Oxford: Oxford University Press.

Lightbown, P., N. Spada, and **L. White.** 1993. 'The role of instruction in second language acquisition'. *Studies in Second Language Acquisition* 15. Special issue.

Liu, D. and **P. Master** (eds.). 2003. *Grammar Teaching in Teacher Education.* Alexandria, Va.: TESOL.

Loewen, S. 2002. 'The occurrence and effectiveness of incidental focus on form in meaning-focused ESL lessons'. PhD Thesis. Applied Language Studies and Linguistics, Auckland, New Zealand: The University of Auckland.

Loewen, S. 2003. 'Variation in the frequency and characteristics of incidental focus on form'. *Language Teaching Research* 7/3: 315–45.

Loewen, S. 2004. 'Uptake in incidental focus on form in meaning-focused ESL lessons'. *Language Learning* 54/1: 153–87.

Loewen, S. 2005. 'Incidental focus on form and second language learning'. *Studies in Second Language Acquisition* 27/3: 361–86.

Loewen, S. and **J. Philp.** 2006. 'Recasts in the adult L2 classroom: characteristics, explicitness and effectiveness'. *The Modern Language Journal* 90/4.

Long, M. 1980. 'Input, interaction, and second language acquisition'. PhD Thesis. University of California, Los Angeles, 1980. *Dissertation Abstracts International* 41/5082.

Long, M. 1981. 'Input, interaction, and second language acquisition' in H. Winitz (ed.). *Native and foreign language acquisition (Vol.) 379: Annals of the New York Academy of Sciences.*

Long, M. 1983. 'Does second language instruction make a difference? A review of research'. *TESOL Quarterly* 17/3: 359–82.

Long, M. 1991. 'Focus on form: a design feature in language teaching methodology' in K. de Bot, R. Ginsberg, and C. Kramsch (eds.). *Foreign Language Research in Cross-cultural Perspective.* Amsterdam: John Benjamins.

Long, M. 1996 'The role of the linguistic environment in second language acquisition' in W. Ritchie and T. Bhatia (eds.). *Handbook of Second Language Acquisition.* San Diego, Calif.: Academic Press.

Long, M. 2000. 'Focus on form in task-based language teaching' in R. Lambert and E. Shohamy (eds.). *Language Policy And Pedagogy: Essays in Honor of A. Ronald Walton.* Philadelphia: John Benjamins.

Long, M. 2006a. 'Recasts in SLA: the story so far' in M. Long (ed.). *Problems in SLA.* Mahwah, N.J.: Lawrence Erlbaum Associates.

Long, M. 2006b. *Problems in SLA.* Mahwah, N.J.: Lawrence Erlbaum Associates.

Long, M., S. Inagaki, and **L. Ortega.** 1998. 'The role of implicit negative evidence in SLA: models and recasts in Japanese and Spanish'. *The Modern Language Journal* 82/3: 357–71.

Long, M. and **P. Robinson.** 1998. 'Focus on form: theory, research and practice' in C. Doughty and J. Williams (eds.). *Focus on Form in Classroom Language Acquisition.* Cambridge: Cambridge University Press.

Loschky, L. and **R. Bley-Vroman.** 1993a. 'Creating structure-based communication tasks for second language development' in G. Crookes and S. Gass (eds.). *Tasks and Language Learning.* Volume 1. Clevedon, UK: Multilingual Matters.

Loschky, L. and **R. Bley-Vroman.** 1993b. 'Grammar and task-based methodology' in G. Crooks and S. Gass (eds.). *Tasks in Integrating Theory and Practice.* Clevedon, UK: Multilingual Matters.

Luria, A. 1973. *The Working Brain: An Introduction to Neuropsychology.* New York: Basic Books.

Luria, A. 1982. *Language and Cognition.* New York: John Wiley and Sons.

Lyster, R. 1998a. 'Negotiation of form, recasts, and explicit correction in relation to error types and learner repair in immersion classrooms'. *Language Learning* 48/2: 183–218.

Lyster, R. 1998b. 'Recasts, repetition, and ambiguity in L2 classroom discourse'. *Studies in Second Language Acquisition* 20/1: 51–81.

Lyster, R. 2001. 'Negotiation of form, recasts, and explicit correction in relation to error types and learner repair in immersion classrooms'. *Language Learning* 51/ Supplement 1: 265–301.

Lyster, R. 2002. 'The importance of differentiating negotiation of form and meaning in classroom interaction' in P. Burmeister, T. Piske, and A. Rohde (eds.). *Papers in Honour of Henning Wode.* Trier: Wissenschaftlicher Verlag.

Lyster, R. 2004. 'Differential effects of prompts and recasts in form-focused instruction'. *Studies in Second Language Acquisition* 26/3: 399–432.

Lyster, R., P. Lightbown, and **N. Spada.** 1999. 'A response to Truscott's "What's wrong with oral grammar correction"'. *Canadian Modern Language Review* 55/4: 457–67.

Lyster, R. and **H. Mori.** 2006. 'Interactional feedback and instructional counter-balance'. *Studies in Second Language Acquisition* 28/2: 269–300.

Lyster, R. and **L. Ranta.** 1997. 'Corrective feedback and learner uptake: negotiation of form in communicative classrooms'. *Studies in Second Language Acquisition* 19/2: 37–66.

Mackey, A. 1999. 'Input, interaction, and second language development: an empirical study of question formation in ESL'. *Studies in Second Language Acquisition* 21/4: 557–87.

Mackey, A. and **R. Oliver.** 2002. 'Interactional feedback and children's L2 development'. *System* 30/4: 459–77.

Mackey, A. and **J. Philp.** 1998. 'Conversational interaction and second language development: recasts, responses and red herrings'. *The Modern Language Journal* 82/3: 338–56.

Macrory, G. and **V. Stone.** 2000. 'Pupil progress in the acquisition of the perfective tense in French: the relationship between knowledge and use'. *Language Teaching Research* 4/1: 55–82.

MacWhinney, B. 1997a. 'Implicit and explicit processes: commentary'. *Studies in Second Language Acquisition* 19/2: 277–82.

MacWhinney, B. 1997b. 'Second language acquisition and the competition model' in A. M. De Groot and J. Kroll (eds.). *Tutorials in Bilingualism: Psycholinguistic Perspectives*. Mahwah, N.J.: Lawrence Erlbaum Associates.

Mangan, B. 1993. 'Taking phenomenology seriously: The "fringe" and its implications for cognitive research'. *Consciousness and Cognition* 2/2: 89–108.

Mantello, M. 2002. 'Error correction in the L2 classroom' in M. Turnbull, J. Bell, and S. Lapkin (eds.). *From the Classroom: Grounded Activities for Language Learning*. Toronto: The Canadian Modern Language Review.

Markova, A. K. 1979. *The Teaching and Mastering of Languages*. White Plains, N.Y.: M. E. Sharpe.

Masuhara, M. 1998. 'Factors influencing the reading difficulties of advanced learners of English as a foreign language when reading authentic texts'. PhD Thesis. University of Luton.

Masuhara, M. 2003. 'Materials for developing reading skills' in B. Tomlinson (ed.). *Developing Materials for Language Teaching*. London: Continuum.

Masuhara, H. 2005. 'Helping learners to achieve multi-dimensional mental representation in L2 reading'. *Folio* 9/2: 6–9.

McAlpine, L. 1989. 'Teacher as reader: oral feedback on ESL student writing'. *TESL Canada Journal* 7/1: 62–7.

McDonough, K. 2005. 'Identifying the impact of negative feedback and learners' responses on ESL question development'. *Studies in Second Language Acquisition* 27/1: 79–103.

McDonough, K. and **A. Mackey.** 2000. 'Communicative tasks, conversational interaction and linguistic form: an empirical study of Thai'. *Foreign Language Annals* 33/1: 82–92.

McKay, P. 2000. 'On ESL standards for school'. *Language Testing* 17/2: 185–214.

McKay, P., C. Hudson, and **M. Sapuppo.** 1994. *ESL Development: Language and Literacy in Schools Project*. Canberra: National Languages and Literacy Institute of Australia.

McLaughlin, B. 1978. 'The monitor model: some methodological considerations'. *Language Learning* 28/2: 309–32.

McLaughlin, B. 1987. *Theories of Second Language Learning*. London: Arnold.

McLaughlin, B. 1990. 'Restructuring'. *Applied Linguistics* 11/2: 113–28.

McLeod, B. and **B. McLaughlin.** 1986. 'Restructuring or automaticity? Reading in a second language'. *Language Learning* 36/2: 109–23.

Mehnert, U. 1998. 'The effects of different lengths of time for planning on second language performance'. *Studies in Second Language Acquisition* 20/1: 83–108.

Meisel, J., H. Clahsen, and **M. Pienemann.** 1981. 'On determining developmental stages in second language acquisition'. *Studies in Second Language Acquisition* 3/2: 109–35.

Milanovic, M., N. Saville, and **S. Shushong.** 1996. 'A study of the decision-making behaviour of composition markers' in M. Milanovic and N. Saville (eds.). *Performance Testing, Cognition, and Assessment: Selected Papers from the 15th Language Testing Research Colloquium (LTRC) Cambridge and Arnhem.* New York: Cambridge University Press.

Mitchell, R. 1998. *Communicative Language Teaching in Practice.* London: CLT.

Mitchell, R. 2000. 'Applied linguistics and evidence-based classroom practice: the case of foreign language grammar pedagogy'. Anniversary article. *Applied Linguistics* 21/3: 281–303.

Mitchell, R. and **F. Myles.** 2004. *Second Language Learning Theories.* Second edition. London: Arnold.

Mohamad, N. 2001. 'Teaching grammar through consciousness-raising tasks: learning outcomes, learner preferences and task performance'. MA Thesis. University of Auckland.

Mohamad, N. 2004. 'Consciousness-raising tasks: a learner perspective'. *ELT Journal* 58/3: 228–33.

Muranoi, H. 2000. 'Focus on form through interaction enhancement: integrating formal instruction into a communicative task in EFL classroom'. *Language Learning* 50/4: 617–7.

Nabei, T. and **M. Swain.** 2001. 'Learner awareness of recasts in classroom interaction: a case study of an adult EFL student's second language learning'. *Language Awareness* 11/1: 43–63.

NALDIC (National Association for Language Development in the Curriculum). 1999. *The Distinctiveness of English as an Additional Language: A Handbook for All Teachers.* NALDIC Working Paper 5. NALDIC (ISBN 1 902 189 004).

Nassaji, H. 1999. 'Towards integrating form-focussed instruction and communicative interaction in the second language classroom: some pedagogical possibilities'. *Canadian Modern Language Review* 55/3: 385–402.

Nassaji, H. 2005, May. 'The relationship between second language acquisition research and language pedagogy: EFL and ESL teachers' perspective'. Paper presented at the Canadian Association of Applied Linguistics (CAAL), University of Western Ontario, London, Ontario, Canada.

Nassaji, H. In press. 'Interactional feedback in dyadic-student teacher interaction: a case for recast enhancement' in C. Gascoigne (ed.). *Assessing the Impact of Input Enhancement in Second Language Education.* Stillwater: New Forums Press.

Nassaji, H. and **A. Cumming.** 2000. 'What's in a ZPD: a case study of a young ESL student and teacher interacting through dialogue journals'. *Language Teaching Research* 4/2: 95–121.

Nassaji, H. and **S. Fotos.** 2004. 'Current developments in the teaching of grammar'. *Annual Review of Applied Linguistics* 24: 126–45.

Nassaji, H. and **M. Swain.** 2000. 'Vygotskian perspective on corrective feedback in L2: the effect of random versus negotiated help on the learning of English articles'. *Language Awareness* 9/1: 34–51.

Nassaji, H. and **J. Tian.** 2005, October. 'Co-production of language forms in task based group work'. Paper presented at Second Language Research Forum (SLRF). Teacher's College, Columbia University, New York City.

Nassaji, H. and **G. Wells.** 2000. 'What's the use of "triadic dialogue"?: an investigation of teacher–student interaction'. *Applied Linguistics* 21/3: 376–406.

Negueruela, E. 2003. 'A sociocultural approach to the teaching and learning of second languages: systemic-theoretical instruction and L2 development'. PhD Dissertation. The Pennsylvania State University, University Park, Pa.

Newman, D., P. Griffin, and **M. Cole.** 1989. *The Construction Zone: Working for Cognitive Change in School.* Cambridge: Cambridge University Press.

Nicholas, H., P. Lightbown, and **N. Spada.** 2001. 'Recasts as feedback to language learners'. *Language Learning* 51/4: 719–58.

Nobuyoshi, J. and **R. Ellis.** 1993. 'Focused communicative tasks and second language acquisition'. *ELT Journal* 47/3: 113–28.

Norris, J. and **L. Ortega.** 2000. 'Effectiveness of L2 instruction: a research synthesis and quantitative meta-analysis'. *Language Learning* 50/3: 417–28.

Norris, J. and **L. Ortega.** 2001. 'Does type of instruction make a difference? Substantive findings from a meta-analytic review'. *Language Learning* 51/ Supplement 1: 157–213.

Odlin, T. 1989. *Language Transfer.* New York: Cambridge University Press.

Odlin, T. 1994. 'Introduction' in T. Odlin (ed.). *Perspectives on Pedagogical Grammar.* Cambridge: Cambridge University Press.

O'Dowd, R. 2003. 'Understanding the "other side": intercultural learning in a Spanish-English e-mail exchange'. *Language Learning and Technology* 7/2: 118–44. http://llt.msu.edu/vol7num2/odowd.

OfSTED (Office for Standards in Education). 2001. *Inspecting Subjects 3–11: Guidance for Inspectors and Schools.* London: HMSO.

O'Grady, W. 2003. 'The radical middle: nativism without Universal Grammar' in C. Doughty and M. H. Long (eds.). *Handbook of Second Language Acquisition.* Oxford: Blackwell Publishing.

Ohta, A. 2001. *Second Language Acquisition Processes in the Classroom: Learning Japanese.* Mahwah, N.J.: Lawrence Erlbaum Associates.

Oliver, R. 1995. 'Negative feedback in child NS–NNS conversation'. *Studies in Second Language Acquisition* 17/4: 459–81.

Oliver, R. and **A. Mackey.** 2003. 'Interactional context and feedback in child ESL classrooms'. *The Modern Language Journal* 87/4: 519–33.

O'Malley, J. and **L. Valdez Pierce.** 1996. *Authentic Assessment for English Language Learners: Practical Approaches for Teachers.* Reading, Mass.: Addison-Wesley Publishing Company.

Ortega L. 1999. 'Planning and focus on form in L2 oral performance'. *Studies in Second Language Acquisition* 21/1: 109–48.

Ortega, L. 2005 'Methodology, epistemology, and ethics in instructed SLA research: an introduction'. *The Modern Language Journal* 89/3: 317–27.

Palley, M. (ed.). 2000. *Sustained Content Teaching in Academic ESL/EFL: A Practical Approach.* Boston: Houghton-Mifflin.

Patrie, J. 1989. 'The use of the tape-recorder in an ESL composition programme'. *TESL Canada Journal* 6/2: 87–90.

Pellettieri, J. 2000. 'Negotiation in cyberspace. The role of chatting in the development of grammatical competence' in M. Warschauer and R. Kern (eds.). *Network-based Language Teaching; Concepts and Practice.* New York: Cambridge University Press.

Pennington, M. 2003. 'Electronic media in second language writing: an overview of tools and research findings' in S. Fotos and C. Browne (eds.). *New Perspectives on CALL for Second Language Classrooms.* Mahwah, N.J.: Lawrence Erlbaum Associates.

Perkins, D. 1993. 'Person-plus: a distributed view of thinking and learning' in G. Salomon (ed.). *Distributed Cognitions: Psychological and Educational Considerations.* Cambridge: Cambridge University Press.

Perl, S. 1979. 'The composing processes of unskilled college writers'. *Research in the Teaching of English.* 13/4: 317–36.

Philp, J. 2003. 'Constraints on "noticing the gap": non-native speakers' noticing of recasts in NS–NNS interaction'. *Studies in Second Language Acquisition* 25/1: 99–126.

Pica, T. 1983. 'Adult acquisition of English as a second language under different conditions of exposure'. *Language Learning* 33/4: 465–97.

Pica, T. 1985. 'The selective impact of classroom instruction on second language acquisition'. *Applied Linguistics* 6/3: 215–22.

Pica, T. 1988. 'Interlanguage adjustments as an outcome of NS–NNS negotiated interaction'. *Language Learning* 38/1: 45–73.

Pica, T. 1991. 'The linguistic context of second language acquisition'. *ITL Review of Applied Linguistics* 105–106: 69–116.

Pica, T. 1994a. 'Questions from the language classroom: research perspectives'. *TESOL Quarterly* 28/1: 49–79.

Pica, T. 1994b. 'Research on negotiation – What does it reveal about 2nd language learning – conditions, process, and outcomes?'. *Language Learning* 44/3: 493–527.

Pica, T. 1996. 'Do second language learners need negotiation?' *International Review of Applied Linguistics* 34/1: 1–21.

Pica, T. 1997. 'Second language research and language pedagogy: a relationship in process'. *Language Teaching Research* 1/1: 48–72.

Pica, T. 2002. 'Subject matter content: how does it assist the interactional and linguistic needs of classroom language learners?' *The Modern Language Journal* 86/1: 1–19.

Pica, T. 2005. 'Classroom learning, teaching, and research: a task-based perspective'. *The Modern Language Journal* 89/3: 339–52.

Pica, T., L. Holliday, N. Lewis, and **L. Morgenthaler.** 1989. 'Comprehensible output as an outcome of linguistic demands on the learner'. *Studies in Second Language Acquisition* 11/1: 63–90.

Pica, T., R. Kanagy, and **J. Falodun.** 1993. 'Choosing and using communication tasks for second language instruction' in G. Crookes and S. Gass (eds.). *Tasks and Language Learning.* Volume 1. Clevedon: Multilingual Matters.

Pica, T., H. Kang, and **S. Sauro.** 2006. 'Information gap tasks: their multiple roles and contributions to interaction research methodology'. *Studies in Second Language Acquisition* 28/2: 301–38.

Pica, T., F. Lincoln-Porter, D. Paninos, and **J. Linnell.** 1996. 'Language learner interaction: how does it address the input, output, and feedback needs of second language learners?' *TESOL Quarterly* 30/1: 59–84.

Pica, T., S. Sauro, and **J. Lee.** In preperation, 'Sustaining the learner's attention over time through task-based interaction'. University of Pennsylvania.

Pienemann, M. 1984. 'Psychological constraints on the teachability of languages'. *Studies in Second Language Acquisition* 6/2: 186–214.

Pienemann, M. 1985. 'Learnability and syllabus construction' in K. Hyltenstam and M. Pienemann (eds.). *Modeling and Assessing Second Language Acquisition.* Clevedon: Multilingual Matters.

Pienemann, M. 1989. 'Is language teachable? Psycholinguistic experiments and hypotheses'. *Applied Linguistics* 10/1: 52–79.

Pienemann, M. 1998. *Language Processing and Second Language Development: Processability Theory.* Amsterdam: John Benjamins.

Pienemann, M., M. Johnston, and **G. Brindley.** 1988. 'Constructing an acquisition based procedure for second language assessment'. *Studies in Second Language Acquisition* 10/2: 217–44.

Poehner, M. and **J. Lantolf.** 2005. 'Dynamic assessment in the language classroom'. *Language Teaching Research* 9/3: 233–65.

Polio, C. and **P. Duff.** 1994. 'Teachers' language use in university foreign language classrooms: a qualitative analysis of English and target language alternation'. *The Modern Language Journal* 78/3: 313–26.

Posner, M. and **S. Peterson.** 1990. 'The attention system of the human brain'. *Annual Review of Neuroscience* 13: 25–42.

Pulvermüller, F. 1999. 'Words in the brain's language'. *Behavioral and Brain Sciences* 22/2: 253–336.

Pulvermüller, F. 2003. *The Neuroscience of Language. On Brain Circuits of Words and Serial Order.* Cambridge: Cambridge University Press.

QCA (Qualifications and Curriculum Authority). 2000. *A Language in Common: Assessing English as an Additional Language.* London: Qualifications and Curriculum Authority.

Qi, D. and **S. Lapkin.** 2001. 'Exploring the role of noticing in a three-stage second language writing task'. *Journal of Second Language Writing* 10/4: 277–303.

Radwan, A. 2005. 'The effectiveness of explicit attention to form in language learning'. *System* 33/1: 69–87.

Rea-Dickins, P. 2001. 'Mirror, mirror on the wall: identifying processes of classroom assessment'. *Language Testing* 18/4: 429–62.

Rea-Dickins, P. 2002. 'Exploring the educational potential of assessment with reference to learners with English as an additional language' in C. Leung (ed.). *Language and Additional/Second Language Issues for School Education: a Reader for Teachers.* York: York Publishing Services.

Rea-Dickins, P. 2006. 'Current and eddies in the discourse of assessment: a learning focused interpretation'. *International Journal of Applied Linguistics* 16/2: 163–88.

Rea-Dickins, P. and **S. Gardner.** 2000. 'Snares or silver bullets: disentangling the construct of formative assessment'. *Language Testing* 17/2: 215–43.

Reber, A. 1976. 'Implicit learning of synthetic languages: the role of instructional set'. *Journal of Experimental Psychology: Human Learning and Memory* 2: 88–94.

Reber, A. 1989. 'Implicit learning and tacit knowledge'. *Journal of Experimental Psychology-General* 118/3: 219–35.

Reber, A. 1993. *Implicit Learning and Tacit Knowledge: an Essay on the Cognitive Unconscious.* Oxford: Clarendon Press.

Reber, A., S. Kassin, S. Lewis, and **G. Cantor.** 1980. 'On the relationship between implicit and explicit modes in the learning of a complex rule structure'. *Journal of Experimental Psychology: Human Learning and Memory* 6/5: 492–502.

Renou, J. 2000. 'Learner accuracy and learner performance: the quest for a link'. *Foreign Language Annals* 33/2: 168–80.

Richards, J. 1999. *Springboard.* New York: Oxford University Press.

Richards, J. 2001. *Curriculum Development in Language Teaching.* New York: Cambridge University Press.

Richards, J. and **D. Bycina.** 1984. *Person to Person.* New York: Oxford University Press.

Richards, J. and **S. Eckstut-Didier.** 2003. *Strategic Reading.* New York: Cambridge University Press.

Richards, J. and **C. Sandy.** 1998. *Passages, 1 and 2.* New York: Cambridge University Press.

Robbins, D. 2003. *Vygotsky's and A. A. Leontiev's Semiotics and Psycholinguistics: Applications for Education, Second Language Acquisition, and Theories of Language.* Westport, Conn.: Praeger Publishers.

Robinson, P. 1995. 'Attention, memory, and the noticing hypothesis'. *Language Learning* 45/2: 283–331.

Robinson, P. 1996. 'Learning simple and complex second language rules under implicit, incidental, rule-search, and instructed conditions'. *Studies in Second Language Acquisition* 18/4: 27–67.

Robinson, P. (ed.). 2001. *Cognition and Second Language Instruction.* Cambridge: Cambridge University Press.

Robinson, P. 2003. 'Attention and memory during SLA' in C. Doughty and M. Long (eds.). *Handbook of Second Language Acquisition.* Oxford: Blackwell Publishing.

Robinson, P. 2005. 'Aptitude and second language acquisition'. *Annual Review of Applied Linguistics* 25: 46–73.

Rumelhart, D. and **J. McClelland** (eds.). 1986. *Parallel Distributed Processing: Explorations in the Microstructure of Cognition.* Volume 2: Psychological and biological models. Cambridge, Mass.: MIT Press.

Russell, J. and **N. Spada.** 2006. 'The effectiveness of corrective feedback for second language acquisition: a meta-analysis of the research' in J. Norris and L. Ortega (eds.). *Synthesizing Research on Language Learning and Teaching.* Amsterdam: John Benjamins.

Sachs, J. 1967. 'Recognition memory for syntactic and semantic aspects of connected discourse'. *Perception and Psychophysics* 2/9: 437–42.

Sacks, H., E. Schegloff, and **G. Jefferson.** 1974. 'A simplest systematics for the organization of turn-taking for conversation'. *Language* 50/4: 696–735.

Salomon, G. (ed.). 1993. *Distributed Cognitions: Psychological and Educational Considerations.* Cambridge: Cambridge University Press.

Samuda, V. 2001. 'Guiding relationships between form and meaning during task performance: the role of the teacher' in M. Bygate, P. Skehan, and M. Swain (eds.). *Researching Pedagogic Tasks: Second Language Learning, Teaching and Testing.* New York: Longman.

SCAA (School Curriculum and Assessment Authority). 1996. *Teaching English as an Additional Language: A Framework of Policy.* London: School Curriculum and Assessment Authority: 2.

Scardamalia, M. and **C. Bereiter.** 1987 'Knowledge telling and knowledge transforming in written composition' in S. Rosenberg (ed.). *Advances in Applied Psycholinguistics.* Volume 2: *Reading, Writing and Language Learning.* Cambridge: Cambridge University Press.

Schachter, J. 1974. 'An error in error analysis'. *Language Learning* 24/2: 205–14.

Schacter, D. 1987. 'Implicit memory: history and current status'. *Journal of Experimental Psychology: Learning, Memory, and Cognition* 13/3: 501–18.

Schmidt, R. 1990. 'The role of consciousness in second language learning'. *Applied Linguistics* 11/2: 129–59.

Schmidt, R. 1992. 'Psychological mechanisms underlying second language fluency'. *Studies in Second Language Acquisition* 14/4: 357–85.

Schmidt, R. 1993. 'Awareness and second language acquisition'. *Annual Review of Applied Linguistics* 13: 206–26.

Schmidt, R. 1995. 'Consciousness and foreign language learning: a tutorial on the role of attention and awareness in language learning' in R. Schmidt (ed.). *Attention and Awareness in Foreign Language Learning*. Honolulu: University of Hawaii Press.

Schmidt, R. 2001. 'Attention' in P. Robinson (ed.). *Cognition and Second Language Instruction*. New York: Cambridge University Press.

Schmidt, R. and **S. Frota.** 1986. 'Developing basic conversational ability in a second language: a case study of an adult learner of Portuguese' in R. Day (ed.). *Talking to Learn: Conversation in Second Language Acquisition*. Rowley, Mass.: Newbury House.

Schwartz, B. 1993. 'On explicit and negative data effecting and affecting competence and linguistic behavior'. *Studies in Second Language Acquisition* 15/2: 147–63.

Scott, C. 2003. 'Interaction in the Literacy Hour: a case study of learners with English as an additional language' in S. Sarangi and T. van Leeuwen (eds.). *Applied Linguistics and Communities of Practice*. London: Continuum.

Scott, C. 2005. 'Washback in the UK primary context with EAL learners: exploratory case studies'. PhD Dissertation. University of Bristol.

Scott, C. and **S. Erduran.** 2004. 'Learning from international frameworks for assessment: EAL descriptors in Australia and the USA'. *Language Testing* 21/3: 409–31.

Scott Kelso, J. 2002. 'The complementary nature of coordination dynamics: self-organization and agency'. *Nonlinear Phenomena in Complex Systems* 5/4: 364–71.

Segalowitz, N. and **S. Segalowitz.** 1993. 'Skilled performance, practice, and the differentiation of speed-up from automatization effects: evidence from second language word recognition'. *Applied Psycholinguistics* 14/3: 369–85.

Shank, R. and **R. Abelson.** 1977. *Scripts, Plans, Goals and Understanding: An inquiry into Human Knowledge Structures*. Hillside, N.J.: Lawrence Erlbaum Associates.

Sharwood Smith, M. 1981. 'Consciousness-raising and second language acquisition theory'. *Applied Linguistics* 2/2: 159–68.

Sharwood Smith, M. 1993. 'Input enhancement in instructed SLA: theoretical bases'. *Studies in Second Language Acquisition* 15/2: 165–79.

Shaw, P. and **E. Liu.** 1998. 'What develops in the development of second language writing'. *Applied Linguistics* 19/2: 225–54.

Sheen, R. 1992. 'Problem solving brought to task'. *RELC Journal* 23/2: 44–59.

Sheen, R. 2002. ' "Focus on form" and "focus on forms" '. *ELT Journal* 56/3: 303–5.

Sheen, Y. 2004. 'Corrective feedback and learner uptake in communicative classrooms across instructional settings'. *Language Teaching Research* 8/3: 263–300.

Sherrington, C. 1941. *Man on his Nature. The Gifford Lectures*. First edition. Cambridge: Cambridge University Press.

Shetzer, H. and **M. Warschauer.** 2001. 'An electronic literacy approach to network-based language teaching' in M. Warschauer and R. Kern (eds.). *Network-based Language Teaching: Concepts and Practice*. Cambridge: Cambridge University Press.

Sinclair, J. and **M. Coulthard.** 1975. *Towards an Analysis of Discourse*. Oxford: Oxford University Press.

Skehan, P. 1996a. 'A framework for the implementation of task-based instruction'. *Applied Linguistics* 17/1: 38–62.

Skehan, P. 1996b. 'Second language acquisition research and task-based instruction' in J. Willis and D. Willis (eds.). *Challenge and Change in Language Teaching*. Oxford: Heinemann.

Skehan, P. 1998. *A Cognitive Approach to Language Learning*. Oxford: Oxford University Press.

Skehan, P. 2001. 'Tasks and language performance' in M. Bygate, P. Skehan, and M. Swain (eds.). *Researching Pedagogic Tasks: Second Language Learning, Teaching and Testing*. New York: Longman.

Skehan, P. 2002. 'Theorising and updating aptitude' in P. Robinson (ed.). *Individual Differences and Instructed Language Learning*. Amsterdam: John Benjamins.

Skehan, P. and **P. Foster.** 1997. 'The influence of planning and post-task activities on accuracy and complexity in task based learning'. *Language Teaching Research* 1/3: 185–211.

Skehan, P. and **P. Foster.** 1999. 'The influence of task structure and processing conditions on narrative retellings'. *Language Learning* 49/1: 93–120.

Skehan, P. and **P. Foster.** 2001. 'Cognition and tasks' in P. Robinson (ed.). *Cognition and Second Language Instruction*. New York: Cambridge University Press.

Skehan, P. and **P. Foster.** 2005. 'Strategic and on-line planning: the influence of surprise information and task time second language performance' in R. Ellis (ed.). *Planning and Task Performance in a Second Language*. Amsterdam: John Benjamins.

Skehan, P. and **P. Foster.** Manuscript. 'The effects of post-task activities on the accuracy of language during task performance'. English Department, Chinese University of Hong Kong.

Skinner, B. and **R. Austin.** 1999. 'Computer conferencing—does it motivate EFL students?' *ELT Journal* 53/4: 270–80.

Sommers, N. 1980. 'Revision strategies of student writers and experienced adult writers'. *College Composition and Communication* 31/4: 378–8.

Sorace, A. 1985 'Metalinguistic knowledge and language use in acquisition-poor environments'. *Applied Linguistics* 6/3: 239–54.

Sotillo, S. 2000. 'Discourse functions and syntactic complexity in synchronous and asynchronous communication'. *Language Learning and Technology* 4/1: 82–119.

Spada, N. 1997. 'Form-focussed instruction and second language acquisition: a review of classroom and laboratory research'. *Language Teaching* 30/2: 73–87.

Spada, N. and **P. Lightbown.** 1999. 'Instruction, first language influence, and developmental readiness in second language acquisition'. *The Modern Language Journal* 83/1: 1–22.

Squire, L. and **E. Kandel.** 1999. *Memory: From Mind to Molecules.* New York: Scientific American Library.

Stadler, M. and **P. Frensch.** (eds.). 1998. *Implicit Learning Handbook.* Thousand Oaks, Calif.: Sage Publications.

Stenhouse, L. 1981. 'What counts as research?' *British Journal of Educational Studies* 29/2: 103–14.

Stenhouse, L. 1983. 'Research as a basis for teaching' in L. Stenhouse (ed.). *Authority, Education, and Emancipation.* London: Heinemann Educational.

Stockwell, G. and **M. Harrington.** 2003. 'The incidental development of L2 proficiency in NS–NNS interactions'. *CALICO Journal* 20/2: 337–59.

Stoller, F. 2004. 'Content-based instruction: perspectives on curriculum planning'. *Annual Review of Applied Linguistics* 24: 261–83.

Swan, M. 2005. 'Legislation by hypothesis: the case of task-based instruction'. *Applied Linguistics* 26/3: 376–401.

Swain, M. 1985. 'Communicative competence: some rules of comprehensible input and comprehensible output in its development' in S. Gass and C. Madden (eds.). *Input in Second Language Acquisition.* Rowley, Mass.: Newbury House.

Swain, M. 1991. 'Manipulating and complementing content teaching to maximize second language learning' in E. Kellerman, R. Phillipson, L. Selinker, M. Sharwood Smith, and M. Swain (eds.). *Foreign/Second Language Pedagogical Research.* Clevedon: Multilingual Matters.

Swain, M. 1995. 'Three functions of output in second language learning' in G. Cook and B. Seidlhofer (eds.). *Principle and Practice in Applied Linguistics.* Oxford: Oxford University Press.

Swain, M. 1998. 'Focus on form through conscious reflection' in C. Doughty and J. Williams (eds.). *Focus on Form in Classroom Second Language Acquisition.* Cambridge: Cambridge University Press.

Swain, M. 2000. 'The output hypothesis and beyond: mediating acquisition through collaborative dialogue' in J. P. Lantolf (ed.). *Sociocultural Theory and Second Language Learning.* Oxford: Oxford University Press.

Swain, M. 2001a. 'Examining dialogue: another approach to content specification and to validating inferences drawn from test scores'. *Language Testing* 18/3: 275–302.

Swain, M. 2001b. 'Integrating language and content teaching through collaborative tasks'. *Canadian Modern Language Review* 58/1: 44–63.

Swain, M. 2005. 'The output hypothesis: theory and research' in E. Hinkel (ed.). *Handbook on Research in Second Language Teaching and Learning*. Mahwah, N.J.: Lawrence Erlbaum Associates.

Swain, M. 2006. 'Languaging, agency and collaboration in advanced language proficiency' in H. Byrnes (ed.). *Advanced Language Learning: The Contributions of Halliday and Vygotsky*. London: Continuum.

Swain, M. and **S. Lapkin.** 1995. 'Problems in output and the cognitive processes they generate: a step towards second language learning'. *Applied Linguistics* 16/3: 371–91.

Swain, M. and **S. Lapkin.** 1998. 'Interaction and second language learning: two adolescent French immersion students working together'. *The Modern Language Journal* 82/3: 320–37.

Swain, M. and **S. Lapkin.** 2001. 'Focus on form through collaborative dialogue: exploring task effects' in M. Bygate, P. Shehan, and M. Swain (eds.). *Researching Pedagogic Tasks; Second Language Learning, Teaching and Testing*. New York: Longman.

Swain, M. and **S. Lapkin.** 2002. 'Talking it through: two French immersion learners' response to reformulation'. *International Journal of Educational Research* 37/3: 285–304.

Swain, M., L. Brooks, and **A. Tocalli-Beller.** 2002. 'Peer–peer dialogue as a means of second language learning'. *Annual Review of Applied Linguistics* 22: 171–85.

Tannen, D. (ed.). 1993. *Framing in Discourse*. New York: Oxford University Press.

Tavakoli, P. and **P. Skehan.** 2005. 'Strategic planning, task structure, and performance testing' in R. Ellis (ed.). *Planning and Task Performance in a Second Language*. Amsterdam: John Benjamins.

Terrell, T. 1991. 'The role of grammar instruction in a communicative approach'. *The Modern Language Journal* 75/1: 52–63.

TESOL (Teachers of English to Speakers of Other Languages). 1997. *ESL Standards for pre-K–12*. Alexandria, Va.: TESOL.

TESOL (Teachers of English to Speakers of Other Languages). 2001. *Scenarios for ESL Standards-based Assessment*. Alexandria, Va.: TESOL.

Tomlin, R. and **V. Villa.** 1994. 'Attention in cognitive science and second language acquisition'. *Studies in Second Language Acquisition* 16/2: 183–203.

Tomlinson, B. 1981. *O-Level Summary and Composition*. Harlow: Longman.

Tomlinson, B. 1990. 'Managing change in Indonesian high schools'. *ELT Journal* 44/1: 25–37.

Tomlinson, B. 1994. 'Pragmatic awareness activities'. *Language Awareness* 3/3: 119–29.

Tomlinson, B. 2000a 'A multi-dimensional approach'. *The Language Teacher Online*: 24/07. July 2000. http://www.jalt-publications.org/tlt/articles/2000/07/tomlinson.

Tomlinson, B. 2000b. 'Materials for cultural awareness; combining language, literature and culture in the mind'. *The Language Teacher* 24/2: 19–21.

Tomlinson, B. 2001. 'Connecting the mind: a multi-dimensional approach to teaching language through literature'. *The English Teacher* 4/2: 104–15.

Tomlinson, B. 2003a. 'Developing principled frameworks for materials development' in B. Tomlinson (ed.). *Developing Materials for Language Teaching.* London: Continuum.

Tomlinson, B. 2003b. 'Materials evaluation' in B. Tomlinson (ed.). *Developing Materials for Language Teaching.* London: Continuum.

Trahey, M. 1996. 'Positive evidence in second language acquisition: some long terms'. *Second Language Research* 12/2: 111–39.

Trenchs, M. 1996. 'Writing strategies in a second language: three case studies of learners using electronic mail'. *Canadian Modern Language Review* 52/3: 464–91.

Truscott, J. 1996. 'The case against grammar correction in L2 writing classes'. *Language Learning* 46/2: 327–69.

Truscott, J. 1999. 'The case for "the case against grammar correction in L2 writing classes": a response to Ferris'. *Journal of Second Language Writing* 8/2: 111–22.

Tyler, A. and **V. Evans.** 2001. 'The relation between experience, conceptual structure and meaning: non-temporal uses of tense and language teaching' in M. Pütz, S. Niemeier, and R. Dirven (eds.). *Applied Cognitive Linguistics I: Theory and Language Acquisition.* Berlin: Mouton de Gruyter.

Ullman, M. 2005. 'A cognitive neuroscience perspective on second language acquisition: the declarative/procedural model' in C. Sanz (ed.). *Mind and Context in Adult Second Language Acquisition. Methods, Theory, and Practice.* Washington, D.C.: Georgetown University Press.

Ur, P. 1988. *Grammar Practice Activities.* Cambridge: Cambridge University Press.

Van den Branden, K. 1997. 'Effects of negotiation on language learners' output'. *Language Learning* 47/4: 589–636.

Van Ek, J. and **L. G. Alexander.** 1980. *Threshold Level English.* Oxford: Pergamon.

Van Handle, D. and **K. Corol.** 1998. 'Extending the dialogue: using electronic mail and the Internet to promote conversation and writing in intermediate level German language courses'. *CALICO Journal* 15/1–3: 129–43.

Van Lier, L. 1998. 'The relationship between consciousness, interaction and language learning'. *Language Awareness* 7/2: 128–45.

Van Lier, L. 2004. *The Ecology and Semiotics of Language Learning: A Sociocultural Perspective.* Boston: Kluwer.

VanPatten, B. 1990. 'Attention to form and content in the input: an experiment in consciousness'. *Studies in Second Language Acquisition* 12/3: 287–301.

VanPatten, B. 2002. 'Processing instruction: an update'. *Language Learning* 52/4: 755–803.

VanPatten, B. and **T. Cadierno.** 1993. 'Explicit instruction and input processing'. *Studies in Second Language Acquisition* 15/2: 225–44.

Vocate, D. R. 1994. 'Self-talk and inner speech: understanding the uniquely human aspects of intrapersonal communication' in D. R. Vocate (ed.). *Intrapersonal Communication. Different Voices, Different Minds.* Hillsdale, N.J.: Lawrence Erlbaum Associates.

Vygotsky, L. 1979. 'Consciousness as a problem in the psychology of behavior'. *Soviet Psychology* 17/4: 3–35.

Vygotsky, L. 1986. *Thought and Language.* Cambridge, Mass.: MIT Press.

Wajnryb, R. 1990. *Grammar Dictation.* Oxford: Oxford University Press.

Warschauer, M. 1995. *E-mail for English Teaching.* Alexandria, Va.: TESOL.

Warschauer, M. 1996. 'Motivational aspects of using computers for writing and communication' in M. Warschauer (ed.). *Telecollaboration in Foreign Language Learning. Proceedings of the Hawai'i symposium.* Technical Report # 21. Honolulu: University of Hawaii Press.

Warschauer, M. and **R. Kern** (eds.). 2001. *Network-based Language Teaching: Concepts and Practice.* Cambridge: Cambridge University Press.

Weinreich, U. 1953. *Languages in Contact.* The Hague: Mouton.

Weir, C. 2005. *Language Testing and Validation.* Basingstoke: Palgrave Macmillan.

Wenger, E. 1998. *Communities of Practice: Learning, Meaning, and Identity.* Cambridge: Cambridge University Press.

Wertsch, J. 1985. *Vygotsky and the Social Formation of Mind.* Cambridge, Mass.: Harvard University Press.

Wertsch, J. 1991. *Voices of the Mind: a Sociocultural Approach to Mediated Action.* Cambridge, Mass.: Harvard University Press.

Wertsch, J. 1998. *Mind as Action.* New York: Oxford University Press.

Wertsch, J. and **P. Tulviste.** 1992. 'L. S. Vygotsky and contemporary developmental psychology'. *Developmental Psychology* 28/4: 548–57.

Wertsch, J., P. Tulviste, and **F. Hagstrom.** 1993. 'A sociocultural approach to agency' in E. Forman, N. Minick, and C. Stone (eds.). *Contexts for Learning: Sociocultural Dynamics in Children's Development.* New York: Oxford University Press.

Wesche, M. and **P. Skehan.** 2002. 'Communicative, task-based, and content based language instruction' in R. B. Kaplan (ed.). *The Oxford Handbook of Applied Linguistics.* New York: Oxford University Press.

West, M. 1953. *A General Service List of English Words.* London: Longman.

White, J. 1998. 'Getting the learners' attention: a typographical input enhancement study' in C. Doughty and J. Williams (eds.). *Focus on Form in Classroom Second Language Acquisition.* Cambridge: Cambridge University Press.

White, L. 1991. 'Adverb placement in second language acquisition: some effects of positive and negative evidence in the classroom'. *Second Language Research* 7/2: 122–61.

Whitley, M. S. 1986. *Spanish/English Contrasts*. Washington, D.C.: Georgetown University Press.

Widdowson, H. G. 1987. 'Aspects of syllabus design' in M.Tickoo (ed.). *Language Syllabuses: State of the Art*. Singapore: Regional Language Centre.

Widdowson, H. G. 1990. *Aspects of Language Teaching*. Oxford: Oxford University Press.

Wilkins, D. 1976. *Notional Syllabuses*. Oxford: Oxford University Press.

Williams, J. 1995. 'Focus on form in communicative language teaching: research findings and the classroom teacher'. *TESOL Journal* 4/4: 12–16.

Williams, J. 1999. 'Learner-generated attention to form'. *Language Learning* 49/4: 583–625.

Williams, J. 2001. 'The effectiveness of spontaneous attention to form'. *System* 29/3: 325–40.

Williams, J. 2005a. 'Form-focused instruction' in E. Hinkel (ed.). *Handbook on Research in Second Language Teaching and Learning*. Mahwah, N.J.: Lawrence Erlbaum Associates.

Williams, J. 2005b. *Teaching Writing in Second and Foreign Language Classrooms*. Boston: McGraw Hill.

Williams, J. and **J. Evans.** 1998. 'What kind of focus and on which forms?' in C. Doughty and J. Williams (eds.). *Focus on Form in Classroom Second Language Acquisition*. Cambridge: Cambridge University Press.

Willis, J. 1996. *A Framework for Task-based Learning*. London: Longman.

Wong, W. 2001. 'Modality and attention to meaning and form in the input'. *Studies in Second Language Acquisition* 23/3: 345–68.

Wright, T. 1991. 'Language awareness in teacher education programmes for non-native speakers' in C. James and P. Garrett (eds.). *Language Awareness in the Classroom*. Harlow: Longman.

Wright, T. 2002. 'Doing language awareness: issues for language study in language teacher education' in H. Trappes-Lomax and G. Ferguson (eds.). *Language in Language Teacher Education*. Amsterdam: John Benjamins.

Wright, T. and **R. Bolitho.** 1993. 'Language awareness: a missing link in language teacher education'. *ELT Journal* 47/4: 292–304.

Wright, T. and **R. Bolitho.** 1997. 'Towards awareness of English as a professional language'. *Language Awareness* 6/2 and 3: 162–70.

Yaroshevsky, M. 1989. *Lev Vygotsky*. Moscow: Progress Press.

Yin, M. 2005. 'A progressively focused qualitative study of teacher thinking in English for academic purposes (EAP) classroom language assessment'. PhD Dissertation. University of Bristol.

Yuan, F. and **R. Ellis.** 2003. 'The effects of pre-task planning and on-line planning on fluency, complexity and accuracy in L2 monologic oral production'. *Applied Linguistics* 24/1: 1–27.

Zamel, V. 1983. 'The composing processes of advanced ESL students: six case studies'. *TESOL Quarterly* 17/2: 165–87.

Index